YEARS OF REGAL RECIPES
1945-1995

... from the kitchens of Regal Ware Employees

Adeline Halfmann, Editor

REGAL®

Regal Ware, Inc.
Kewaskum, Wisconsin

First Edition

Library of Congress Catalog Card Number: 95-77716

ISBN: 0-942495-49-7

For additional copies of this book, contact:

Regal Ware, Inc.
1675 Reigle Drive
Kewaskum, Wisconsin 53040

Printed by
Palmer Publications, Inc.
PO Box 296
Amherst, Wisconsin 54406

All recipes in this book were tested in the homes of the named employees or retirees of Regal Ware, Inc. and its subsidiaries. Recipes have been edited for clarity and style.

—Adeline Halfmann, Editor

CONTENTS

REGAL WARE, INC.
A privately-held corporation celebrating 50 years of excellence

Three generations of leadership

J.O. Reigle, Founder
President: 1945-1965

James D. Reigle
Chairman of the Board
President: 1965-1991

Jeffrey A. Reigle
President and Chief Executive Officer
1991-

The history of what is today Regal Ware, Inc. began on August 6, 1945, when James O. Reigle of Massillon, Ohio, along with two associates—L.N. Peterson and Edna Oster—purchased the Kewaskum Aluminum Company located in Kewaskum, Wisconsin. In its earliest years the company was named Kewaskum Utensil Company and in 1951 the Reigle family chose to rename the company Regal Ware, Inc.

The first two saucepans, made of stainless steel, 1945

From a two saucepan line, just 47 employees, and an 18,000 square-foot building, the company has grown to become a world leader in housewares. Today, the name Regal is a mark of quality found on cookware and small appliances in homes in more than 100 countries around the world.

Shortly after the purchase of the company, World War II ended and so did the company's government contracts to make

"The golden opportunity of the future belongs to those who are willing to think and plan, and work. Let us move forward together."

—J.O. Reigle, Founder

81 millimeter mortar shells. The founders had to scramble to convert the facility to peacetime operations. Aluminum was scarce and they decided to begin producing saucepans out of stainless steel since that was the only metal available. In the ensuing months, after locating aluminum supplies, the focus turned to manufacturing aluminum cookware.

The Cheerio Beverage Set included colorful anodized aluminum pitcher and tumblers

In the fifties a line of anodized aluminum serveware was introduced in cherry red, gold, blue and green. This distinct diversion from polished aluminum utilitarian pots and pans included an assortment of tumblers, pitchers, two- and three-tiered trays, popcorn bowls and large serving trays.

It was in the early sixties that Regal Ware took another giant step forward with the introduction of the Poly Perk® coffeemaker, which quickly became America's number one selling percolator. Original color offerings of the Poly Perk were persimmon, lemon yellow and white. After dozens of color changes and several style modifications, the Poly Perk still remains an affordable coffeemaker that delivers a good cup of coffee.

The early sixties also marked the beginning of the nonstick era when DuPont Company brought Teflon to the housewares industry. Regal Ware was the first U.S. company to produce and market matched cookware sets with the slippery interiors. Since then the company has produced rangetop cookware with a myriad of nonstick interior coatings and today one would be hard-pressed to find a line of aluminum cookware without some type of nonstick coating on the interior.

The seventies brought renewed emphasis on small appliances at Regal Ware with the introduction of a wide assortment of drip coffeemakers. The company also introduced decorator stripes to the cookware industry.

A further expansion of the company's electrics assortment occurred in the early eighties with the addition of the LaMachine® food processor line. In the mid-eighties this was complemented by the addition of the company's first automatic breadmaker offering; the company continued to market these machines as the bread-making trend flourished well into the nineties.

America's No. 1 selling percolator—the Poly Perk® coffeemaker—introduced in 1963

Regal's commitment to innovation was the driving force behind the company's development of a patented application process that created a superior nonstick coating for cookware with a lifetime warranty.

This dedication to innovation in housewares has set the pace for the company's growth for the latter half of the nineties and beyond.

The company has enjoyed continuity in upper levels of management, owing in large part to the involvement of three generations of Reigles in the history of the company. James D. Reigle, the second company president, laid the groundwork for a multiplicity of employee programs promulgating the goals of his father. He, too, has guided the company through acquisitions, expansions and product diversifications that earned Regal Ware's reputation as a world class housewares source.

Automatic breadmakers enjoyed consumer acceptance for the past decade

With the increasing complexity of Regal Ware's operations in recent decades, the development of self-motivated, independent employees has become more crucial than ever—a philosophy passed on through the generations of company executives by its founder, J.O. Reigle. Management remains committed to providing opportunities for all employees to develop their talent to the fullest and supports continuing education at all levels.

"Our past is but a base from which we will build a successful future. We shall continue to build on the success of the first 50 years through a total dedication to passionately serving our customers."

—Jeffrey A. Reigle, President and CEO

The dedicated and responsible workforce has enjoyed a stake and sense of ownership at the company, exhibited in part in their remarkable staying power. The company's 25-year club presently includes more than 200 members. It is not unusual to have three or four members of a single family working at Regal Ware. Through the past five decades, the company has employed two and three generations of more than a handful of families.

Early polishing operations

The kind of mutually beneficial relationship that has existed between Regal Ware and its employees has also prevailed between the company and the community of Kewaskum, Wisconsin. Although the company has grown considerably, and manufacturing, marketing and sales facilities are located in other areas of the country, corporate headquarters remain firmly planted in the small village of Kewaskum.

Settled in 1849, Kewaskum was named after a chief of the Potawatomi Indians whose name has been interpreted as meaning "the turner," or "one who is able to turn fate whichever way he pleases." A publication of the Wisconsin State Historical Society indicated that the chief "stood on friendly and honorable terms with the settlers who reciprocated in righteousness and good feeling."

A pastoral scene as viewed from the fourth floor of the Administration Center in the 1980s

The village of Kewaskum, in keeping with its noble name, has provided a "friendly and honorable" environment over the past half-century, and its stability has contributed to the success of Regal Ware, Inc.

The inspiring story of Regal Ware's five decades is not a cause for nostalgia because the story of its past is really about its present and its future. It is said that trees and skyscrapers can grow skyward to the extent that their roots and foundations are developed below ground. In this sense, Regal Ware's past 50 years suggest a rich sense of promise for the future: "the past is prologue," as Shakespeare asserted. Or, in the words of James O. Reigle, "Remember, the past is only a stepping stone into the glorious future."

With acknowledgement to Jerry E. Burns, Marian College, Fond du Lac, Wisconsin, for excerpts from his written company history.

PROLOGUE

As one of the leading housewares producers, it is only fitting that we celebrate our 50 years of success with this commemorative cookbook. The recipes were submitted by the employees and retirees of Regal Ware, Inc. with the same pride and dedication they have devoted to producing the world's finest cookware for homes around the world.

OLD FAVORITES

Regal's first electric percolator, introduced in 1949

DANDELION WINE

A 1918 recipe from my great-grandmother.

1 full quart dandelion blooms
1 gallon water
2 unpeeled lemons, sliced
2½ pounds sugar

Put all ingredients into a large kettle and boil 5 minutes. Then pour into a clean jar. When cool add 2 tablespoons of yeast. Keep in warm place three days until it ferments. Strain into bottles and cork tightly. After 3 to 6 months start nipping!

Judy Bowater, Sales Dept.
—Kewaskum

HOMEMADE GRAPENUTS

My great-grandmother's favorite breakfast cereal.

½ cup buckwheat flour
3¼ cups whole wheat flour
2 cups brown sugar
1 teaspoon baking soda
1 teaspoon salt
2 cups buttermilk or sour milk

In a large bowl mix all dry ingredients. Add buttermilk; beat until smooth. Spread on greased cookie sheet and bake in 350° oven until golden brown. Let stand overnight in cool place. When dry put through a food chopper (coarse grind).

Judy Bowater, Sales Dept.
—Kewaskum

APPLE PANCAKES

This is an old German favorite that my mother-in-law passed on to me.

2 eggs, well beaten
1 cup milk, divided
½ cup sugar
1 cup flour
½ teaspoon salt
1 to 2 cups thinly sliced, peeled apples
2 tablespoons vegetable oil for frying

In medium bowl, mix eggs, ½ cup milk and sugar. Add flour to make stiff batter. Stir in remaining half-cup milk to make thin batter. Stir in salt and apples. Heat 2 teaspoons oil in large fry pan or griddle over medium-high heat. Drop batter onto hot griddle, about ¼ cup at a time. Cook until edges begin to look dry and pancake is browned. Turn and brown other side. Add more oil as needed to bake remaining pancakes.

Marianne Staehler, Creative Services Dept.
—Kewaskum

BUTTERMILK PANCAKES

I watched my friend Val's grandma very carefully when she would make this recipe. Whenever I asked for this recipe she would say, "Just add a large spoonful of this and a dash of that until it looks like this!"

3 cups all-purpose flour
1½ teaspoons baking soda
1 teaspoon sugar
1 teaspoon salt
3 cups buttermilk
3 eggs, separated
¼ cup butter, melted

Mix together flour, baking soda, sugar and salt. Fold in buttermilk, beaten egg yolks and butter until flour mixture is moistened (batter will be lumpy). In a clean bowl beat egg whites until stiff; fold into batter. Pre-heat griddle until a few drops of water skitter around. Lightly oil griddle surface. Pour about ½ cup batter onto griddle. Cook pancakes until puffy and edges begin to look dry. Turn and cook other side until golden.

Makes about 12 4" pancakes

Susan Portmann Anderson, Marketing
—Kewaskum

SPEEDY ROLL DOUGH

I use this recipe for Parker House, Clover Leaf and Butter Horn rolls, as well as Frosted Coconut Coffee Cake, Sticky Buns, etc. I've used this at least 50 years!

2 cups warm milk
⅓ cup sugar
1 or 2 packages dry yeast
2 teaspoons salt
6½ cups flour, divided
2 eggs
⅓ cup plus 1 tablespoon solid
    shortening, melted and cooled

In large bowl, combine milk, sugar and yeast; stirring to dissolve yeast. Add salt and 2 cups flour. Beat with electric mixer 2 minutes. Add eggs and shortening. Beat 1 minute. With a large spoon, stir in remaining flour, until smooth. Let dough rest 20 minutes. Shape into desired rolls or coffee-cakes. Cover; let rise in warm place until almost doubled in size. Bake at 375° for 15 to 18 minutes.

Marvin (and Minerva) Martin, Retired
—Kewaskum

BANANA NUT BREAD

This recipe has been in my family since before my great-great-grandmother. It originally used cake flour instead of all-purpose flour. We serve this at all holidays or special occasions.

2 cups sugar
1 cup shortening
6 ripe bananas
4 eggs
2½ cups flour
1 teaspoon salt
2 teaspoons baking soda
1½ cups chopped pecans

Grease and flour two loaf pans. Preheat oven to 350°. In large bowl cream together sugar and shortening. Set aside. On a plate, mash bananas with a fork until runny. Beat eggs. Add bananas and eggs to sugar and shortening. Do not over mix; batter will be lumpy. In separate bowl mix together flour, salt and baking soda. Blend wet and dry ingredients together, but do not over mix. Stir in pecans. Pour into prepared loaf pans. Bake at 350° for 40 to 50 minutes.

Virginia Mashewski, Dept. 10
—Jacksonville

CRANBERRY NUT BREAD

This is my mother's recipe that's been around for more than 50 years. She loves to bake several loaves for gifts at Christmas time.

2 cups sifted flour
1 cup sugar
1½ teaspoons baking powder
½ teaspoon baking soda
1 teaspoon salt
Juice of one orange, boiling water added
    to make 1 cup
Rind of one orange, ground
2 tablespoons Crisco
1 egg, beaten
1 cup cranberries, cut in half
1 cup chopped walnuts

Sift together flour, sugar, baking powder, soda and salt. Combine orange juice, rind and shortening. Stir in dry ingredients. Add beaten egg. Stir only until flour is blended. Add cranberries and nuts. Pour into greased bread pan. Let stand for 20 minutes. Bake at 350° for 60 to 70 minutes.

Jim Myre, Sales
—California

PICKLED APPLES

A specialty of Aunt Jo's; in the family for more than 50 years.

5 cups sugar
4 cups water
3 cups vinegar
2 whole cloves
2 sticks cinnamon
10 pounds honey crab apples

Mix all but apples in 10-quart kettle. Add apples and bring to boil. Cook in syrup until tender. Put into pint or quart jars. Process in hot water bath for 10 minutes.

Marty Polzean, Retired
—Kewaskum

GERMAN POTATO SALAD

This is my great-grandmother's recipe. It has been in the family for at least 75 years.

5 pounds salad potatoes
1 medium onion, chopped
Salt and pepper to taste
½ pound bacon
1 cup sugar
1 cup water
1 cup white vinegar

Boil potatoes until done. Peel and slice potatoes; add chopped onion, salt and pepper. Cut bacon in small pieces, fry until crispy, drain and return to pan. Add water, sugar and vinegar, bring to a boil. Cool and pour over potatoes. Mix well.

Brenda Pikulik, 1600 CDT Drip
—Kewaskum

MOLDED CHICKEN SALAD

This recipe is over 50 years old. It was given to Jean Myers by her mother Madge Johnson.

2 envelopes unflavored gelatin (Knox)
1 cup cold water
1 10½-ounce can cream of celery soup
½ teaspoon salt
2 tablespoons lemon juice
1 teaspoon minced onion
1 cup salad dressing
2 tablespoons diced pimiento
1 cup diced celery
2 cups diced cooked chicken

Sprinkle gelatin over water in medium saucepan. Place over low heat; stir constantly until gelatin dissolves, about 4 minutes. Remove from heat; stir in celery soup, salt, lemon juice, onions and salad dressing; beat with rotary beater until smooth. Chill; stirring occasionally, until mixture mounds when dropped from a spoon. Add pimiento, celery and chicken. Turn into a 6-cup loaf pan or mold. Chill until firm.

6 servings

Dick (and Jean) Meyers, Retired
—Kewaskum

CORN-TOMATO DISH

This recipe has been a family favorite for more than 50 years.

1 medium onion, diced
16 ounces frozen corn
14 ounces stewed tomatoes, juice drained
¾ cup crushed cracker crumbs OR
    1 cup bread crumbs or croutons
5 tablespoons butter, melted, divided
Salt and pepper to taste

Saute onion in 2 tablespoons butter until golden. In buttered 1-quart dish or a little larger, mix corn, tomatoes and onions. Mix well. Mix crumbs in remaining butter. Remove ¼ cup buttered crumbs and set aside. Add remaining buttered crumbs to corn and tomato mixture. Add salt, pepper or anything you like to taste. Top with reserved crumbs. Cover and bake at 350° for 30 minutes. Uncover for last 10 minutes.

Marvin (and Minerva) Martin, Retired
—Kewaskum

DUMPLINGS

This is a recipe from my 81-year old mother-in-law and the trick is the "no peeking." She got the recipe when she was a Girl Scout.

1 cup sifted flour
2 teaspoons baking powder
½ teaspoon salt
1 egg
½ cup milk

Mix and sift dry ingredients. Beat the egg and milk; add to flour mixture. Mix only enough to moisten flour. Drop batter by spoonfuls over hot stew. Cover tightly to hold steam. Boil gently for 15 minutes. No peeking!

Marianne Staehler, Creative Services
—Kewaskum

STEW DUMPLINGS

My grandmother, Mary Seefeldt (1869-1953) made these. They were used to stretch a pot of stew to feed more farm hands.

4

1½ cups flour
2¼ teaspoons baking powder
¾ cup milk

In medium bowl, mix flour and baking powder. Add milk; mix well. Drop by spoonfuls onto hot stew. On low boil, cook covered for 20 minutes. Serve with butter, if desired.

Bethana Herriges, Outlet Store
—Kewaskum

OLD FASHIONED CHICKEN AND NOODLES

This recipe is at least 50 years old, possibly 75. My grandmother's Aunt Joe used to make this for our family whenever we went to visit her in Sauk City. She would triple the recipe and then some. I have always liked this casserole and it's a great way to use leftover chicken.

1 10¾-ounce can cream of chicken soup
⅓ cup milk
1½ cups diced cooked chicken
1½ cups cooked noodles
1 cup cooked corn
¼ cup finely chopped onion
⅓ teaspoon paprika
Generous dash of pepper
¼ cup buttered bread crumbs
1 hard cooked egg, sliced

In 1½-quart casserole, blend soup and milk. Stir in chicken, noodles, corn, onion, paprika and pepper. Top with bread crumbs. Bake at 350° for 30 minutes or until hot. Garnish with egg.

Makes about 4½ cups

Denise Braatz, Oil Core Line
—Kewaskum

NOODLE DISH

This recipe has been in the family for over 50 years. My mother made it often because all the kids liked it so much. I add fresh green beans from my garden!

1½ pounds ground beef
1 onion, chopped
2 cans vegetarian vegetable soup
1 can tomato soup
16-ounce package egg noodles
1 green pepper, chopped and boiled, optional

Boil noodles in salt water for 10 minutes. Drain; set aside. Fry meat and onions until brown. Add soups. Mix in the noodles. Add green pepper. Preheat oven and bake at 250° for 2½ hours, stirring after 1 hour.

Arlene Herriges, Dept. 15EE
—Kewaskum

HASENPFEFFER

This was always served with a baked potato. I got this recipe from my mother-in-law. The recipe is over 100 years old.

1 wild rabbit, cut in serving pieces
1 teaspoon salt
Water
¼ teaspoon pepper
1 medium onion, sliced
1 bay leaf
Pinch of ground cloves
⅓ cup vinegar
¼ cup flour dissolved in ½ cup cold water

In a large kettle, place rabbit meat. Add salt and water to cover. Cook until water foams. Skim off foam—skimming may have to be repeated. Add pepper, onion, bay leaf, cloves and vinegar. Cook until meat is tender. Thicken with flour or cornstarch and water mixture.

Valeria Baier, Dept. 16EL
—Kewaskum

ROMANIAN SARMALE
(Stuffed Cabbage Rolls with Sauerkraut)

This recipe was given to my wife, Aurelia, by her mother when she first learned to cook. Her mother used this recipe before she came to America from Romania.

2 **pounds ground beef or turkey**
1 **large onion, chopped**
¼ **cup finely chopped celery**
2 to 3 **cloves garlic, chopped**
¼ **cup chopped parsley**
¼ **cup fresh dill or 1 tablespoon dried dill**
2 **tablespoons sweet ground paprika**
¼ **teaspoon ground allspice**
¼ **teaspoon salt and pepper or to taste**
3 **egg whites plus 1 egg**
½ **cup washed dry rice**
4 **pounds fresh cabbage**
2 **pounds sauerkraut, rinsed and drained**
3 **tablespoons pearl barley**
2 **tablespoons caraway seeds**
2 **tablespoons sugar - brown or white**
2 **smoked pork hocks, turkey wings, or ribs**
4 **cups tomato juice, water or 10-ounce can tomato soup diluted with water**

In large bowl, mix together first 11 ingredients. Set aside. Take core out of cabbage. Parboil cabbage to loosen leaves with fork. Drain and rinse in cold water. Cut large vein in leaf. Spoon heaping tablespoon of meat mixture onto each leaf. Fold, roll and tuck ends in securely.

In a large 6-quart stock pot or roasting pan, layer sauerkraut, 1 tablespoon pearl barley, 1 tablespoon caraway seeds, 1 tablespoon white or brown sugar. Place cabbage rolls close together on top of sauerkraut. Add some smoked meat. Continue to layer sauerkraut, barley, caraway seeds and sugar. Pour water, tomato juice or diluted tomato soup on top of rolls, just to cover. Cover and place in 275-300° oven; bake for 1½ to 2 hours.

Serves 8-10 and can be prepared several days ahead and refrigerated. It also freezes well.

Lawrence F. Beck, Retired Chief Electrician, Club Products—Cleveland

EASTER LOAF

My grandmother on my mother's side was Bohemian. She said she remembers making the Easter Loaf in the 1930s. She doesn't know why the family only made it at Easter, but it was always a special treat for everyone.

6 **eggs, beaten**
1 **cup bread crumbs**
½ **cup evaporated milk**
¼ **teaspoon allspice**
½ **teaspoon baking powder**
2 **cups cooked ham, cut in small pieces**
1 **cup cooked veal, cut in small pieces**
Salt and pepper to taste

Preheat oven to 350°. In large bowl, mix eggs and bread crumbs. Add milk and mix well. Add baking powder and allspice. Add ham, veal, salt and pepper; mix thoroughly. Place mixture in greased loaf pan. Bake 45 to 60 minutes or until a knife inserted in center comes out clean.

Makes 10-12 side dish servings

Linda Ertl, Q.C. Dept. —Kewaskum

HONEY COOKIES

This recipe is from my great-grandmother, Augusta Shroeter Rosenthal (1852-1920), who gave it to my grandmother Hulda Rosenthal Seyfert (1885-1963), who passed it on to my mother Hilda Seyfert Seefeldt (1916-). Honey Cookies are still a family favorite.

1 **pint honey**
4 **cups flour**
2 **eggs**
1 **cup sugar**
½ **teaspoon cloves**
½ **teaspoon cinnamon**
½ **teaspoon grated lemon rind**
½ **teaspoon baking soda**
Few drops anise oil

In large saucepan, bring to boil honey. Cool. Stir in flour. Add remaining ingredients; mix well. Drop on greased cookie sheets. Bake at 325° until lightly browned.

Tips from 1870s - Bake these only on a clear day, no rain. Bake a sample cookie. If too flat, add more flour.

1995 Tip: Heat honey in the microwave until boiling.

Bethana Seefeldt Herriges
Outlet Store Sales
—Kewaskum

MOLASSES COOKIES

This recipe was given to my mother, Mary Hron, by Mrs. J.O. Reigle many years ago.

1 cup shortening
2 cups brown sugar
1 cup molasses
1 egg
5 cups flour
1 teaspoon salt
1 teaspoon cinnamon
½ teaspoon ginger
⅔ cup hot water
1 teaspoon baking soda

Preheat oven to 375°. Cream shortening with sugar and molasses. Add egg and beat. Sift flour with seasonings and add alternately with hot water in which the soda has been dissolved. Drop by teaspoonfuls onto greased cookie sheets. Bake for 8 to 10 minutes. Frost with a thin powdered sugar icing while they are still warm.

John (and Patty) Coulter, Retired
—Kewaskum

ANGEL CRISP COOKIES

This recipe was my mother-in-law's and is over 50 years old.

½ cup sugar
½ cup brown sugar
1 cup shortening
1 egg
1 teaspoon vanilla
2 cups flour
½ teaspoon salt
1 teaspoon baking soda
1 teaspoon cream of tartar

Cream sugars, shortening, egg and vanilla. Add sifted dry ingredients. Form into balls the size of walnuts. Dip top half in water and then in sugar. Place on greased cookie sheet, sugar side up, and flatten with a fork handle. Bake at 375° for 10 minutes.

Makes 30-36 cookies.

Joyce Werbelow, Outlet Store-Sales
—Oshkosh, WI

BUTTERSCOTCH COOKIES

This recipe is well over 50 years old. Jim's mother, Ruth Reigle, made these cookies at Christmas time. She always used large cookie cutters, iced them with powdered sugar icing, and sprinkled them with colored sugar. Today we use Crisco instead of lard and sometimes margarine instead of butter. Seven cups of flour is quite a load for the mixer so it may be easier to cut the recipe in half and do it in two batches.

½ cup butter
¼ cup lard
4 cups brown sugar
4 eggs
2 tablespoons milk
1 tablespoon vanilla
7 cups flour
1 tablespoon cream of tartar
1 tablespoon baking soda
1 tablespoon salt

Cream shortenings and brown sugar; add eggs, milk and vanilla. Add sifted dry ingredients and mix well. Chill and roll out on lightly floured surface. Cut with cookie cutters. Bake on greased cookie sheet at 325° for 10 minutes.

Jim (and Patty) Reigle, Chairman of the Board
—Kewaskum

PEANUT BUTTER COOKIES

This is my grandma's recipe out of her favorite cookbook.

1 cup shortening
¾ cup sugar
1 cup brown sugar
2 eggs, beaten
3 cups flour
1½ teaspoons baking soda
½ teaspoon salt
1 cup peanut butter

Cream shortening and sugars. Add remaining ingredients. Mix well. Roll into balls and flatten in criss-cross manner with fork. Bake on greased cookie sheet at 400° for 5 to 10 minutes.

Cheri Baird, Finance
—Kewaskum

PIE CRUST COOKIES

This recipe has been in the family more than 100 years.

4 cups flour
¾ cup sugar
1 teaspoon salt
3 teaspoons baking powder
1¼ cups lard
¼ cup milk
½ teaspoon cinnamon

Preheat oven to 375°. Mix dry ingredients. Work in the lard. Add milk; 1 teaspoon more might be needed depending on dough mixture. Chill thoroughly; overnight if desired. On floured board, roll dough ¼-inch thick (if too thin they break easily). Cut into desired shapes. Arrange on ungreased cookie sheet. Bake at 375° for 10 to 12 minutes. Frost with egg white and powdered sugar frosting.

Marvin (and Minerva) Martin, Retired
—Kewaskum

SNICKERDOODLES

My grandmother's recipe which is over 50 years old.

1 cup shortening
1½ cups sugar
2 eggs
2¾ cups flour
2 teaspoons cream of tartar
1 teaspoon baking soda
¼ teaspoon salt

Cream shortening and sugar together. Add eggs; beat well. Sift together dry ingredients and mix with creamed mixture. Roll into balls. Then roll in a mixture of sugar and cinnamon. Bake at 400° until light brown—about 8 to 10 minutes.

Cheri Baird, Finance
—Kewaskum

CHOCOLATE PEANUT BUTTER COOKIES

This recipe has been in my family for 40 years. Anytime we get together for a family event or holiday, someone will request it. They are very easy to make and are a great first cooking experience for young people.

2 sticks margarine
6 tablespoons cocoa
4 cups sugar
1 cup milk
1 cup peanut butter
5 cups oatmeal
1 teaspoon vanilla
1 cup chopped pecans, optional

In large pan (6 or 8 qt.) mix margarine, cocoa, sugar and milk. Cook over medium heat until mixture comes to boil, stirring frequently. Boil 1½ minutes. Remove from heat and immediately add peanut butter, oatmeal, vanilla and pecans. Mix well. Stir until thick and drop onto waxed paper to cool. Makes 3-5 dozen, depending on size.

Note: Boiling time is very important—not long enough and the batter won't thicken, too long and it will be dry.

Cheryl Shipley
Saladmaster Payroll/Personnel Dept.
—Arlington, TX

ADRIENNE'S EASY FUDGE

Submitted by Adrienne's daughter, Kay M. Fuller of Beaumont, Texas from her mother's collection of family favorites.

Pinch of salt
2 cups sugar
1 tablespoon cocoa
1 cup milk
1 tablespoon butter
1 teaspoon vanilla or other flavoring

Mix salt, sugar and cocoa in 2-quart saucepan. Add milk. Cook over medium heat just until boiling point, stirring often or until mixture forms a soft ball in cold water, about 30 minutes. Add butter and vanilla; beat until it starts to form peaks. Pour onto buttered plate. Cut into squares when almost firm.

Adrienne Evans (deceased), Retired
Club Aluminum
—Cleveland

TOFFEE BARS

This is my mother-in-law's recipe and is at least 50 years old.

½ cup butter
1 cup sugar
2 eggs, separated
½ teaspoon almond extract
1½ cups sifted flour
1 teaspoon baking powder
¼ teaspoon salt
½ cup chopped nuts
2 cups brown sugar

In large bowl cream butter and sugar. Add egg yolks and almond extract; mix well. Mix together flour, baking powder and salt. Add to creamed mixture; mix well. Stir in nuts. Spread into greased and floured 9 x 13" pan. Beat egg whites until foamy. Gradually add brown sugar; beat until stiff. Spread on top of batter. Bake at 350° for 30 minutes.

Joyce Werbelow, Outlet Store Sales
—Oshkosh, WI

NO BAKE CHOCOLATE BARS

This recipe came from my great-grandma and was given to me by my grandma.

½ cup sugar
½ cup white syrup
½ cup peanut butter
1 teaspoon vanilla
5 cups Special K cereal
1 cup butterscotch chips
1 cup chocolate chips
Chopped Nuts, optional

Boil sugar and syrup. Remove from heat; add peanut butter and vanilla. Mix well. Put cereal in large bowl; pour sugar/syrup mixture over and mix. Spread into 9 x 13" pan. In double boiler, melt butterscotch and chocolate chips. Spread on top of cereal. Sprinkle nuts on top if desired. Cool.

Jill Zimdahl, Dept. 1500
—Kewaskum

CHOCOLATE GRAHAM ICE BOX CAKE

This recipe has been in my family for as long as I can remember. Having 5 brothers and sisters, it was quite economical and fast to prepare. It has been a favorite of mine and my family and now my grandchildren enjoy it.

¼ cup cocoa
⅓ cup sugar
1 cup whipping cream
½ teaspoon vanilla
16 graham crackers

Mix cocoa and sugar in small bowl and set aside. In medium bowl, whip cream until slightly thickened. Add cocoa mixture gradually; add vanilla. Whip until stiff. Spread over graham crackers and stack on a plate. Stand crackers on their side; frost sides and top with cream mixture. Refrigerate for at least 4 hours. Cut into slices. May be topped with additional plain whipped cream, a drizzle of chocolate syrup, and a maraschino cherry.

Gordon Leavens, Dept. 900
—Kewaskum

BUNS OR COFFEE CAKE

This recipe was my Grandma McMullen's recipe and is more than 100 years old.

1 pint milk, scalded and cooled
1 ounce compressed yeast, dissolved in warm water
2 eggs, beaten
⅓ cup sugar
⅓ cup shortening, melted and cooled
1 tablespoon salt
6 cups flour

Mix together all ingredients, except flour. Stir in flour to make a stiff dough. Knead until it leaves sides of pan. Grease top, cover and let rise until double in size—about 1 ½ hours. Knead down 2 or 3 times during rising. Makes about 40 buns or three coffee cakes. Let rise again. Bake 20 or 25 minutes at 375°.

Jeanne Staehler, Retired
—Kewaskum

BANANA CAKE

A family favorite for 4 generations.

1¼ cups sugar
½ cup butter, softened
1 teaspoon vanilla
2 cups flour
1 teaspoon baking powder
2 eggs, separated
2 bananas, mashed
1 teaspoon baking soda
1 cup sour cream or buttermilk

In large bowl, cream sugar and butter. Add vanilla. In small bowl mix flour and baking powder. Blend bananas with beaten egg yolks. Dissolve baking soda in sour cream and mix with banana/yolk mixture. Alternately add dry ingredients and sour cream mixture to creamed sugar and butter. In medium bowl, beat egg whites until stiff but not dry. Fold into batter. Spread batter into greased and floured 9 x 13" pan. Bake at 350° for 35 to 40 minutes.

Broiled Icing:
1 cup brown sugar
4 tablespoons sweet cream
6 tablespoons soft butter
1½ to 2 cups flaked coconut

Mix all ingredients and spread over top of warm cake. Place under broiler until well browned. For a special treat, make 1½ batches for a 9 x 13" cake.

Jim (and Helen) Portmann, Retired-Sales
—Minnesota

APPLE KUCHEN

This recipe was used by my mother and grandmother and is probably over 100 years old.

½ cup sugar
¾ cup milk
1½ tablespoons shortening
1 egg
1 teaspoon salt
1 teaspoon baking powder
1½ cups flour
6 to 8 tart apples, peeled and sliced ½" thick
¾ cup sugar
½ teaspoon cinnamon
2 tablespoons butter

In medium bowl, mix first 7 ingredients together. Pour batter into greased 9 x 13" pan. Press apples into dough in rows. Top apples with ¾ cup sugar. Sprinkle with cinnamon and dot with butter.

Bake at 350° for 40 to 50 minutes, until apples are tender. For added richness and flavor, use sour cream instead of butter.

Valeria Baier, Dept. 1600EL
—Kewaskum

CRUMB CAKE

This recipe has been in our family for over 50 years. It was given to me by my mother-in-law.

½ cup shortening
2 cups brown sugar
2 cups flour
¼ teaspoon salt
1 teaspoon baking soda
1 egg
1 cup sour milk
1 teaspoon vanilla

Blend shortening, brown sugar, flour and salt thoroughly. Measure ¾ cup crumb mixture and set aside for topping. To remaining mixture add baking soda, egg and sour milk. Add vanilla and stir. Pour batter into greased 8 x 11" cake pan. Sprinkle reserved crumb mixture on top of batter. Bake at 350° for 40 minutes.

Laura Hammes, Retired
—Kewaskum

DATE MATE

This recipe came from my great-grandmother. Make for your date to find a mate.

4 squares chocolate
4 tablespoons butter
2 cups flour
2 cups sugar
1 teaspoon salt
2 teaspoons baking soda
2 cups milk
2 eggs
2 teaspoons vanilla

Preheat oven to 350°. In small saucepan, over low heat, melt chocolate and butter together. Mix all ingredients together in mixing bowl. Pour into 9 x 13" pan and bake for 30 minutes.

Tricia Arnold
—Kewaskum

GRANDMA'S HICKORY NUT CAKE

This is an old recipe. My mother and grandmother always made it for special occasions.

2 cups sugar
⅔ cup butter
3 eggs
1 cup milk
⅛ teaspoon salt
2 teaspoons baking powder
2½ cups all-purpose flour
1 teaspoon vanilla extract
1 cup hickory nuts, chopped (reserve a few halves for garnish)

Cream together sugar and butter. Add eggs; beat on medium speed of mixer for 2 minutes. Mix dry ingredients and add alternately with milk. Mix well. Stir in vanilla and nuts. Pour into greased and floured 9 x 13" pan, or two 8" round pans. Bake at 325° for 45 to 50 minutes.

Penuche frosting:
½ cup butter
1 cup packed brown sugar
¼ cup milk or cream
2 cups confectioners sugar
1 teaspoon vanilla
½ cup chopped hickory nuts, optional

Melt butter in a medium saucepan. Add brown sugar; boil 2 minutes. Add milk; bring to boil. Remove from heat and cool to lukewarm. Beat in sugar and vanilla. Add hickory nuts, if desired.

Serves 16

Marianne Wondra, Retired
—Kewaskum

REGAL CARAMEL CAKE

This recipe is from my mother-in-law's cookbook.

2 cups sifted Swans Down Cake Flour
2 teaspoons baking powder
½ teaspoon salt
⅔ cup butter or other shortening
1 cup sugar
3 eggs, well beaten
6 tablespoons milk
1 teaspoon vanilla

Sift flour once, measure, add baking powder and salt, and sift together 3 times. Cream butter thoroughly. Add sugar gradually, and cream together until light and fluffy. Add eggs and beat well. Add flour, alternately with milk, a small amount at a time. Beat after each addition until smooth. Add flavoring. Bake in two greased 9" layer pans at 375° for 25 minutes or until done. Spread caramel frosting between layers and on top and sides of cake. Double recipe to make three 10" layers. Sprinkle chopped nuts on sides of cake if desired.

Viola Fritz, Retired
—Kewaskum

SALTED PEANUT CAKE

This recipe is over 75 years old.

1 cup sugar
½ cup shortening
2 egg yolks
1 cup sour milk
1 teaspoon baking soda
1½ cups flour
1 teaspoon vanilla
1 cup ground salted peanuts

Mix in order listed. Spoon into greased and floured 9 x 13" pan. Bake at 375° for about 30 minutes. Cool on rack.

Frosting:
5 tablespoons brown sugar
3 tablespoons butter
3 tablespoons cream
1 cup powdered sugar
1 teaspoon vanilla
1 cup ground salted peanuts

Jeanne Staehler, Retired
—Kewaskum

SPONGE CAKE

This recipe has been in the family more than 50 years.

5 eggs, separated
1½ cups sugar
½ cup hot water
1½ cups flour
1 teaspoon baking powder
1 teaspoon vanilla

Beat eggs yolks until thick, at least 10 minutes. Add sugar and mix well. Add water and beat until it thickens again. Add sifted flour and baking powder. Beat egg whites until stiff and fold into batter. Bake in dry angel food cake pan for 1 hour at slow heat (325°). Invert pan onto bottle to cool.

Susie Batzler, Dept. 1600EL
—Kewaskum

HUSBAND-TESTED CHEESE CAKE

This recipe has been in the family 40 years.

28 graham crackers
¼ pound margarine, softened
1 3-ounce package lemon gelatin
1 cup boiling water
1 cup sugar
1 8-ounce package cream cheese
1 teaspoon vanilla
1 can well chilled evaporated milk

Crush crackers fine. Mix with margarine and spread on bottom of 9 x 13" pan, reserving ½ cup to sprinkle on top. Mix gelatin with boiling water and let stand for 15 minutes. Cream sugar, cheese and vanilla for 5 minutes. Add cooled gelatin and blend for 2 minutes. In a separate bowl, whip evaporated milk until stiff. Add cheese mixture and spread over crust. Sprinkle remaining crumbs on top and chill for at least 4 hours.

Bonny Murphy, Retired
Maintenance Dept.
—Wooster

CHEESE KUCHEN

This recipe has been in the family more than 50 years.

1 pound cottage cheese
1 cup sugar
1 tablespoon cornstarch
1 cup milk
2 eggs, beaten
½ teaspoon salt
1 teaspoon vanilla
⅔ cup raisins, optional
Pastry shell (9 x 13")
2 tablespoons butter
Cinnamon

Mix all ingredients except butter and cinnamaon together. Pour into pastry shell. Dot with butter and sprinkle with cinnamon. Bake at 375° until set and crust is lightly browned, about 40 minutes.

Valeria Baier, Dept. 16EL
—Kewaskum

MOSS TORTE

This recipe was my mother's who died three days before her 100th birthday.

½ cup butter
2 cups sugar
4 egg yolks, beaten
1 cup milk
2 cups flour
2 teaspoons baking powder
1 bar sweet chocolate, grated
½ cup walnuts

Beat egg whites until stiff. Mix all ingredients together, folding in beaten egg whites last. Put in 9 x 13" pan. Bake at 375° for 30 minutes, or until toothpick comes out clean.

Jeanne Staehler, Retired
—Kewaskum

BLITZ TORTE

Cake:
2 cups sifted cake flour
3 teaspoons baking powder
½ teaspoon salt
½ cup butter
1 cup sugar
4 egg yolks
½ teaspoon lemon extract
¼ teaspoon almond extract
⅔ cup milk

Meringue:
½ teaspoon cream of tartar
½ teaspoon salt
4 egg whites
1 cup sugar

Topping:
1 tablespoon sugar
½ cinnamon
½ up chopped nuts

Sift together cake flour, baking powder and salt; set aside. Cream butter; add sugar gradually and continue creaming until fluffy. Beat egg yolks until thick; add butter mixture and mix. Add extracts to milk. Add sifted ingredients alternately with milk to butter mixture, mixing just enough after each addition to keep batter smooth. Pour into two 9" round cake pans lined with waxed paper.

Combine egg whites, cream of tartar and salt; beat until foamy. Gradually add sugar and beat until meringue will hold its shape. Spread on cake batter.

Combine topping ingredients and sprinkle over top of meringue. Bake in preheated 350° oven for 45 minutes. Cool 5 minutes; remove from pans and continue cooling on racks. Put layers together with meringue topping up; custard filling can be put in between layers.

Susie Batzler, Dept. 1600EL
—Kewaskum

COTTAGE CHEESE TORTE

This recipe has been in the family more than 60 years.

Crust:
2 cups graham cracker crumbs
½ cup butter
⅓ cup sugar

Filling:
2 pounds cottage cheese
1 cup sugar
4 eggs
2 tablespoons cornstarch
1 tablespoon flour
½ cup whipping cream or half and half cream
1 teaspoon vanilla

Mix crumbs, butter and sugar together; press into greased 9" springform pan. In large bowl, mix all filling ingredients together. Beat until mixed; do not beat until smooth. Bake at 350° for 50 minutes.

(You may use creamed cottage cheese, but then there's no need to add whipping cream.)

Jan Kumrow, Retired
—Kewaskum

CARAMEL TORTE

6 eggs, separated
1½ cups sugar
1 teaspoon baking powder
1 teaspoon almond extract
2 teaspoons vanilla
2 cups graham cracker crumbs
1 cup nuts

Beat egg whites until stiff. Beat egg yolks; add sugar, baking powder, almond extract and vanilla. Fold yolk mixture into egg whites. Fold in cracker crumbs and nuts. Pour mixture into two 9" round pans lined with waxed paper. Bake at 325° for 30 minutes. Cool.

Sauce for topping:
1 egg, beaten
1 tablespoon flour
¼ cup orange juice
1 cup brown sugar
¼ cup butter
¼ cup water
½ teaspoon vanilla
1 pint whipping cream

In a saucepan, combine first 6 ingredients and cook until thickened; add vanilla. Cool. Whip cream until stiff peaks form. Spread cream between layers and on top. Spoon sauce on top of whipped cream.

Susie Batzler, Dept. 1600EL
—Kewaskum

PINEAPPLE TORTE

This is my mother-in-law's recipe and is at least 50 years old.

Crust:
20 graham crackers, crushed
¼ cup sugar
½ cup butter, melted
Dash of cinnamon

Filling:
¾ pound marshmallows
1 cup milk
1 cup drained crushed pineapple
½ pint cream, whipped

Mix together crust ingredients in small bowl. Remove ½ cup crumb mixture and

set aside. Press into bottom and up sides of buttered 9 x 13" cake pan. Chill in refreigerator.

In 2-quart saucepan, bring milk to boil; add marshmallows. Cook and stir over low heat until marshmallows are melted. Chill until partially set. Stir until well blended. Fold in pineapple and whipped cream. Pour into graham cracker crust. Sprinkle top with reserved graham cracker crumbs. Chill in refrigerator until ready to serve.

You may use bananas, chocolate chips, etc. instead of pineapple.

Joyce Werbelow, Outlet Store Sales
—Oshkosh, WI

BAKED BUTTERSCOTCH PIE

This recipe has been in the family more than 50 years.

1 cup brown sugar
½ cup sugar
1 tablespoon flour
¼ teaspoon salt
2 eggs, well beaten
1¼ cups milk
2 tablespoons butter, melted
1 teaspoon vanilla
1 9" pie shell

Combine ingredients and pour into unbaked pie shell. Bake at 350° until it rises, about 35 to 45 minutes.

Naoma P. Butts, Retired
—Wooster

LEMON CAKE PIE

1 cup sugar
2 rounded tablespoons flour
2 tablespoons butter, melted
2 egg yolks
1 cup milk
Juice of 1 lemon
Grated rind of 1 lemon
2 egg whites, stiffly beaten
9" unbaked pie crust

Mix sugar and flour; add butter, egg yolks and milk, stir until smooth. Add lemon juice and rind; fold in stiffly beaten egg whites. Pour into pie shell and bake 15 minutes at 450°; reduce heat to 350° and bake another 20 minutes, or until done.

Naoma P. Butts, Retired
—Wooster

OLD FASHIONED CUSTARD PIE

2 eggs, beaten light
⅛ teaspoon salt
½ cup sugar
2 cups rich milk

Season with nutmeg and pour into unbaked 9″ pie shell. Bake slowly in moderate oven.

Naoma P. Butts, Retired
—Wooster

MINCE MEAT

Specialty of Grandma Beatrice; over 60 years old.

2 pounds ground venison or beef cooked
¼ pound beef suet, ground
4 pounds cored, unpeeled apples, ground
2 pounds raisins
4 pounds sugar
¾ cup vinegar
1½ cups sour wine
2 tablespoons cinnamon
1 tablespoon nutmeg
1 tablespoon ground cloves

Mix well and put into 1 quart freezer containers with tight fitting lids. Freeze.

Note: 1 quart will be enough for a 9″ pie.

Marty Polzean, Retired
—Kewaskum

OLD FASHIONED COBBLER

This recipe was given to me by my grandmother and given to her by her mother.

1 stick (½ cup) butter
2 16-ounce cans any flavor fruit, drained
1 cup sugar
1 cup milk
1 cup self-rising flour

Preheat oven to 450°. In 9 x 13″ glass baking dish place butter. Place in oven to melt. In medium bowl, mix together sugar, milk and flour. Set aside. After butter has melted, pour fruit on top of butter. Pour batter over fruit. Bake at 450° for 30 minutes or until top is brown.

This can also be made with fresh fruit.

Linda Hodges
—Pigeon Forge, TN

GRANDMA MORR'S BAKED APPLES

This recipe came from Lester's grandmother and is at least 50 years old. Originally, the apples were baked in the oven, all flour was used to thicken it; there were no mini-marshmallows or coconut. His mother changed it and started using the microwave version about 10 years ago.

6 large apples, peeled and sliced
2 cups milk
2 heaping tablespoons cornstarch
2 heaping tablespoons flour
1 cup miniature marshmallows
3 tablespoons coconut

Put sliced apples in a round, glass 8″ dish. Add ¼ cup of water. Microwave, uncovered, at full power 14-16 minutes or until tender; giving dish a half turn once.

In a saucepan over medium heat, cook milk, cornstarch and flour until thickened. When apples are done, arrange mini-marshmallows on top. Pour pudding on top. Sprinkle with coconut. Cool.

Lester Morr, Sr., Retired, Deceased
—Wooster
Submitted by his daughter-in-law,
Pamela Morr

PRALINES

This recipe, from a family friend, is more than 50 years old.

2 cups brown sugar
1 cup evaporated milk
1 teaspoon vanilla
1 tablespoon butter
1 cup pecans

Cook sugar and milk together until a soft ball is formed when tested in a cup of water. Remove from heat and cool slightly. Add remaining ingredients and mix together. Drop onto a greased surface.

Makes 15 3" pralines

Dick (and Jean) Myers, Retired
—Kewaskum

CHAPTER II

SALADS

Aluminum colander from the early fifties

COTTAGE CHEESE SALAD

1 24-ounce carton cottage cheese
1 6-ounce package gelatin (orange is good)
1 8-ounce container Cool Whip
1 15-ounce can fruit cocktail, drained

Pour cottage cheese in large bowl. Sprinkle gelatin over top. Add Cool Whip and fruit cocktail. Mix well and refrigerate.

8 to 10 servings

Lucy Horton, Drips CDT
—Kewaskum

COTTAGE CHEESE SALAD

2 cups cottage cheese
1 3-ounce package orange gelatin
1 11-ounce can mandarin oranges, drained
1 cup miniature marshmallows, optional
1 8-ounce container Cool Whip

Combine cottage cheese with dry gelatin, oranges and marshmallows; mix well. Fold in Cool Whip; refrigerate.

6 servings

Michael Hendricks, Dept. 900
and
Viola Fritz, Retired
—Kewaskum

EASY SALAD

1 3-ounce package orange gelatin
1 8-ounce can crushed pineapple
1 11-ounce can mandarin oranges, drained
1 12-ounce carton cottage cheese
1 9-ounce container Cool Whip

Mix together dry gelatin, pineapple and oranges. Add cottage cheese and Cool Whip. May be served immediately or refrigerated.

4 to 6 servings

Shari Bickell, Dept. 2000
—Jacksonville

LIME ICE CREAM SALAD

2 3-ounce packages lime gelatin
2 cups boiling water
2 teaspoons unflavored gelatin
⅔ cup cold water
2 pints vanilla ice cream, slightly softened
1 16-ounce can crushed pineapple, drained
2 cups miniature marshmallows
6 tablespoons milk
⅔ cup sour cream

Dissolve lime gelatin in boiling water. Dissolve unflavored gelatin in cold water; combine with lime gelatin. While still hot, add ice cream and stir until melted. Add pineapple. Combine milk and marshmallows and stir over medium heat until marshmallows are melted. Remove from heat and fold in sour cream. Add this mixture to gelatin/ice cream mixture. Pour into 2-quart mold. Chill overnight.

10 to 12 servings

Diane Schraufnagel, Dept. 8300-1
—Kewaskum

ORANGE JELLO SALAD

1 12-ounce carton Cool Whip
1 pint sour cream
1 3-ounce package orange gelatin
1 8-ounce can crushed pineapple, drained
2 11-ounce cans mandarin oranges, drained
1½ cups grated Cheddar cheese
1 cup miniature marshmallows, optional
½ cup coconut, optional

Mix Cool Whip and sour cream together lightly. Add dry gelatin and mix. Fold in pineapple, oranges and cheese, and marshmallows and coconut if desired. Chill overnight.

6 to 8 servings

Barbara Hanson, Retired
—California Sales Office

RUSSIAN CREAM

¾ cup sugar
1½ cups water
1 envelope unflavored Knox gelatin
1 cup sour cream
1 teaspoon vanilla
1 cup whipping cream, whipped
1 package thawed frozen strawberries, drain and reserve juice
1 package strawberry Junket (Danish Dessert Glaze)

Dissolve sugar, water and gelatin over medium heat. Boil 5 minutes. Remove from heat and cool to room temperature. Add water mixture gradually to sour cream to avoid lumps. Stir in vanilla. Chill until almost set. Fold in whipped cream. Pour into mold or bowl. Chill.

Prepare junket according to package directions for pie filling using juice from thawed berries. Fold berries into junket. Cool. Spread junket on top of white mixture or spoon into center of mold.

6 to 8 servings

Annie Shaske
—Kewaskum

STRAWBERRY-CREME SQUARES

2 3-ounce packages strawberry gelatin
2 cups boiling water
2 10-ounce packages frozen strawberries
1 13.5-ounce can crushed pineapple, drained
2 large bananas, finely diced
1 cup sour cream

Dissolve gelatin in 2 cups boiling water, add strawberries; stir until strawberries are thawed. Add pineapple and bananas. Pour ½ mixture into 9 x 13" pan, chill until firm. Spread evenly with sour cream. Pour remaining gelatin on top. Chill until firm. Cut into squares.

18 to 24 servings

Diane Schneider, Sales Dept.
—Kewaskum

COOL RASPBERRY JELLO

2 3.4-ounce packages raspberry gelatin
1½ cups boiling water
1 pint frozen raspberries
2 cups chunky applesauce
Whipped cream, optional

Dissolve gelatin in boiling water. Add raspberries, stirring until thawed. Stir in applesauce. Refrigerate until set. Top with whipped cream, if desired.

6 to 8 servings

Bill (and Lucy) McCarty, Retired
—Kewaskum

FLUFFY JELLO

1 11-ounce can mandarin oranges, drain and reserve juice
Water
1 3.4-ounce package orange gelatin
1 3.4-ounce package vanilla pudding (not instant)
1 3.4-ounce package tapioca pudding
2 envelopes Dream Whip
Milk

Combine reserved juice with water to make 3 cups. Bring to boil and dissolve gelatin and puddings. Cook until thickened. Cool to room temperature.

Prepare Dream Whip according to package directions; fold into cooled pudding mixture. Add mandarin oranges.

Variation: Strawberry gelatin with frozen strawberries, or raspberry gelatin with frozen raspberries can be used in place of oranges.

6 to 8 servings

Byrdell Schulz, Retired
—Kewaskum

WATERGATE SALAD

1 20-ounce can crushed pineapple, undrained
1 11-ounce can mandarin oranges, drained
1 3-ounce package pistachio pudding
.1 cup miniature marshmallows
1 12-ounce container Cool Whip

Combine undrained pineapple and oranges in large bowl. Add remaining ingredients. Refrigerate at least 1 hour before serving.

6 to 8 servings

Marilyn Loomis, 15 East Line
—Kewaskum

PISTACHIO PUDDING SALAD

2 8-ounce containers Cool Whip
2 3.4-ounce package instant pistachio pudding
1 15-ounce can crushed pineapple, drained
1 cup miniature marshmallows
¾ cup chopped pecans, optional
¾ cup shredded coconut, optional

Transfer Cool Whip to large mixing bowl. Stir in dry pudding and pineapple. Mix well. Add marshmallows, pecans and coconut if desired.

6 to 8 servings

Carolyn Lessley, Saladmaster, Inc.
—Arlington, TX

MOUNTAIN DEW SALAD

1 6-ounce package lemon gelatin
1 cup boiling water
1 12-ounce can cold Mountain Dew soda
1 15-ounce can pineapple chunks, drain and reserve juice
1 3.4-ounce package lemon pudding (not instant)
1 cup whipped cream or Cool Whip
1 cup colored miniature marshmallows

Dissolve gelatin in boiling water; add soda and reserved pineapple juice. Chill just until thickened. Cook pudding according to package instructions; cool.

Mix together gelatin, pudding and whipped cream. Add pineapple and marshmallows. Pour into large serving bowl and chill.

10 to 12 servings

Bonnie Will, Personnel Dept.
—Kewaskum

APPLE TAFFY SALAD

1 8-ounce can crushed pineapple, drain and reserve juice
2 tablespoons vinegar
½ cup sugar
1 tablespoon flour
1 12-ounce carton Cool Whip
4 cups bite-size apple chunks
1 cup salted peanuts

Boil pineapple juice, vinegar, sugar and flour until light and fluffy; cool. Fold in Cool Whip. Add apples, peanuts and pineapple. Serve immediately or chill.

6 to 8 servings

Leah Hartmann, International Division
—Kewaskum

FRESH APPLE SALAD

Dressing:
Reserved pineapple juice
¼ cup butter
¼ cup sugar
1 tablespoon lemon juice
2 tablespoons cornstarch
2 tablespoons water
1 cup mayonnaise, or ½ cup reduced calorie mayonnaise and ½ cup plain yogurt

8 cups chopped, unpeeled tart red apples
1 20-ounce can pineapple chunks, drained (reserve juice)
2 cups seedless green grapes
1 to 2 teaspoons poppy seeds, optional
1½ cups toasted pecans

Make dressing by combining reserved pineapple juice, butter, sugar and lemon juice in small saucepan. Heat to boiling. Combine cornstarch and water to make a smooth paste; add to hot mixture. Cook until thick and smooth. Chill completely before stirring in mayonnaise.

Combine apples, pineapple, grapes and poppy seeds in large glass bowl. Add chilled dressing; refrigerate until time to serve. Stir in pecans before serving for maximum crunchiness.

16 servings

> *Marion Erdmann, Retired*
> *—Kewaskum*

TAFFY APPLE SALAD

2 cups powdered sugar
1 cup butter (not margarine), softened
2 eggs
1 12-ounce container Cool Whip
3 Granny Smith apples, chopped
1 cup well drained crushed pineapple
1 8-ounce package crushed dry roasted peanuts

Beat together sugar and butter. Add eggs and beat well with mixer for 5 minutes until creamy. Blend in Cool Whip. Add chopped apples and pineapple. Blend in ½ to ¾ of chopped peanuts. Top with remainder of peanuts. Chill at least ½ hour.

6 to 8 servings

> *Laura Wollerman, Direct Sales*
> *—Kewaskum*

TOFFEE APPLE SALAD

1 8-ounce can crushed pineapple with juice
1 tablespoon flour
½ cup sugar
1 egg, beaten
2 tablespoons apple cider vinegar
1 8-ounce container Cool Whip
4 cups chopped, unpeeled apples
½ cup Honey Roasted peanuts*

Combine first 5 ingredients and cook over medium heat until thickened. Refrigerate to cool. To cooled mixture, add remaining ingredients and mix well. Garnish with additional peanuts.

*Substitute 2 cups salted cocktail peanuts

6 servings

> *Anna Schaeffer, Dept. 15WW*
> *and*
> *Janet Backhaus, M.I.S. Dept.*
> *—Kewaskum*

TASTY CHERRY SALAD

1 15-ounce can cherry pie filling
1 12-ounce container Cool Whip
1 cup drained, crushed pineapple
1 can (14-ounce) Eagle Brand condensed milk
1 cup chopped pecans
1 cup miniature marshmallows

Combine all ingredients. Mix well. Chill for several hours before serving.

8 to 10 servings

> *John Howard, Draftsman*
> *—Jacksonsville*

CRANBERRY SALAD

1 6-ounce package raspberry gelatin
1 6-ounce package lemon gelatin
1½ cups boiling water
2 10-ounce packages frozen raspberries
2 10-ounce packages frozen cranberry-orange relish
2 cups 7-Up soda

Dissolve gelatin in boiling water. Add fruit and soda. Stir together and pour into 9 x 13" pan. Refrigerate.

18 to 24 servings

> *Mary Ann Miller, Dept. 15WW*
> *—Kewaskum*

GRAPE SALAD

2 3-ounce packages grape gelatin
2 cups boiling water
1 20-ounce can crushed pineapple, drained
1 20-ounce can blueberry pie filling

Topping:
1 8-ounce package cream cheese, softened
½ cup sour cream
½ cup sugar
½ cup chopped nuts
1 teaspoon vanilla

Dissolve gelatin in boiling water. Let cool; add pineapple and pie filling. Pour into 9 x 13″ pan; chill until set.

Combine topping ingredients; spread on top of gelatin mixture.

18 to 24 servings

Harriet Michaels, Retired
—Kewaskum

FRUIT SALAD

1 6-ounce can frozen orange juice, thawed, undiluted
1¼ cups milk
1 3.4-ounce package instant vanilla pudding
¼ cup sour cream
6 to 8 cups fruit

Combine orange juice, milk and pudding. Beat with electric mixer until smooth. Stir in sour cream. Pour over fresh or drained canned fruit. Chill 2 hours.

6 to 8 servings

Rich Yahr, Purchasing
—Kewaskum

FRUIT SALAD

1 16-ounce can fruit cocktail
Water
1 3.4-ounce package lemon gelatin
1 4-ounce package cream cheese
1 cup miniature marshmallows
¾ cup chopped celery
½ pint whipping cream

Drain fruit cocktail, reserving juice. Add water to juice to make 1 cup liquid. Heat to boiling and dissolve gelatin, cheese and marshmallows. (A blender may be used to mix.) Cool. Add fruit and celery as mixture starts to set. Beat whipping cream until stiff; fold into fruit mixture. Refrigerate.

6 to 8 servings

Ruth Raether, Retired
—Kewaskum

FROZEN FRUIT SALAD

2½ cups boiling water
¾ cup sugar
1 6-ounce can frozen lemonade
1 6-ounce can frozen orange juice
1 10-ounce package frozen strawberries
3 bananas, peeled and sliced
1 13-ounce can crushed pineapple with juice
1 12-ounce can 7-Up soda

Dissolve sugar in boiling water; add remaining ingredients except 7-Up in order given. Freeze in individual serving bowls.

Remove from freezer 1 hour before serving and pour warm 7-Up over the top.

12 servings

Pat Buechel, 1600 PrCDT
—Kewaskum

QUICK FRUIT SALAD

1 21-ounce can peach pie filling
3 firm bananas, sliced
2 cups strawberries, halved
1 cup green seedless grapes

Combine all ingredients in bowl. Refrigerate until serving.

6 to 8 servings

Jan Kumrow, Retired
—Kewaskum

HOT FRUIT SALAD

1 large can sliced pears, drained
1 large can sliced peaches, drained
1 large can pineapple chunks or tidbits, drained
1 large can bing or dark sweet cherries
12 coconut macaroons, crumbled
¼ cup butter, melted
¼ cup brown sugar
½ cup cooking sherry
¼ cup slivered almonds, or more if desired

In 2½-quart buttered casserole, place fruit and cookie crumbs in layers, ending with cookie crumbs. Combine butter, brown sugar and wine; drizzle over fruit and top with slivered almonds. Bake at 350° for 20 to 25 minutes or until hot. Serve hot. Can be made ahead of time and put in oven 25 minutes before eating.

16 to 20 servings

Bonnie Will, Personnel Dept.
—Kewaskum

BEET AND RED ONION SALAD

1½ pounds fresh beets, trimmed and washed
2 whole cloves
2 whole allspice
1 bay leaf
Salt and freshly ground pepper to taste
½ teaspoon sugar
2 teaspoons red wine vinegar
2 tablespoons chopped Italian parsley
1 large red onion, about 8 ounces, sliced

Place beets in saucepan and cover with water. Add cloves, allspice, bay leaf, salt and pepper. Bring to boil and simmer for about 20 minutes or until tender throughout. Let cool in cooking liquid.

Remove beets and peel. Slice beets and place in mixing bowl. Add salt, pepper, sugar, vinegar, parsley and onion. Toss well to blend and serve.

4 servings

Kim Peterson
—Kewaskum

BLACK BEANS IN TOMATO VINAIGRETTE

2 tomatoes, peeled, seeded and chopped
½ cup sliced scallions
¼ cup chopped cilantro
2 tablespoons olive oil
2 tablespoons vinegar
Salt and pepper
2 cups cooked or 1 (16-ounce) can unseasoned black beans
Lettuce leaves, optional

In bowl, combine tomatoes, scallions, cilantro, olive oil and vinegar. Season to taste with salt and pepper. Drain beans and rinse lightly. Drain thoroughly. Add to tomato mixture and toss to combine. Serve on lettuce leaves, if desired.

4 servings

Skip Hillary, Sales
—Texas

BROCCOLI SALAD

2 bunches broccoli, cut in bite-size pieces
1 yellow onion, chopped
1 cup yellow raisins
10 to 12 slices bacon, cooked crisp, drained and crumbled
1 cup Miracle Whip salad dressing
3 tablespoons vinegar
¼ cup sugar

Combine all ingredients and store in refrigerator.

10 to 12 servings

Ruby J. Morrison, Dept. 2000
—Jacksonville

BROCCOLI SALAD

2 bunches (about 3 pounds) broccoli, stems and flowers cut into bite-size pieces
1 small red onion, thinly sliced
1 cup mayonnaise or salad dressing
1 cup sour cream
3 tablespoons vinegar
2 tablespoons sugar
½ to 1 pound bacon, cooked, drained and crumbled

Toss broccoli and red onion in large salad bowl. In medium mixing bowl, combine mayonnaise, sour cream, vinegar and sugar; mix thoroughly. Pour over vegetables and toss. Sprinkle bacon over salad. Refrigerate until served.

6 to 8 servings

Susan Portmann-Anderson, Marketing
—Kewaskum

CAULIFLOWER-BROCCOLI SALAD

1 large head cauliflower
1 large head broccoli
1 10-ounce package frozen peas, thawed
1 cup chopped celery
1 large sweet onion, chopped
Cherry tomatoes, optional

Dressing:
2 cups Miracle Whip salad dressing
1 cup sour cream
⅓ cup sugar
1 teaspoon garlic salt
1 teaspoon Spice Island Beau Monde seasoning
1 teaspoon black pepper

Cut cauliflower and broccoli into bite-size pieces. Lightly toss together all vegetables.

Combine all dressing ingredients; mix well. Gently pour over vegetables; toss until well coated. Let stand several hours before serving.

10 to 12 servings

Mary Ann Miller, Dept. 15WW
—Kewaskum

BROCCOLI-CAULIFLOWER-BACON SALAD

1 head cauliflower, uncooked, cut into bite-size pieces
1 head broccoli, uncooked, cut into bite-size pieces
½ medium to large-size red onion, cut in half rings
1 cup shredded Cheddar cheese
1 pound bacon, cut in small pieces, fried crisp and drained

Dressing:
2 cups mayonnaise
1 cup sugar
4 tablespoons vinegar

Combine salad ingredients in large bowl. Combine dressing ingredients in separate bowl. Pour over salad and stir to mix. Serve.

Shredded carrots, chopped celery, or frozen peas (thawed) may be added to salad if desired.

10 to 12 servings

Lester (and LaVerne) Schaub, Retired
—Kewaskum

CAULIFLOWER SALAD

1 head cauliflower, broken into buds
1 red onion, sliced thin
2 cups Miracle Whip salad dressing
⅓ cup sugar
¼ cup Parmesan cheese
1 pound bacon, cooked crisp and crumbled
1 head lettuce

Mix cauliflower, onion, Miracle Whip, sugar, Parmesan cheese and bacon. Refrigerate overnight for best flavor. Just before serving, shred lettuce and toss with cauliflower.

10 to 12 servings

Mary Belcher, Dept. 2000
—Jacksonville

CARROT SALAD

5 cups carrots, cut in small pieces
1 medium onion, chopped
1 small green pepper, chopped (or any other raw vegetables)
1 can tomato soup
½ cup oil
1 cup sugar
¾ cup vinegar
1 teaspoon mustard
1 teaspoon Worcestershire sauce
1 teaspoon salt
Pepper to taste

Cook carrots until tender; drain and cool. Add remaining ingredients. Marinate for 12 hours.

8 to 10 servings

Virginia Wendorff, Retired
—Kewaskum

CORN SALAD

2 15-ounce cans white corn
1 15-ounce can yellow corn
2 to 3 tomatoes, chopped
4 to 5 green onions, chopped
1 tablespoon mayonnaise

Drain corn and mix together with other ingredients. Chill before serving. Great for picnics or potlucks.

10 to 12 servings

Hank Craig
—Jacksonville

HOMINY SALAD

1 16-ounce can yellow hominy
1 16-ounce can white hominy
1 cup diced celery
2 medium green peppers, diced
2 or 3 tomatoes, cut in small pieces
½ cup chopped onions

Dressing:
1 package Italian dressing mix
2 tablespoons Worcestershire sauce
¼ teaspoon lemon pepper, optional

Combine all salad ingredients and toss lightly. Chill.

Prepare Italian dressing as directed on package replacing water with Worcestershire sauce and lemon pepper. Shake well. Pour over vegetables. Keeps well in refrigerator for several days.

8 to 10 servings

Debbie Brumbaugh, Dept. 8200
—Jacksonville

GUACAMOLE SALAD

2 ripe avocados
1 large tomato, chopped
¼ cup chopped onion
1 tablespoon vinegar
Salt and pepper to taste
Shredded lettuce
Tortilla chips

Peel and pit avocados. Process avocados, tomato and onions in food processor on high until smooth. Add vinegar, salt and pepper. Mix well. Spoon onto shredded lettuce and serve with tortilla chips.

4 to 6 servings

Donna Lindesmith, Dept. 8400
—Jacksonville

GERMAN POTATO SALAD

1 pound bacon
6 tablespoons flour
1½ cups sugar
1½ cups vinegar
1½ cups water
Salt and pepper to taste
5 pounds potatoes, cooked, peeled and sliced
1 large onion, chopped

Cut up and fry bacon. Remove bacon. To reserved grease, add flour and sugar; stir. Add vinegar and water; cook until thick. Add salt and pepper to taste. Pour over potatoes, onions and bacon. Toss lightly. Serve warm.

10 to 12 servings

Carol Darmody
—Kewaskum

FRENCH POTATO AND BEET SALAD

2 tablespoons herb or white wine
  vinegar
Salt and pepper to taste
½ cup olive oil
1½ pounds or 4 medium beets, including
  leaves
2 pounds small red potatoes
2 tablespoons dry white wine
1 tablespoon herb or white wine vinegar
1 tablespoon olive oil
Salt and pepper to taste
2 scallions, finely chopped
2 tablespoons chopped parsley

Vinaigrette: Combine herb or white wine vinegar with salt and pepper. Gradually whisk in oil; set aside.

Remove leaves from beets, leaving ½" stem. Put beets in large saucepan with cold, salted water to cover and bring to boil. Cover, reduce heat to low, and cook until just tender, about 35 minutes. Drain and cool. Peel and cut beets into ⅜" dice; set aside.

Put unpeeled potatoes in large saucepan with cold, unsalted water to cover and bring to boil. Cover and boil until potatoes are just tender, about 25 minutes. Do not overcook. Drain. While still hot, set potatoes on a cutting board and use a paring knife to peel. Cut potatoes into ⅜" dice and put into a large bowl.

In a small bowl, whisk together wine vinegar, oil and salt and pepper. Pour over potatoes, toss until thoroughly mixed. Add scallions and parsley and cool to room temperature. Rewhisk vinaigrette and add 80% to potato mixture, tossing gently. Bring vegetables to room temperature if made ahead. Adjust seasonings. Add beets to potato salad, with rest of vinaigrette. Serve at room temperature.

4 servings

Kim Peterson
—Kewaskum

GERMAN POTATO SALAD

18 small potatoes
1 onion, sliced
3 slices bacon, diced
1 rounded tablespoon flour, or
  1 level tablespoon cornstarch
1 tablespoon butter
¾ cup water
¼ cup vinegar
¼ cup sugar*
1 tablespoon salt
½ teaspoon pepper
2 or 3 hard cooked eggs, sliced, optional

Cook potatoes until done; do not overcook. Peel and slice. Add onion. Fry bacon until golden brown. Remove from pan. To bacon fat, add butter and flour. Stir and add water, vinegar, sugar, salt and pepper. Bring to boil and pour over potatoes. Stir gently. Sprinkle diced bacon on top. Garnish with egg if desired.

If using cornstarch instead of flour, add the cornstarch to some of the water and stir until smooth. To the bacon fat, add butter, vinegar, remaining water, sugar, salt and pepper. Bring to a boil and add the dissolved cornstarch and water mixture. Boil until clear and pour over potatoes.

* For diabetic salad, substitute ¼ cup Sugar Twin sweetener for the sugar.

4 to 6 servings

Laura Hammes, Retired
Gertrude Wondra, Retired
and
LaVern Geidel, Retired
—Kewaskum

ONION SALAD

1 cup sugar
½ cup vinegar
½ cup water
2 tablespoons cornstarch
1 tablespoon butter
1 pint sour cream
4 cups sliced onions

In 2-quart saucepan, over medium heat combine sugar, vinegar, water, cornstarch and butter. Cook and stir until clear and thick; cool. Stir in sour cream.

Place onions in serving bowl and pour sauce on top. Toss lightly. Refrigerate.

8 to 10 servings

Mary Ann Miller, Dept. 15WW
—Kewaskum

SPINACH-STRAWBERRY SALAD

1 pound fresh spinach
2 teaspoons butter, melted
½ cup pecan halves
1 pint strawberries, halved

Dressing:
⅓ cup raspberry vinegar
1 teaspoon salt
½ cup sugar
1 teaspoon dry mustard
1 cup oil
1½ tablespoons poppy seeds

Wash, drain and dry spinach leaves; store in plastic bag until ready to serve. Drizzle butter over pecans in shallow pan; stir to coat. Bake at 350° for 10 minutes, stirring once. Cool. Mix all ingredients in large bowl.

Blend all dressing ingredients, except poppy seeds, in blender. Stir in poppy seeds. Pour over salad and lightly toss.

6 to 8 servings

Bob Branston, Creative Services Dept.
—Kewaskum

VEGETABLE SALAD

1 16-ounce package frozen mixed vegetables
1 8-ounce package frozen green beans
½ green pepper, finely chopped
3 stalks celery, finely chopped
1 medium onion, chopped

Sauce:
¾ cup sugar
1 tablespoon cornstarch
½ cup vinegar
Dash salt
1 tablespoon mustard

Cook mixed vegetables and green beans according to directions; drain. In 3-quart bowl, combine cooked vegetables with green pepper, celery and onion.

In saucepan, combine sauce ingredients; cook and stir until thick and clear. Pour over vegetables and toss lightly. Refrigerate.

6 to 8 servings

Marty Polzean, Retired
—Kewaskum

SIMPLY DELICIOUS SALAD

1 head lettuce, finely cut
½ cup chopped red onion
½ cup chopped celery
½ cup chopped green pepper
½ cup sliced fresh mushrooms
Diced cucumber, optional
1 10-ounce package frozen peas
1 pint Hellmann's mayonnaise
1 tablespoon sugar
¾ cup grated Swiss or sharp Cheddar cheese
10 slices bacon, cooked and crumbled

In 9 x 13" pan, layer lettuce, onion, celery, green pepper, mushrooms and cucumber. Spread peas over top. Cover with layer of mayonnaise, sealing to edge of bowl. Sprinkle sugar over mayonnaise; top with grated cheese and bacon. Cover tightly and refrigerate up to 24 hours. Toss and serve.

8 servings

Eugene S. Klepek, Retired
Club Aluminum

THE PERFECT SALAD

3 heads assorted greens
Salt and pepper
Parmesan cheese, optional
Croutons, optional

Creamy Garlic Dressing:
1 large clove garlic, chopped
¼ teaspoon salt
1 tablespoon mayonnaise
1 tablespoon white wine vinegar
1½ teaspoons Dijon mustard
Pinch pepper
⅓ cup vegetable or olive oil

Cut out core or stem from lettuce; separate leaves. In cold water, gently swish leaves to clean well. Place leaves in colander or towel, shaking off excess water. Discard any wilted leaves; tear off any discolored parts. Loosely fill salad spinner half-full with greens; spin. Blot leaves gently with towel to remove any remaining moisture. Layer greens loosely between dry towels; roll up and place in plastic bag. (Greens can be prepared to this point and refrigerated for up to 5 days.)

In bowl and using back of spoon, mash garlic with salt to form paste. Whisk in mayonnaise, vinegar, mustard and pepper. Gradually whisk in oil in slow steady stream until blended. (Vinaigrette can be covered and refrigerated for up to 5 days. Whisk to reblend.) Tear enough greens into bite-size pieces to make 12 cups loosely packed. Place in salad bowl. Drizzle with dressing; toss gently just until leaves are coated and glistening. Taste and adjust seasoning with salt and pepper. Sprinkle with cheese and croutons. Serve immediately.

8 to 10 servings

Fern Vanin, Purchasing
—Orangeville

COLESLAW

1 head cabbage, cored
1 carrot

Dressing:
2½ tablespoons grated onion
2 tablespoons lemon juice
1 cup salad oil
¼ cup vinegar
2 teaspoons salt
1 tablespoon honey
2 tablespoons sugar

Shred cabbage and carrot. Put all dressing ingredients into a pint jar. Shake until mixed well. Add enough dressing to coat slaw. Chill and serve.

This recipe is from my husband's aunt who made this recipe in large quantities for weddings, banquets and such as she catered for all occasions. Through trial and error, I got it down to a family-size portion.

8 to 10 servings

Marianne Staehler, Creative Services
—Kewaskum

CABBAGE COLESLAW

2 packages Ramen chicken-flavored noodles
1 16-ounce package shredded cabbage
1 2-ounce package slivered almonds
½ cup sunflower hearts

Dressing:
1 cup oil
¾ cup sugar
½ cup white vinegar
2 seasoning packets from Ramen noodles

Break up Ramen noodles and cook according to package directions. Drain and cool. Mix together with remaining ingredients.

Dissolve sugar in oil; add remaining ingredients. Pour over coleslaw and mix well. Refrigerate.

6 to 8 servings

Pat Buechel, 16 PrCDT
—Kewaskum

BOK CHOY SALAD

2 large or 4 small bok choy
3 green onions
½ cup butter
3 or 4 3-ounce bags Ramen noodles*
¼ cup sesame seeds
½ cup sliced almonds
1 cup oil
1 cup sugar
¼ cup vinegar
2 tablespoons soy sauce

Chop bok choy and dice green onions. Put in large bowl and set aside. In 12" fry pan, melt butter. Add Ramen noodles (broken up), sesame seeds and sliced almonds. Over medium heat, fry until brown. Cool Mix together in large bowl bok choy and Ramen noodle mixture. In separate bowl, mix together oil, sugar, vinegar and soy sauce. Toss with bok choy mixture 15 minutes before serving.

* The seasoning packets included are not used; reserve for use in soups or casseroles.

6 to 8 servings

Diane Schneider, Sales Dept.
—Kewaskum

NAPPA SALAD

2 large heads nappa cabbage or romaine lettuce
1 small red onion
1 cup butter
3 packages Ramen snack noodles, reserving 1 seasoning packet (oriental)
½ cup sesame seeds
¼ cup slivered almonds
1 cup oil
3 tablespoons soy sauce
1 cup sugar
½ cup vinegar

Cut nappa in ¼" strips or tear lettuce in small pieces (different kinds of lettuce may be used, including spinach). Dice onion; mix with greens and chill.

In fry pan, melt butter over low heat. Add broken up noodles, sesame seeds, almonds and 1 seasoning packet from Ramen noodles; lightly brown. Cool before adding to salad greens.

Blend oil, soy sauce, sugar and vinegar in quart jar. Mix well. Store in refrigerator until ready to use.

6 to 8 servings

Lloyd (and Joyce) Gatzke, Industrial Engineer
—Kewaskum

VEGGIE SPAGHETTI SALAD

1 pound spaghetti
1 head broccoli, broken into flowerets
1 head cauliflower, broken into flowerets
1 small bag radishes, chopped
1 medium onion, chopped
1 pound Cheddar cheese, cubed
3 medium carrots, peeled and sliced
1 16-ounce bottle Zesty Italian dressing
Parmesan cheese

Cook spaghetti as directed; drain and rinse with cold water. Drain well. In large bowl, mix spaghetti, vegetables and Cheddar cheese. Mix well and refrigerate. Just before serving, add dressing; mix well. Sprinkle with Parmesan cheese.

8 to 10 servings

Heidi Ewerdt, Dept. 1400
—Kewaskum

SPAGHETTI SALAD

1 16-ounce package spaghetti
1 to 2 ripe tomatoes, chopped
6 to 10 radishes, chopped
4 to 6 green onions, chopped
1 to 2 bell peppers, chopped
1 to 2 cucumbers, chopped
1 16-ounce bottle Italian dressing

Cook spaghetti; drain and rinse with cool water. Drain well. Add vegetables. Pour dressing over mixture and toss well. Serve warm or chilled.

10 to 12 servings

Connie Trahern, Dept. 8300
—Jacksonville

KENT'S INCREDIBLE PASTA SALAD

1 pound penne or rotini pasta
1 bottle (approx. 2 cups) Ranch dressing
2 teaspoons Dijon mustard
½ teaspoon garlic powder
½ teaspoon dried oregano
½ teaspoon dried basil
Juice of 1 large lemon
1 medium cucumber, peeled and cut in small chunks
1 medium red bell pepper, seeded and cut in small chunks
1 medium green or yellow pepper, seeded and cut in small chunks
1 medium white or red onion, peeled and cut in small chunks
1 small bunch green onions, tops only, thinly sliced
1 can pitted black olives, thinly sliced

Cook pasta in large pot until al dente (tender but firm). Drain and rinse under cold water. Set over cooking pot until completely drained. Empty any water from pot and pour in drained pasta.

In large bowl, pour in dressing, mustard and spices. Pour lemon juice into dressing bottle and shake. Add juice to bowl and mix well. Pour dressing mixture into pasta and toss thoroughly. The vegetables can now be tossed with pasta or added just before serving.

Refrigerate 2 to 4 hours to combine flavors. Stir well just before serving.

8 to 10 servings

> *Sallie (and Kent) Myers, Receptionist*
> *—Orangeville*

GLORIFIED RICE

1 cup rice, cooked and cooled
½ cup sugar
1½ cups drained, crushed pineapple
½ teaspoon vanilla
1 cup whipped cream or Cool Whip
1 cup miniature marshmallows
Maraschino cherries, optional
Chopped nuts, optional

Mix in order given. Put cherries and nuts on top or mix in salad.

6 to 8 servings

> *Therese Rohlinger, Consumer Service*
> *—Kewaskum*

CRABBY PASTA

1 box jumbo macaroni shells
1 8-ounce package cream cheese, softened
1 12-ounce package imitation crab meat
¼ cup milk
½ cup mayonnaise or salad dressing
1 small onion, chopped
2 to 3 teaspoons horseradish sauce
Dash of Worcestershire sauce
Paprika

Cook macaroni according to directions. In mixing bowl, combine remaining ingredients; set aside. Rinse shells under cold water; place on platter and stuff each with cream cheese mixture. Sprinkle paprika on top of each shell. Garnish with greens and radish flowerets if desired.

8 to 10 servings

> *Heide Ewerdt, Dept. 1400*
> *—Kewaskum*

CRAB SALAD

1 pound spiral noodles (rotini)
1 cup peas
1 cup sliced water chestnuts, drained
1 cup chopped celery
1 pound crab meat, cut into ½" pieces
3 cups mayonnaise
1 cup water
4 teaspoons seasoned salt
2 teaspoons celery seed
Dash pepper

Boil noodles until tender; drain and rinse. Mix noodles with peas, water chestnuts, celery and crab meat. In medium bowl, combine mayonnaise, water, seasoned salt, celery seed and pepper. Mix well and refrigerate.

12 to 15 servings

> *Byrdell Schulz, Retired*
> *—Kewaskum*

WARM SALAD OF SEARED SCALLOPS AND BEANS

½ pound haricots verts (thin French green beans) trimmed*
1 pound sea-scallops
⅓ cup extra-virgin olive oil, divided
3 yellow bell peppers, cut into 2 x ¼" strips
3 orange bell peppers, cut into 2 x ¼" strips
2 large shallots, minced
3 tablespoons Sherry vinegar
½ teaspoon sugar
3 tablespoons walnut oil**
Salt
4 heads radicchio, outer leaves only
⅓ cup walnuts, toasted lightly and chopped

* available at specialty produce markets
** available at specialty food shops and some supermarkets

In saucepan of boiling, salted water, boil green beans until crisp and tender, 2 to 3 minutes. Drain beans in colander and re-fresh in cold water to stop cooking. Pat beans dry and wrap in kitchen towel. Beans may be prepared 1 day ahead and chilled, covered.

Remove tough muscle from side of each scallop if necessary. Halve scallops horizontally and pat dry. Season scallops with salt and pepper.

In a non-stick skillet large enough to hold scallops in one layer, heat 1 tablespoon olive oil over moderately high heat and saute scallops until golden, about 2 minutes on each side. Transfer scallops with a slotted spoon to a large bowl.

In skillet, heat 1 tablespoon remaining olive oil until hot but not smoking and saute bell peppers stirring until crisp-tender. Transfer bell peppers with slotted spoon to bowl with scallops.

In skillet, cook shallots in 1 tablespoon remaining olive oil over moderate heat, stirring until softened. Add vinegar, sugar, walnut oil, remaining olive oil, and salt to taste and simmer 1 minute. Remove skillet from heat and let vinaigrette cool 5 minutes.

Divide radicchio among eight plates. Add beans and vinaigrette to scallop mixture and toss gently. Divide salad among plates and sprinkle with walnuts.

8 servings

L.N. (and Pat) Peterson
Founder Chairman of the Board

CALICO CHICKEN SALAD

Dressing:
½ cup mayonnaise
1 4-ounce package cream cheese
2 tablespoons oil
2 teaspoons lemon juice
1 teaspoon dry Italian seasoning
¼ teaspoon black pepper

Salad:
5 chicken leg quarters
1 quart water
4 chicken bouillon cubes
½ teaspoon salt
½ teaspoon garlic powder
½ cup chopped green bell pepper
5 green onions, sliced (tops included)
¼ cup sliced pimientos
¼ cup sliced ripe olives
1 4.5-ounce sliced mushrooms, drained

Garnish:
Curly lettuce leaves
1 medium tomato cut into 12 wedges
13 ripe olives

In blender, combine all dressing ingredients; mix well. Refrigerate until needed.

Boil chicken in water with bouillon, salt, and garlic powder until tender. Cool, de-bone and cut into bite-size pieces; enough for 3 cups. Add vegetables and toss with dressing. On round platter, place lettuce leaves on bottom, spoon salad into center and place tomato wedges around edge. Put one olive on top of salad and arrange remaining olives between the tomato wedges.

4 servings

Jack (and Betty) Stivers, Purchasing Agent
—Jacksonville

CURRY CHICKEN SALAD

4 cups cooked and diced chicken
1 cup diced celery
½ cup toasted broken pecans
2 cups cold cooked rice
⅔ cup salad dressing
⅓ cup creamy French dressing
½ teaspoon salt
Dash of pepper
1 teaspoon curry powder
2 11-ounce cans mandarin oranges,
   drained

Combine chicken, celery, pecans and rice; set aside. Mix together salad dressing, French dressing, salt, pepper and curry powder; pour over chicken mixture and stir well. Chill several hours. Just before serving, fold in oranges.

8 to 10 servings

Jim (and Helen) Portmann, Retired-Sales
—Minneapolis

TEXAS TACO SALAD

1½ pounds ground beef
Salt and pepper to taste
1 onion, minced
1 large can ranch-style beans, drained
1 16-ounce can Spanish rice
1 4-ounce can diced green chiles
2 tablespoons Picante sauce
1 cup cubed American processed cheese
Tortilla chips

Brown meat seasoned with salt, pepper and onion. Add beans, rice, chiles and Picante sauce. Mix well. Stir in cheese. Let simmer until cheese is melted. Serve on tortilla chips.

10 to 12 servings

Donna Lindesmith, Dept. 8400
—Jacksonville

DORITOS SALAD

1 large bag Doritos
1 large head lettuce, bite-size pieces
3 tomatoes, diced
1 8-ounce package shredded Cheddar
   cheese
1 15-ounce can whole kernel corn,
   drained
1 16-ounce bottle Catalina salad dressing

In large mixing bowl, crumble Doritos; add lettuce, tomatoes and cheese. Just before serving, add corn and top with dressing.

10 to 12 servings

Anita Cassidy, Dept. 8400
—Jacksonville

TACO SALAD

1 to 1½ pounds ground chuck
1 1¼-ounce package taco seasoning
⅔ cup water
1 head lettuce
2 to 3 large tomatoes
1 16-ounce can pitted black olives
1 medium-size bag Frito corn chips
1 medium-size bag Kraft shredded
   medium Cheddar cheese
1 16-ounce can refried beans
1 12-ounce container sour cream
1 12-ounce jar salsa

In large skillet, brown ground chuck on medium heat; drain grease. Add taco seasoning and water and bring to boil; turn heat to low and simmer for 10 minutes.

Shred lettuce, dice tomatoes and slice olives. In large bowl, layer bottom with corn chips. Top with 2 to 3 heaping spoonfuls of ground chuck, followed by layers of cheese, lettuce, tomatoes and black olives. Repeat until all of corn chips and ground chuck is used. Serve with heated refried beans, sour cream and salsa.

10 to 12 servings

Linda Hodges
—Pigeon Forge, TN

TACO SALAD

1½ pounds ground beef
¼ cup water
1 1¼-ounce package dry taco seasoning
1 head lettuce, cut into 1" pieces
1 tomato, chopped
1 16-ounce can medium black olives, pitted, drained
1 medium onion, diced
¼ cup chopped green pepper
1 16-ounce bottle Western salad dressing
1 12-ounce package shredded Cheddar cheese
1 12-ounce package taco chips, slightly crushed

In fry pan, brown ground beef. Add water and taco seasoning; mix well and cool. Add remaining ingredients and serve immediately.

10 to 12 servings

Leo and Bev Emmer
—Kewaskum

KITTY'S TACO SALAD

2 pounds ground beef
2 onions, diced
2 1¼-ounce packages taco seasoning (Lawry's)
Salt and pepper to taste
1 head lettuce, cut up
1 pound mild Brick cheese, grated
1 16-ounce can kidney beans, drained
1 4-ounce can sliced black olives, drained
1 green pepper, diced
3 tomatoes, cut up
1 8-ounce package corn chips, crumbled
Western French dressing

Brown hamburger, onions and seasoning. Add salt and pepper to taste. Cool. Add lettuce, cheese, kidney beans, black olives, green pepper, tomatoes and chips. Mix with dressing until moist.

8 to 12 servings

Kitty Krueger, Retired
—Kewaskum

FRESH CRANBERRY RELISH

1 12-ounce package cranberries
1 medium orange
2 medium Cortland apples
¾ to 1 cup sugar

Cut unpeeled orange and apples into eighths. Remove seeds and cores. In food processor, process cranberries, orange and apples, one-half at a time, pulsing until evenly chopped. Transfer to 1½-quart bowl. Repeat with remaining cranberries, orange and apple slices. Stir in sugar, or sugar substitute, to desired sweetness.

Makes about 3 cups

Ernie Haegler, Retired
—Kewaskum

PICKLED CARROTS

18 carrots
1 tablespoon canning salt
1 quart water
4 cups sugar
¼ cup prepared mustard
1 tablespoon pickling spices
2 cups vinegar

Cut carrots in quarter lengths. Put in kettle with salt and water and boil until tender. Drain, reserving 1 pint liquid. In large soup pot, combine reserved liquid, sugar, mustard, spices and vinegar; bring to boil. Add carrots and boil for 15 minutes. Spoon into sterilized jars; seal and cool to room temperature.

Makes 2 quarts

Margaret Schneider, Retired
—Kewaskum

CREAMY PARMESAN PEPPERCORN SALAD DRESSING

2 cups mayonnaise (not salad dressing)
1 cup grated Parmesan cheese
1 cup buttermilk
2 tablespoons red wine vinegar
2 to 3 teaspoons coarsely cracked peppercorns
2 teaspoons lemon juice
1 teaspoon minced garlic
1 teaspoon Worcestershire sauce

In large bowl, combine all ingredients. Cover and refrigerate.

Makes 1 quart

Susan Portmann-Anderson, Marketing
—Kewaskum

COOKED SALAD DRESSING

3 tablespoons flour
1 teaspoon salt
½ teaspoon dry mustard
½ teaspoon paprika
2 eggs, well beaten
½ cup vinegar
½ cup water

Mix dry ingredients together and add to eggs. Add vinegar and water slowly. Stir and cook until thick and smooth. Cool.

(Use on favorite greens or vegetable salads.)

Makes about 1 cup

Rita Felton, Retired
—Wooster

HOT HONEY-BACON SALAD DRESSING

1 cup sugar
½ teaspoon dry mustard
½ teaspoon paprika, optional
⅜ teaspoon salt
1½ tablespoons lemon juice
¾ tablespoon celery seed
½ tablespoon grated onion
½ cup honey
½ cup vinegar
1½ cups oil
6 slices bacon, cooked crisp and crumbled

Mix together sugar and mustard. Add remaining ingredients; stirring slowly as oil is added. Put in jar and store in refrigerator. Use with spinach salad.

Makes about 1 quart

Darlene Pesch
—Kewaskum

C H A P T E R   I I I

VEGETABLES & SIDE DISHES

*Concave covers on early pans ensured
easy stackability*

POPPED ASPARAGUS

1 to 1½ pounds asparagus
1 tablespoon Accent food enhancer
1 tablespoon soy sauce
1 tablespoon oil

Cut asparagus into 1" pieces; set aside. In large fry pan or wok, combine remaining ingredients. Heat pan over medium-high heat, about 2 to 3 minutes. Add asparagus and stir-fry until crispy-tender, 3 to 4 minutes.

4 to 5 servings

Susan Portmann-Anderson, Marketing
—Kewaskum

CALICO BEANS

½ pound bacon, cut up
½ pound ground beef
1 cup chopped onion
1 clove garlic or ¼ teaspoon garlic powder
½ cup catsup
¾ cup brown sugar
½ cup sugar
2 teaspoons vinegar
2 tablespoons molasses
1 16-ounce can lima beans, drained
1 16-ounce can Great Northern beans, drained
1 16-ounce can pork and beans with juice

Cook bacon until crispy; drain. Brown meat with onion and garlic. Mix together with remaining ingredients; spoon into large baking dish. Bake at 350° for 1 hour or in slow cooker on high for 3 hours.

10 to 12 servings

Jean Prost, Sales
—Kewaskum

SWEET AND SOUR BEANS

This recipe belonged to our grandmother and is still a family favorite. A great recipe with a pork or beef dinner.

1 quart French-cut green beans
¼ pound bacon
1 teaspoon salt
¼ teaspoon pepper
¾ cup vinegar
¾ cup sugar
¼ cup water

Cook beans over low heat and drain. Cut bacon into small ¼ x ¼" pieces; fry over low heat. When crisp, pour beans into fry pan (do not remove grease). Add remainder of ingredients. Mix well.

Note: We do not use Heinz vinegar, the flavor is too strong.

4 to 6 servings

Lloyd and Lewis Gatzke
—Kewaskum

DUFFY'S BLACK-EYED PEA CASSEROLE

1 pound ground beef
Accent seasoning to taste
Salt and pepper to taste
2 16-ounce cans black-eyed peas
2 16-ounce cans black-eyed peas with jalapeno peppers
1 10-ounce can cream of chicken soup
1 10-ounce can cream of mushroom soup
1 8-ounce jar mild picante sauce
1 12-ounce bag Doritos corn chips
2 cups shredded Cheddar cheese

Lightly brown and season ground beef; set aside. Drain all juice from black-eyed peas. In large mixing bowl, combine peas, soups, picante sauce and ground beef. Place in casserole dish; crush or layer corn chips on top of mixture; top with cheese. Bake at 300° for 30 minutes, until cheese melts.

8 to 10 servings

Katherine Duffy, Saladmaster, Inc.
—Arlington, TX

GREEN BEAN CASSEROLE

1 10¾-ounce can cream of mushroom
  soup
¼ to ½ cup milk
1 teaspoon soy sauce
Dash pepper
4 cups cooked, cut beans (2 16-ounce
  cans, drained) OR
  1 16 or 20-ounce bag frozen green
  beans, cooked
1 2.8-ounce can Durkee French fried
  onions, divided

In 1½ quart casserole, combine soup, milk,
soy sauce and pepper. Stir in beans and ½
can onions. Bake at 350° for 25 minutes or
until hot and bubbling; stir. Top with
remaining fried onions and bake 5 minutes
until onions are golden brown.

6 servings

Catherine Speer, Dept. 9500
—Jacksonville
and
Anna Schaeffer, Dept. 15WW
—Kewaskum

HAMBURGER WITH
BAKED BEANS

2 strips bacon, cut in small pieces
1 medium onion, chopped
1 pound ground beef
3 16-ounce cans pork and beans
½ cup molasses
½ cup catsup
½ teaspoon dry mustard
Salt to taste
Worcestershire to taste

Saute bacon and onion; add ground beef
and brown. Drain well. In mixing bowl,
combine beef, pork and beans, molasses,
catsup, dry mustard, salt and Worcestershire. Mix and pour into casserole and bake
at 375° for 30 minutes.

12 to 16 servings

Kathy (and Rick) Zugel, Sales
—Atlanta

BAKED BEANS
WITH GROUND BEEF

1½ pounds ground chuck
1 medium onion, finely chopped
Salt, pepper and garlic powder to taste
2 16-ounce cans Van Camps pork and
  beans
2 16-ounce cans ranch-style beans
¼ cup light brown sugar
¼ cup sorghum molasses
2 tablespoons prepared yellow mustard
¾ cup catsup

In fry pan, brown ground chuck, onion and
seasonings; set aside to cool. Combine
remaining ingredients; mixing well. Add
meat mixture. Pour into 4-quart casserole
and bake at 350° for 45 minutes.

10 to 12 servings

Carolyn Lessley, Saladmaster, Inc.
—Arlington, TX

BROCCOLI CASSEROLE

1 cup diced celery
1 medium onion, diced
1 cup diced green pepper, optional
2 tablespoons margarine
1 16 to 20-ounce package frozen chopped
  broccoli
1 10-ounce can cream of mushroom soup
1 10-ounce can cream of chicken soup
1 cup Minute rice, uncooked
Grated Cheddar cheese

Saute celery, onion and green pepper in
margarine until lightly browned. Mix in
frozen broccoli, soups and rice. Pour into
buttered casserole dish and top with
cheese. Bake at 350° for 45 minutes.

8 to 10 servings

Gord McLauchlin, Vice President-Sales
—Canada

BROCCOLI-RAVIOLI BAKE

1 40-ounce can Chef Boyardee beef
  ravioli
1 8-ounce container sour cream
1 10-ounce package chopped broccoli
1 cup shredded Mozzarella cheese

Mix together ravioli and sour cream. Place broccoli in lightly oiled baking dish and cover with ravioli mixture. Top with cheese. Bake at 375° for 25 minutes.

6 to 8 servings

Michael Hendricks, Dept. 900
—Kewaskum

BROCCOLI RICE CASSEROLE

1 medium onion, chopped
1 10-ounce package frozen chopped
  broccoli
½ cup margarine
1 10¾-ounce can cream of chicken soup
½ cup Cheez Whiz
½ cup milk
1½ cups quick cooking rice

In skillet, saute onion and broccoli in margarine. Stir occasionally, cooking until onion is transparent and broccoli is thawed. Add soup, Cheez Whiz and milk; blend well and remove from heat. Cook rice according to package directions; add to broccoli mixture. Pour into buttered 2½-quart casserole and bake at 350° for 30 minutes.

6 to 8 servings

Shari Bickell, Dept. 2000
—Jacksonville

BROCCOLI RICE BAKE

1 10-ounce package frozen chopped
  broccoli
2 tablespoons water
½ teaspoon salt
½ cup chopped onions
1 tablespoon butter
1 10-ounce can cream of mushroom soup
2 cups cooked rice
1 cup grated Cheddar cheese

Place broccoli, water and salt in saucepan and cook until tender; drain. Saute onions in butter until soft but not brown. In large mixing bowl, combine broccoli, soup and rice; mix well. Pour into buttered 1½ quart casserole dish. Top with cheese. Bake at 350° for 30 minutes.

6 servings

Jean Dippel, Retired
—Kewaskum

BROCCOLI AND CAULIFLOWER
with Horseradish Bread Crumbs

1½ bunches broccoli (about 1½ pounds)
1 large head cauliflower (about 2
  pounds)
1 tablespoon oil
3 tablespoons unsalted butter, divided
2 cups very coarse dry bread crumbs
2 tablespoons drained bottled
  horseradish

Trim broccoli and cauliflower and cut flowerets into 1" pieces. (There should be at least 5 cups each.)

In large saucepan of boiling, salted water, cook vegetables until crisp-tender, 3 to 5 minutes. In a colander, drain vegetables and refresh under cold water to stop cooking. Drain vegetables well. Vegetables may be prepared up to this point 1 day ahead and chilled, covered.

In large heavy skillet, heat oil and 2 tablespoons butter over moderately high heat until foam begins to subside and saute bread crumbs, stirring until golden. Stir in horseradish and salt to taste and saute, stirring, until crisp. Bread crumbs may be prepared 3 days ahead and kept in an airtight container.

Preheat oven to 350°. In skillet, melt remaining tablespoon butter over moderate heat and add vegetables with salt and pepper to taste. Sprinkle vegetables with bread crumbs and toss to combine. Transfer mixture to a baking dish and bake uncovered 10 minutes or until just heated through.

8 servings

Pat (Mrs. L.N.) Peterson
—Kewaskum

CAULIFLOWER AND BROCCOLI CASSEROLE

½ pound fresh broccoli or 1 10-ounce package frozen
½ medium head cauliflower, in florets
3 tablespoons butter, divided
½ cup chopped onion
2 tablespoons flour
¼ teaspoon salt
¼ teaspoon pepper
1 cup milk
½ cup grated Cheddar cheese
½ cup bread crumbs

Steam or cook broccoli and cauliflower just until tender; drain. In saucepan, melt 2 tablespoons butter; saute onion until tender. Stir in flour, salt and pepper; gradually stir in milk. Cook, stirring until thickened and bubbly.

Place broccoli and cauliflower in 6-cup casserole dish. Pour sauce over and mix lightly. Sprinkle with cheese and bread crumbs. Dot with remaining butter. Bake at 350° for 20 minutes or until top is golden.

6 servings

Fern Vanin, Purchasing
—Orangeville

BROCCOLI-CAULIFLOWER CASSEROLE

1 16-ounce package frozen broccoli
1 16-ounce package frozen cauliflower
1 4-ounce can sliced water chestnuts
1 10-ounce can cream of chicken soup
1 10-ounce can cream of celery soup
1 8-ounce jar Cheez Whiz
1 2.8-ounce can Durkee French fried onions

Steam broccoli and cauliflower until tender; drain. Combine vegetables, water chestnuts, soups and Cheez Whiz; pour into casserole dish and top with fried onions. Bake at 350° for 20 to 30 minutes.

10 to 12 servings

Rose Ketter, Retired
—Kewaskum

CAULIFLOWER CASSEROLE

1 head cauliflower, broken into bite-size pieces
1 large onion, sliced and split into rings
1 cup sliced fresh mushrooms
1 cup butter, divided
½ cup grated Cheddar cheese
¼ cup flour
1 teaspoon salt
1 teaspoon dry mustard
2 cups milk

Cook cauliflower in salt water until tender; drain. Saute onions and mushrooms in ½ cup butter until tender. Remove onions and mushrooms; melt remaining butter in drippings. Blend in flour, salt and mustard. Add milk and cook until thick. Arrange cauliflower in 1½ quart casserole dish; top with half the sauce and sprinkle with half the full amount of cheese. Add onion and mushroom mixture and top with remaining sauce and cheese. Bake at 350° for 25 minutes.

6 to 8 servings

Pat Buechel, 16 PR-CDT
—Kewaskum

SERBIAN CABBAGE

1 medium cabbage, about 3 pounds, shredded
1 13-ounce can evaporated milk
1 teaspoon salt
¼ teaspoon pepper
1 cup dry bread crumbs
⅓ cup butter

Place cabbage in shallow, greased 4-quart casserole. Pour milk over cabbage; sprinkle with salt, pepper and bread crumbs. Dot with butter. Cover and bake at 350° for 30 minutes. Uncover and bake another 30 minutes, until cabbage is tender and crumbs are browned.

8-10 servings

Adeline Halfmann, Retired
—Kewaskum

ROTKOHL MIT APFELN
(Cabbage with Apples)

2½ pounds red cabbage
⅔ cup red wine vinegar
2 tablespoons sugar
2 teaspoons salt
2 tablespoons bacon fat or lard
2 medium cooking apples, cored and cut into ⅛" wedges
½ cup finely chopped onions
1 whole onion stuck with 2 whole cloves
1 small bay leaf
4 cups boiling water
3 tablespoons dry red wine
3 tablespoons red currant jelly, optional

Wash cabbage under cold running water; remove tough outer leaves and cut cabbage in quarters. Cut out core and slice quarters crosswise into ⅛" wide strips or shreds. Drop cabbage into large mixing bowl. Sprinkle with vinegar, sugar and salt; toss with a spoon to coat evenly. In large casserole, melt lard; add apples and onions and cook, stirring frequently for 5 minutes or until apples are lightly browned.

Add cabbage, whole onion and bay leaf; stir thoroughly and pour in boiling water. Bring to a boil over high heat, stirring occasionally, and reduce heat to low. Cover and simmer for 1½ to 2 hours, or until cabbage is tender. Check from time to time to make sure that cabbage is moist. If it seems dry, add a tablespoon of boiling water.

When cabbage is done, there should no liquid left in the casserole. Just before serving, remove onion and bay leaf and stir in wine and jelly. Taste for seasoning and serve.

6 servings

Kim Peterson
—Kewaskum

ZIPPY BAKED CARROTS

1 onion, minced
½ cup butter, divided
5 tablespoons flour
Salt and pepper to taste
2 cups milk
5 cups peeled and sliced carrots, cooked
1 cup shredded Cheddar cheese
1 pound bacon, diced and fried crisp
2 cups soft bread cubes

Saute onion in ¼ cup butter for 2 to 3 minutes; remove from heat and add flour, salt and pepper. Gradually add milk. Cook on low heat until thickened, stirring frequently. Place half the carrots in casserole dish, top with half the white sauce; repeat layers. Sprinkle cheese and bacon over top. Mix together bread cubes and remaining ¼ cup melted butter; spread over top. Bake at 350° for 15 to 20 minutes or until golden brown.

6 to 8 servings

Jill Zimdahl, Dept. 1500
—Kewaskum

RUTABAGA AND CARROTS GRATIN

4 cups diced rutabaga, ¾" dice
3 medium carrots, peeled, ¼" slices
1 teaspoon grated gingerroot
1 large clove garlic, minced
1½ cups water
2 tablespoons butter
3 tablespoons flour
2 cups milk or light cream
Salt and pepper
⅓ cup shredded Swiss cheese
⅓ cup fresh white bread crumbs
1 tablespoon minced fresh parsley

Steam-cook rutabaga, carrots, ginger and garlic, using 1½ cups water for 10 minutes until nearly tender. With slotted spoon, remove vegetables to greased 2½-quart casserole. Boil the cooking liquid until reduced to ¼ cup.

In heavyweight 2-quart saucepan, over medium heat, melt butter. Stir in flour and cook until bubbly, about 2 minutes. Remove from heat and stir in hot vegetable liquid and milk. Simmer 2 minutes. Season to taste. Pour over vegetables in casserole, mixing to coat vegetables. Top with cheese, bread crumbs and parsley. Bake, covered at 325° for 1 hour; remove cover and continue baking 30 to 40 minutes.

6 to 8 servings

Adeline Halfmann, Retired
—Kewaskum

CORN CASSEROLE

1 16-ounce can creamed corn
1 16-ounce can kernel corn
1 10-ounce package frozen chopped broccoli, thawed and drained
½ cup butter, melted
1½ cups crushed Chicken-in-a-Biscuit crackers, divided
Salt and pepper to taste

Combine creamed corn, kernel corn and broccoli. Add butter and mix well. Stir in half of the crackers; salt and pepper to taste. Pour into a buttered casserole dish and sprinkle remaining crackers on top. Bake at 350° for 30 minutes.

6 to 8 servings

Bill (and Lucy) McCarty, Retired
—Kewaskum

MUSHROOM CASSEROLE

1 pound fresh mushrooms
2 cups seasoned croutons
½ cup butter, divided
1 small onion, chopped
1 10-ounce can cream of mushroom soup
1 cup grated Parmesan cheese

Save some mushroom caps for topping. Cut remainder of mushrooms into large pieces. Brown the croutons in half the butter. Spread in ungreased 8 x 8" pan. Saute onion and mushrooms in remaining butter. Spread evenly over croutons. Spread undiluted soup evenly over top. Arrange mushroom caps over top of this. Sprinkle heavily with Parmesan cheese. Bake uncovered at 350° for 30 to 40 minutes. Let stand 5 minutes before serving.

6 to 8 servings

Doris Wesenberg, Retired
Janine Matenaer, Credit Dept.
and
Henrietta Gremminger, Retired
—Kewaskum

COUSCOUS AND MUSHROOMS

2½ cups water
1 teaspoon salt
1¾ cups couscous
2 tablespoons olive oil, divided
6 to 8 green onions, sliced
½ cup thinly sliced celery
¼ cup chopped green bell pepper
¼ cup chopped red bell pepper
1 tablespoon butter
8 ounces fresh mushrooms, sliced
¼ cup minced parsley

In 3-quart saucepan, bring water to boil. Stir in salt and couscous; return to boil. Cover, remove from heat and let stand 7 minutes.

In 10" fry pan, heat 1 tablespoon olive oil over medium-high heat. Saute onions, celery and peppers until crisp-tender, stirring frequently. Add remaining olive oil, butter and mushrooms. Cook and stir until mushrooms are opaque. Fluff couscous with fork; add vegetable mixture and parsley. Toss with fork to mix well. Serve hot.

6 servings

Adeline Halfmann, Retired
—Kewaskum

BAKED ONION DELIGHT

6 large Texas sweet onions, sliced
1 3.75-ounce bag potato chips, crushed
8 ounces shredded Wisconsin Cheddar
  cheese
2 10-ounce cans cream of mushroom
  soup
½ cup milk
⅛ teaspoon cayenne powder (red pepper)

In greased 9 x 13" baking pan, layer half the onions, chips and cheese; repeat layers with remainder. Mix soup and milk together; spoon over layers. Sprinkle red pepper over top. Bake at 350° for 35-45 minutes.

8 to 10 servings

Skip Hillary, Sales
—Texas

ONION CASSEROLE

3 to 4 large Vidalia onions, chopped
¼ cup butter or margarine
20 Ritz crackers, crushed
1 cup shredded Parmesan cheese

Saute onions in butter. Layer in casserole dish half the amount of onions, half the amount of crackers and half the amount of cheese. Repeat layers. Bake at 325° for 30 minutes or until golden brown.

6 to 8 servings

Rose Ketter, Retired
—Kewaskum

BAKED POTATO CHUNKS

1 pound red potatoes, cut into small
  chunks
⅓ cup oil
½ package onion soup mix

Put all ingredients in plastic bag and shake to coat potatoes. Spread potatoes in baking dish; bake at 450° for 30 to 40 minutes.

4 to 6 servings

Jill Zimdahl, Dept. 1500
—Kewaskum

GOLDEN POTATO BAKE

1 cup cornflake crumbs
½ teaspoon salt
4 to 6 medium potatoes, peeled
2 tablespoons butter, melted

Preheat oven to 375°. Mix cornflakes and salt. Brush potatoes with butter and coat with crumbs. Arrange potatoes in 9 x 9" pan. Bake at 375° for 1 hour or until tender.

4 to 6 servings

Marilyn Loomis, 15 East Line
—Kewaskum

CHEESEY SCALLOPED POTATOES

2 tablespoons flour
2½ cups milk
2 tablespoons butter
1½ teaspoons salt
1 10¾-ounce can Cheddar cheese soup
1 tablespoon chopped onion, optional
8 medium-size potatoes, thinly sliced
  (about 8 cups)

In 2-quart saucepan, whisk flour and milk until blended. Add butter, salt, soup and onion. Cook over medium heat until sauce thickens; stirring constantly. Add potatoes and heat with occasional stirring until sauce boils again. Pour potatoes and sauce into greased casserole, cover and bake at 350° for 30 minutes or until potatoes are tender. Or cook potatoes in a slow cooker for 3 to 4 hours.

6 to 8 servings

Philip Zingsheim, Retired
—Kewaskum

CHEESEY POTATOES

6 large potatoes
⅓ cup butter
¼ cup flour
½ cup grated Parmesan cheese
¾ teaspoon salt
Pepper to taste

Pare and quarter potatoes. Melt butter in 9 x 13" pan. Combine flour, cheese, salt and pepper in plastic bag; add potatoes and shake until well coated. Arrange in pan. Bake at 375° for 1 hour.

6 to 8 servings

In memory of James Lance, Millwright
—Wooster

BAKED MASHED POTATOES

10 to 12 medium potatoes
1 8-ounce carton sour cream
1 8-ounce package cream cheese, softened
Garlic salt
3 to 4 tablespoons milk
1 2.8-ounce can French fried onions

Cook potatoes, mash and add all above ingredients, except fried onions. Spoon into buttered baking dish. Bake uncovered at 350° for 1 hour. Top with fried onions for last 5 minutes of baking.

6 to 8 servings

Randy Gartman
—Kewaskum

POTATO CASSEROLE

8 large red potatoes
1 cup milk
½ pint whipping cream (not whipped)
1 teaspoon dry mustard
1½ teaspoons salt
Pepper to taste
½ cup chopped onion
4 ounces shredded Cheddar cheese
4 ounces shredded mild cheese
Paprika

Boil potatoes with skins on until almost tender, but not soft; cool. Peel and shred potatoes into greased 9 x 13" baking dish. Preheat oven to 325°.

In saucepan over low heat, cook remaining ingredients, except paprika, until cheese melts; stir frequently. Pour over potatoes;

sprinkle with paprika. Bake 1 hour.

8 to 10 servings

Barbara Nelson, Nationwide Acceptance Corp.
—Arlington, TX

CHEESEY POTATOES

2 pounds frozen hash brown potatoes
½ cup chopped onions
1 cup butter, divided, melted
1 10-ounce can cream of chicken soup
1 8-ounce jar Cheez Whiz
1 cup sour cream
2 cups crushed cornflakes

Spread potatoes and onions in 9 x 13" pan. Drizzle ½ cup melted butter over top. In bowl, mix soup, cheese and sour cream; pour over potatoes and onions. Mix corn-flakes with remaining melted butter and spread over top. Bake at 350° for 45 minutes.

10 to 12 servings

Cindy L. Molter, 16 DR-CDT-M-Line
—Kewaskum

VERY GOOD POTATOES

2 pounds frozen hash brown potatoes
½ cup butter, melted
1 pint sour cream
1 10-ounce can cream of chicken soup
8 ounces shredded Cheddar cheese
2 cups crushed cornflakes
2 tablespoons butter, melted

Combine potatoes, ½ cup butter, sour cream, soup and cheese; pour into 9 x 13" pan. Top with cornflakes; drizzle butter over top. Bake at 350° for 1½ hours.

10 to 12 servings

Philip Zingsheim, Retired
—Kewaskum

T & T's FAVORITE BREAKFAST DISH

1 12-ounce package frozen hash browns (can use fresh diced potatoes)
6 eggs
⅓ cup cream or milk
1 cup (4 ounces) shredded cheese
2 tablespoons chopped onion
Salt and pepper to taste
1 cup chopped ham

Put potatoes in 8" square pan and cover with plastic wrap. Microwave 6 to 7 minutes; stir once. In mixing bowl, combine eggs and cream; beat well. Add cheese, onions, salt, pepper and ham; pour over potatoes and mix well. Cover with waxed paper and microwave on medium (50%) for 12 minutes; rotate dish once. Adjust temperature to high for 3 to 4 minutes or until set and cooked through. Let stand in oven 5 minutes; remove and cut into squares. Hint: This can be cooked a day ahead and reheated.

6 to 8 servings

Annie Shaske
—Kewaskum

POTATO CASSEROLE

½ cup plus 2 tablespoons melted margarine, divided
1 can cream of chicken soup
½ 12-ounce can evaporated milk
1 pint sour cream
½ cup chopped onions
9 cups hash brown potatoes
2 cups grated cheese
1 cup crushed cornflakes

Grease 9 x 13" pan and put half the hash browns on bottom. Mix together ½ cup melted margarine, soup, milk, sour cream and onions. Pour half this mixture over potatoes. Sprinkle half the grated cheese over onion layer. Add remaining hash browns and pour remaining sauce over top. Sprinkle with remaining cheese. Top with cornflakes and drizzle with 2 tablespoons

melted butter. Bake at 350° for 45 to 50 minutes.

10 to 12 servings
Lloyd Teeselink, Retired-Shipping Dept.
—Kewaskum

POTATO CASSEROLE

¾ cup butter, divided
2 pounds frozen hash brown potatoes
2 cups shredded Cheddar cheese
½ cup chopped onion
1 16-ounce carton sour cream
2 10-ounce cans cream of chicken soup
½ teaspoon salt
2 cups crushed cornflakes

Melt ½ cup butter and pour over potatoes in shallow 9 x 13" dish. Combine remaining ingredients except ¼ cup butter and cornflakes; mix. Pour over potatoes. Melt remaining ¼ cup butter and mix with cornflakes; spread on top. Bake uncovered at 350° for 1 hour.

10 to 12 servings
Anita Cassidy, Dept. 8400—Supervisor
—Jacksonville

BAKED HASH BROWNS

2 pounds frozen hash browns, thawed
2 10¾-ounce cans cream of celery or mushroom soup
1 cup sour cream or sour half & half
½ cup chopped onion
1 tablespoon dried parsley flakes
¾ teaspoon salt
½ teaspoon pepper
1 cup (4 ounces) shredded Cheddar cheese

Preheat oven to 325°. Spread potatoes into greased 9 x 13" pan. In large mixing bowl, combine soup, sour cream, onion, parsley flakes, salt and pepper. Spread evenly over potatoes. Sprinkle cheese on top. Bake uncovered for 1 to 1½ hours.

Hint: This casserole can be made ahead, covered and refrigerated up to 24 hours.

8 to 10 servings
Susan Portmann-Anderson, Marketing
—Kewaskum

SOUTHERN POTATOES

1 2-pound bag frozen southern hash
  browns
½ cup chopped onion
1 10-ounce can cream of chicken soup
1 pint sour cream
½ cup butter, melted
1 cup (or more) grated sharp Cheddar or
  Colby cheese

Topping:
1 cup crushed cornflakes
¼ cup butter, melted

Mix together hash browns, onion, soup,
sour cream, butter and cheese. Put into
greased 9 x 13" pan. Top with cornflakes
and butter. Bake at 350° for 1 hour.

10 to 12 servings

Randy Gartman
—Kewaskum

ZUCCHINI FRITTERS

1½ cups flour
2 teaspoons baking powder
¾ teaspoon salt
1 cup milk
1 egg, beaten
1 cup shredded zucchini
Oil for deep frying

In bowl, mix flour, baking powder and salt.
Mix milk, egg and zucchini. Add to dry
ingredients. Mix until moistened. Drop by
tablespoonfuls into deep, hot oil. Fry 3 to 4
minutes until golden brown. Serve hot; top
with butter or cheese sauce.

Makes 24

Nancy White, Nationwide Acceptance
—Arlington, TX

ZUCCHINI CASSEROLE

1 large or 2 small zucchini, sliced
3 tablespoons butter
4 tablespoons flour
2 cups chopped tomatoes
1 small green pepper, diced
1 medium onion, chopped
1 teaspoon salt
Pepper to taste
Parmesan cheese

Place squash in greased baking dish. In fry
pan, melt butter; add flour, tomatoes,
green pepper, onion, salt and pepper. Cook
5 minutes. Pour over squash. Dot with
butter and sprinkle with cheese. Bake at
350° for 45 minutes.

6 to 8 servings

Mary Ann Miller, Dept. 15WW
—Kewaskum

ZUCCHINI SURPRISE

½ cup chopped onion
1 cup Bisquick baking mix
½ cup Parmesan cheese
2 tablespoons parsley flakes
½ teaspoon salt
½ teaspoon oregano
½ teaspoon seasoned salt
½ cup vegetable oil
4 eggs, slightly beaten
Dash pepper and garlic
3 cups thinly sliced, unpeeled zucchini (2
  medium-sized)

Mix together all ingredients except zucchini. Stir in zucchini. Place in greased 9 x
13" baking dish. Bake uncovered at 350° for
20 to 25 minutes or until golden brown.

8 to 10 servings

Rhonda Ivey, Sales Dept.
—Orangeville

VEGETABLE HARVEST CASSEROLE

Here's my adaptation of a vegetable sidedish recipe that appeared in Southern Living Magazine about 10 years ago. Make two and freeze one for later use. I don't recommend baking all in one large roaster because the vegetables would not bake evenly.

4 large onions, sliced ¾" thick, separated into rings
3 large bell peppers, cut in ¼" strips (red, green or yellow)
¼ canola or olive oil
2 cups water
1 cup barley
2 tablespoons beef bouillon granules, optional
6 large carrots, ½" chunks
3 small zucchini, 1½" chunks
3 small yellow summer squash, 1½" chunks
1½ pounds green beans, 1" pieces
1 small bunch broccoli, 1" chunks, split stems
1 small head cauliflower, 1" chunks
⅓ cup lemon juice
3 garlic cloves, minced
1 tablespoon salt
2 teaspoons paprika
½ teaspoon ground black pepper
½ cup minced fresh parsley

In large fry pan over medium heat, brown onions and bell peppers in oil for 7 to 8 minutes, stirring occasionally. Coat two 9 x 13" baking dishes with vegetable spray. In each combine 1 cup water, ½ cup barley, 1 tablespoon bouillon. Top each with half the vegetables, then half the onion and pepper mixture. In cup, combine lemon juice and garlic; pour half over each pan. Sprinkle each with half the salt, paprika and pepper. Cover pans with aluminum foil and bake at 375° for 1 hour. If freezing one pan for later use, remove and cool on a rack. Continue baking the second pan for another 30 minutes until barley and vegetables are tender but not mushy. Stir half the parsley into each.

Cool the pan for the freezer about 30 minutes; seal and freeze. When ready to use, thaw overnight in refrigerator; bake at 350° for 1 hour.

8 to 10 servings per pan

Adeline Halfmann, Retired
—Kewaskum

VEGETABLE CASSEROLE

1 10-ounce package frozen broccoli
1 10-ounce package frozen cauliflower
1 10-ounce package frozen Brussels sprouts
1 cup cubed Velveeta cheese
8 ounces fresh or canned mushrooms
¼ cup slivered almonds
1 10-ounce can cream of mushroom soup
½ cup milk

Cook vegetables according to package instructions; drain. In a large bowl, toss vegetables with cheese, mushrooms and almonds. Pour mixture into greased casserole. Heat to blend soup and milk, stirring to blend; pour over vegetables. Bake at 325° for 1 hour.

6 to 8 servings

Viola Fritz, Retired
—Kewaskum

VEGETABLE CHEESE MEDLEY

3 20-ounce packages Midwestern Blend frozen vegetables
1 2.8-ounce can French fried onions
1 10-ounce can Cheddar cheese soup, undiluted
1 cup sour cream
¼ teaspoon pepper
½ teaspoon marjoram, or to taste
1 tablespoon parsley flakes

Cook vegetables until just tender; drain. Mix ½ can onions with vegetables; transfer to shallow 3-quart baking dish. Blend soup, sour cream, pepper, marjoram and parsley;

spoon over vegetables, mixing lightly to coat. Top with remaining onions. Bake at 350° for 30 to 45 minutes, until hot and bubbly.

12 to 14 servings

Donna Tessar, Retired
—Kewaskum

FRIED SPAGHETTI

Oil
1 8-ounce package spaghetti
Salt

Heat oil in skillet on medium heat. Break spaghetti in half and place in hot oil. Remove when spaghetti turns light brown. Place on paper towels. Salt as desired.

4 servings

Kenny Fariss, Dept. 2000
—Jacksonville

OVEN RICE

1⅓ cups Minute rice, uncooked
1 4-ounce can mushroom pieces with liquid
1 14.5-ounce can chicken broth or consomme
2 to 4 green onions, chopped
2 tablespoons soy sauce
2 tablespoons oil

Place all ingredients in a casserole and mix well. Bake covered at 350° for 35 minutes. Check at 25 minutes and stir.

6 servings

Rhonda Ivey, Sales Dept.
—Orangeville

SAUSAGE DRESSING

1 pound mild or hot sausage
1 large onion, chopped
2 stalks celery, chopped
½ cup butter
2½ cups corn bread stuffing or crumbled corn bread
2½ cups (8-ounce package) bread crumbs
1 tablespoon poultry seasoning
1 teaspoon salt
¼ teaspoon pepper
2 14½-ounce cans chicken broth

Brown sausage; drain. Cook onion and celery in butter until tender. Mix together stuffing, bread crumbs and seasonings. Stir in broth, celery, onion and sausage. Mix well. Stuff 14- to 20-pound turkey or dressing may be baked separately in an uncovered pan at 350° for 30 to 35 minutes.

8 to 10 servings

Donna Zindesmith, Dept. 8400
—Jacksonville

CRACKER DRESSING

Ruth (Mrs. J.O.) Reigle was an excellent cook and this dressing was a particular favorite of her children and grandchildren. She always served this with fried chicken and often would add a can of chicken broth to the pan drippings to make a large batch of gravy.

¼ pound soda crackers
2 or 3 celery stalks, finely chopped
2 or 3 green onions, finely chopped
1 or 2 hard boiled eggs, finely chopped
Chicken gravy

Finely crush soda crackers with a rolling pin; add celery, onions and eggs. Add just enough hot chicken gravy to hold mixture together. Be sure to make enough gravy to serve with the dressing as you would mashed potatoes.

4 to 6 servings

James D. and Patty Reigle
—Kewaskum

POULTRY DRESSING

1 pound ground turkey
1 pound ground beef
½ cup chopped onion
¾ cup chopped celery
Liver, gizzard and heart (giblets) from
    turkey or chicken, chopped or ground
¾ cup minced fresh parsley, or 2
    tablespoons dried
1½ cups butter, divided
3 eggs
1 cup milk
1 teaspoon salt
1 teaspoon pepper
1 teaspoon Durkees poultry seasoning
2 1½ pound loaves white bakery-style
    bread, dried or toasted

Saute turkey, beef, onion, celery, giblets
and parsley in ½ cup butter until cooked;
set aside to cool. In mixing bowl, combine,
eggs, milk, salt, pepper and poultry seasoning; mix well and set aside. Break bread into
small pieces, wet with tepid water and mix
until bread is moist. Add egg and meat
mixture; mix well. Brown 1 cup butter in
large fry pan until dark brown; stir into
dressing. Add more salt, pepper and poultry seasoning to taste. Pour into 2 large
buttered bread pans; bake at 300° for 1
hour.

16 to 20 servings

Ken Stuart, Retired Superintendent
—Kewaskum

MEATS & MAIN DISHES

The Regal Chef, a multi-use electrical appliance,
with fry pan above and Dutch oven at the base,
late fifties

CHEESE STRATA

¼ cup butter or margarine, softened
8 slices bread, crust trimmed
3 cups (12 ounces) shredded Cheddar
   cheese
¼ cup finely chopped onion
2½ cups milk
4 eggs
1 teaspoon salt
½ teaspoon pepper
¼ teaspoon dry mustard

Butter bread, cut into 1" cubes. Place bread in 9 x 13" ungreased pan. Sprinkle cheese and onion over bread. In medium mixing bowl, beat milk, eggs, salt, pepper and mustard. Pour egg mixture over cheese. Cover and refrigerate at least 3 hours, but no longer than 24 hours.

Preheat oven to 350°. Uncover strata and bake until knife inserted in center comes out clean, about 60 minutes. Let stand 10 minutes before serving.

Variation: Spanish Strata
Drain 1 can (4 ounces) chopped green chiles and sprinkle over cheese and onion. At serving time have ready: 1 can (16 ounces) stewed tomatoes heated to boiling. Mix 1 tablespoon cornstarch with 2 tablespoons water. Stir into tomatoes; boil 1 minute. Serve over strata.

8 servings

Susan Portmann-Anderson, Marketing
—Kewaskum

SCRUMPTIOUS EGGS

12 ounces sliced mushrooms
½ cup chopped onion
¼ cup butter
1½ pounds shredded Monterey Jack
   cheese
1 cup lean, cubed ham
7 large eggs
1¾ cups milk
½ cup flour
1 tablespoon chopped parsley
1 tablespoon seasoned salt, or to taste

In skillet, saute mushrooms and onions in butter over medium heat until moisture from mushrooms evaporates. This is an important step; if moisture is allowed to remain, the dish will be watery.

Put ½ cheese in bottom of greased 9 x 13" glass dish. Distribute mushroom and onion mixture evenly over cheese. Top with ham and remaining cheese; refrigerate until ready to bake, up to 24 hours in advance. When ready to bake, break eggs in blender and add milk, flour, parsley and salt. Blend 30 seconds. Pour over cheese in pan. Bake at 350° for 45 minutes.

8 to 10 servings

Tom Hoffman, Purchasing
—Kewaskum

MUSHROOM QUICHE

½ pound Italian sausage
¼ pound fresh mushrooms, sliced or
   1 4-ounce can
1 tablespoon butter or margarine
⅔ cup half-and-half or milk
3 eggs, slightly beaten
⅛ teaspoon salt
⅛ teaspoon pepper
1 cup (4 ounces) shredded Monterey Jack
   cheese
1 Deep Dish Pet-Ritz 9" pie crust

Preheat oven and cookie sheet to 375°. In skillet, brown sausage; drain. Saute mushrooms in butter. Mix together cream, eggs, salt and pepper. Combine sausage and mushrooms with egg mixture. Sprinkle cheese on bottom of pie shell. Gradually pour meat mixture over cheese. Place pie pan on preheated cookie sheet; bake for 35 to 40 minutes, until knife inserted in center comes out clean.

8 servings

Steven Seefeldt, Maintenance
—Kewaskum

SCRAMBLED EGGS AND PEPPERS MEXICANA

½ medium onion, coarsely cut
1 clove garlic
2 green peppers, seeded and cut into strips
½ cup tomato puree
1 teaspoon pepper
6 eggs
3 tablespoons butter

Combine all ingredients, except butter, in blender and blend on high for 3 seconds. In skillet, heat butter. Add eggs and stir over low heat until eggs are the consistency of heavy cream. Serve on toast or tortillas.

3 servings

Colleen Fisher, Dept. 8400
—Jacksonville

COMPANY BREAKFAST

10 eggs
1 teaspoon salt
2 cups milk
½ cup butter, melted
12 slices bread, divided
1 cup shredded Cheddar cheese
1 pound bacon or 1 pound ham, cooked and diced
1 medium onion, diced
1 green pepper, diced
8 ounces fresh mushrooms, sliced or 2 4-ounce cans, drained

Mix together eggs, salt, milk and butter. Line a greased 9 x 13" pan with 6 slices bread; spread cheese, meat, onion, green pepper and mushrooms over top. Put on 6 more slices of bread. Pour milk mixture over all and refrigerate overnight. Bake uncovered at 375° for 45 minutes.

8 to 10 servings

Phyllis Faber, Electrics
—Kewaskum

BREAKFAST CASSEROLE

1 pound pork sausage
6 slices white bread
¾ to 1 pound grated cheese
4 eggs, slightly beaten
2 cups milk
1½ teaspoons salt
½ teaspoon dry mustard

Fry sausage and drain off grease. Butter one side of bread and place evenly on bottom of well greased 9 x 13" pan. Sprinkle cheese evenly over bread. Combine eggs, milk, salt, and mustard and pour over bread. Sprinkle sausage over top. Cover and refrigerate overnight. Bake covered at 325° for 1 hour; uncover and bake 15 minutes longer.

6 to 8 servings

Pat Buechel, 16PR-CDT
—Kewaskum

BREAKFAST HAM RING

10 eggs, divided
1 pound fully cooked ham, ground
1 pound bulk pork sausage
1½ cups soft bread crumbs
½ cup milk
2 tablespoons parsley flakes
1 tablespoon prepared horseradish

Glaze:
½ cup brown sugar
2 tablespoons vinegar
1 tablespoon mustard
1 tablespoon water

In large bowl, lightly beat 2 eggs. Add ham, sausage, bread crumbs, milk, parsley and horseradish. Mix well. Press into greased 6 cup ring mold. Bake at 350° for 1¼ hours.

Combine all glaze ingredients and mix well. Pour over ham ring the last 15 minutes of baking time.

Scramble remaining 8 eggs; season to taste. Remove ring from oven and drain juices; place on serving platter. Fill center with hot scrambled eggs; serve immediately.

8 servings

Marty Polzean, Retired
—Kewaskum

CRAB SOUP

1 49-ounce can chicken broth
1 pound imitation crab, cut up
1 medium onion, chopped
½ cup butter or margarine
½ cup flour
5 slices American cheese

Boil broth, crab meat and onion for 10 minutes. Strain broth from crab and onion; save broth, crab and onion. Melt butter; add flour to make paste. Add broth slowly, stirring constantly until thickened. Stir in crab, onion and cheese. Heat thoroughly and serve.

6 to 8 servings

Harriet Michaels, Retired
—Kewaskum

SEAFOOD CHEESE CHOWDER

1 20-ounce package frozen California-
   style vegetables
4 chicken bouillon cubes
½ cup chopped onion
½ cup chopped celery
½ cup butter
1 cup flour
2 cups milk
1 pint half and half cream
1 pound Velveeta cheese, cubed
1 6-ounce can shrimp, drained (or fresh
   or frozen)
1 12-ounce package imitation crab
   chunks

In large saucepan, cook vegetables as directed on package. Drain vegetables; reserve liquid. Add enough water to reserved liquid to make 6 cups. Add bouillon cubes and heat until dissolved.

In heavyweight soup kettle, saute onion and celery in butter. Add flour and blend. Using wire whisk, add milk and cream; stir until smooth. Add water and liquid from vegetables; cook and stir until thick and smooth.

Add cubed cheese and heat until melted. Chop cooled vegetables, shrimp and crab, and stir into soup.

8 to 10 servings

Laura Wollerman, Direct Sales
—Kewaskum

GUMBO

1 chicken, cut up and deboned
1 cup oil
1½ pounds sausage, cut into ½" pieces
1 cup flour
4 cups chopped onions
2 cups chopped celery
2 cups chopped green pepper
1 tablespoon chopped garlic
8 cups chicken stock
Salt to taste
Cayenne pepper to taste
2 cups chopped green onions

In very large pot, season and brown chicken in oil over medium-high heat. Add sausage and saute with chicken. Remove both from pot. Make roux in same pot over medium-high heat by mixing equal parts of oil and flour until it reaches desired brownish color. Add onions, celery and green pepper to roux. Stir continuously until vegetables reach desired tenderness. Add garlic to roux.

Return chicken and sausage to pot and cook with vegetables, continuing to stir frequently. Gradually stir in liquid and bring to boil. Reduce to simmer and cook 1 hour or more. Season to taste. Approximately 10 minutes before serving, add green onions.

Variations:
-Add 1 pound shrimp when adding green
   onions
-Add 4 to 6 cups cut okra to vegetables,
   saute and cook together with roux
-Serve over cooked rice
-Place sherry at table for individuals to add
   if they wish
-Place filé at table (¼ to ½ teaspoon per
   serving is recommended)

Filé is a fine green powder that is young, dried and ground sassafras leaves. Used in gumbo for flavor and thickening. The word filé means to twist or make threads.

15 to 20 servings

Cindy DeMarb, M.I.S.
—Kewaskum

AUTUMN SOUP

1½ pounds ground beef
1 cup diced celery
1 cup diced onion
1 quart tomatoes
1½ quarts water
4 cups diced potatoes
6 beef bouillon cubes
2 bay leaves
1½ teaspoons basil
Salt and pepper to taste

In fry pan, brown meat. Drain grease and pour meat into soup pot. Add remaining ingredients; simmer 1 hour.

About 8 to 10 servings

Irene Haddy, Retired
—Kewaskum

ALL DAY CHILI

1 pound ground beef
1 29-ounce can tomato puree
1 15-ounce can Hunt's special tomato sauce
1 14-ounce can beef broth
1 16-ounce can kidney beans
Chili powder to taste
Red hot sauce to taste
Worcestershire sauce to taste
2 tablespoons sugar
3 cups cooked elbow macaroni

Brown ground beef in large kettle. Drain off grease and add remaining ingredients, except macaroni. Simmer all day. Fifteen minutes before serving add macaroni.

8 to 10 servings

Janet Backhaus, M.I.S. Dept.
—Kewaskum

CHILI CON CARNE
with Beans

3 pounds lean ground beef or ground chuck*
1 medium onion, chopped
Salt, pepper and garlic powder to taste
3 8-ounce cans tomato sauce
3 16-ounce cans chili beans or ranch-style beans
3 tablespoons chili powder
1 teaspoon ground cumin
¼ teaspoon red pepper
1 46-ounce can tomato juice

Brown meat and onion in 6- or 7-quart Dutch oven; season to taste. Add remaining ingredients and simmer for 45 minutes before serving.

* Or ground venison, or a combination

10 to 12 servings

Carolyn Lessley, Saladmaster, Inc.
—Arlington, TX

CHILI

1 pound ground beef
1¼ cups chopped onion
1 16-ounce can Mexican stewed tomatoes
1 16-ounce can cajun stewed tomatoes
1 16-ounce can kidney beans, drained
1 15-ounce can chili beans
1 16-ounce can pinto beans, drained
2 15-ounce cans Mexican tomato sauce

In heavyweight Dutch oven, brown meat and onion; drain fat. Add remaining ingredients; mix well. Simmer on low heat for 15 minutes, then serve. Can also be frozen.

10 to 12 servings

Colleen Fisher, Dept. 8400
—Jacksonville

BARBECUED HAMBURGER

1 cup chopped onion
2 tablespoons butter
4 pounds ground beef
1 cup water
¼ cup lemon juice
1 tablespoon Worcestershire sauce
2 teaspoons vinegar
½ teaspoon dry mustard
1 14-ounce bottle catsup
½ cup chopped celery
2 tablespoons brown sugar
1 tablespoon salt
1 teaspoon Accent seasoning

In heavyweight Dutch oven, brown onion in butter. Add ground beef; brown and drain off fat. Add remaining ingredients and simmer 30 minutes.

Makes 20 to 22 sandwiches

Carol Wiskirchen
—Kewaskum

JUICE FOR BURGERS

1 green pepper, chopped
1 onion, chopped
1 tomato, chopped
1 envelope Lipton onion soup mix
2 cups beef broth

Mix all ingredients together, adding enough water to make juice. Simmer 1 hour with brats and hamburgers.

Anne Quackenboss, M.I.S.
—Kewaskum

ONE OUTSTANDING BURGER

2 pounds extra lean ground beef
2 eggs
1 large onion, finely chopped
½ cup barbecue sauce
1 tablespoon hot pepper sauce
2 teaspoons garlic powder
2 teaspoons ground black pepper
Fine bread crumbs

Mix all ingredients in large bowl, adding bread crumbs slowly and just enough to bind mixture. Form into burgers and barbecue on medium heat until done.

This recipe also makes a delicious and moist meatloaf. Bake at 350° for 1 hour. Spread more barbecue sauce over top of meatloaf and bake 30 minutes more.

8 servings

Sallie (and Kent) Myers, Receptionist
—Orangeville

PIZZA BURGERS

½ cup chopped onion
2 tablespoons shortening
1 pound ground beef
1 10-ounce can tomato soup
½ cup shredded sharp cheese, any kind
⅛ teaspoon oregano
Dash pepper
12 small hamburger buns, split and toasted
Mozzarella cheese, cut in strips

Brown onions in shortening. Add beef; cook until browned. Stir often to separate meat particles. Add soup, shredded cheese, oregano and pepper; simmer 10 minutes. Spread mixture on buns; place strips of Mozzarella cheese on top. Broil until cheese melts.

12 servings

Helene Benzing, Retired
—Kewaskum

BAR-B-Q HAM

1½ cups catsup
1 medium onion, chopped
1 medium green pepper, chopped, optional
4 tablespoons margarine
⅓ cup brown sugar
⅓ cup prepared mustard
1 tablespoon Worcestershire sauce
4½ pounds shredded ham

Combine sauce ingredients in saucepan; simmer 15 minutes. Pour over ham in casserole or baking dish; bake covered at 350° for 1 hour. Serve on buns. Can be prepared day before; also freezes well.

Makes 20 to 24 sandwiches

Allen (and Bonnie) Koepke
—Kewaskum

PASTY

1 **package pie crust mix**
2 **pounds round steak, cubed**
3 or 4 **potatoes, sliced very thin**
1 **onion, chopped**
2 **tablespoons butter**
Salt and pepper

Roll out 2 crusts; place pie crust in pie pan or on cookie sheet. Combine meat, potatoes, onion and pour into crust. Add butter, salt and pepper. Cover with crust; cut vents in top with knife. Bake at 350° for 1¼ hours, or until potatoes are tender.

6 to 8 servings

Skip Hillary, Sales
—Texas

SPAGHETTI SAUCE

2 **large onions, chopped**
2 **large green peppers, chopped**
⅓ **cup oil**
2 **cloves garlic, minced**
12 to 16 **large tomatoes, peeled, cored, chopped**
1 **12-ounce can tomato paste**
2 **envelopes instant beef broth**
4 **teaspoons basil**
2 **bay leaves**
2 **teaspoons salt**
2 **cups water**

Combine all ingredients, mix well. Simmer 2 to 3 hours. Remove bay leaves and discard. Put in containers and freeze, or seal in jars and process 15 minutes in pressure cooker with 10-pound pressure.

Carol Wiskirchen
—Kewaskum

SPAGHETTI SAUCE
and Meatballs

Sauce:
1 **46-ounce can tomato juice**
1 **8-ounce can tomato sauce**
1 **6-ounce can tomato paste**
1 **teaspoon onion powder**
1 **teaspoon garlic powder**
1 **teaspoon celery salt**
1 **bay leaf**
¼ **teaspoon thyme**
¼ **teaspoon oregano**
¼ **teaspoon basil**
¼ **teaspoon rosemary**
¼ **teaspoon marjoram**
1 **tablespoon parsley**

Meatballs:
½ **cup oatmeal**
1 **pound ground beef**
3 **tablespoons milk, optional**
¼ **teaspoon onion powder**
¼ **teaspoon salt**
¼ **teaspoon thyme**
¼ **teaspoon basil**

Combine all sauce ingredients in slow cooker; do not cover. Simmer on #4 setting for 6 hours. Cover and refrigerate overnight. Serve next day.

To make meatballs, combine oatmeal and hamburger; add milk to moisten, if necessary. Add spices; mix well. Form into balls and fry. When done add to spaghetti sauce.

Karen Sparks, Accounts Payable
—Kewaskum

PESGHETTI PIZZA

1 16-ounce package spaghetti
1 cup milk
½ teaspoon salt
¾ teaspoon garlic powder
4 cups shredded Mozzarella cheese, divided
1 32-ounce jar spaghetti sauce
1 8-ounce package sliced pepperoni

Break spaghetti into pieces and cook according to package directions. Drain and rinse. Mix with milk, salt, garlic powder and 2 cups cheese. Put in greased 9 x 13" pan. Bake at 400° for 15 minutes. Remove from oven and reduce heat to 350°. Spread spaghetti sauce over pasta mixture. Top with remaining 2 cups cheese and pepperoni. Bake for 30 minutes. Let stand for 5 minutes before serving.

8 servings

Art Martin
—Jacksonville

CRAZY CRUST PIZZA

1 pound pork sausage or ground beef
1 cup flour
1 teaspoon salt
1 teaspoon oregano
⅛ teaspoon pepper
2 eggs
⅔ cup milk
1 cup pizza sauce
¼ cup chopped onion
1 cup sliced mushrooms
Grated Mozzarella cheese

Brown meat; drain and set aside. Combine flour, salt, oregano, pepper, eggs and milk; mix well and pour into greased cookie sheet. Bake at 325° for 10 to 15 minutes. Remove from oven and spread sauce, meat, onion and mushrooms over crust. Top with cheese. Bake at 425° for 15 minutes.

8 servings

Alice Raether, Retired
—Kewaskum

SPICY STIR-FRY

3 tablespoons black bean sauce
½ teaspoon sesame or peanut oil
1 pound skinless, boneless chicken breasts or lean steak/roast beef, thinly sliced
¾ cup low-salt chicken/beef broth
1½ tablespoons low sodium soy sauce
2¼ teaspoons cornstarch
2 teaspoons Dijon mustard
3 teaspoons peanut oil
1½ cups bite-size broccoli florets
1½ cups bite-size cauliflower florets
2 medium onions, cut in chunks
2 cloves garlic, minced
¼ cup unsalted peanuts, chopped
⅛ teaspoon red pepper flakes
¼ teaspoon ground black pepper

Combine black bean sauce and ½ teaspoon oil; blend well. Marinate chicken or beef for 2 to 3 hours. Cook meat and marinade in wok until done; set aside.

Combine broth, soy sauce, cornstarch and mustard; stir until cornstarch is dissolved. Warm 3 teaspoons peanut oil in wok over medium-high until hot. Add broccoli, cauliflower, onion and garlic and stir-fry for 4 to 5 minutes. Add meat, peanuts, pepper flakes and black pepper. Stir sauce again and add to wok. Stir-fry until sauce thickens and meat is warmed through, approximately 2 to 4 minutes. Serve over rice.

4 to 6 servings

Sallie (and Kent) Myers, Receptionist
—Orangeville

CHICKEN STIR-FRY

½ cup olive oil
½ teaspoon red pepper flakes
¼ teaspoon garlic salt
1 bunch green onions, chopped
2 to 3 boneless, skinless chicken breasts, or meat of choice
1 bunch broccoli
3 carrots
2 stalks celery
1 small head cabbage
1 to 1½ cups water
3 tablespoons brown sugar
1 cup soy sauce
3 tablespoons cornstarch, dissolved in ½ cup water

Slice meat into very thin slices. Cut vegetables in bite-size pieces. Heat wok; add olive oil, red pepper, garlic salt and onions. Cook until onions are lightly browned. Add chicken and cook until no longer pink. Add vegetables and water. Cook covered about 5 minutes. Combine sugar and soy sauce. Mix gently with chicken mixture. Add cornstarch mixture and continue to cook, stirring carefully until mixture has thickened. Serve over rice.

8 to 10 servings

Mary Belcher, Dept. 2000
—Jacksonville

EASY MACARONI AND CHEESE CASSEROLE

3 tablespoons butter
2½ cups macaroni, uncooked
1 teaspoon salt
¼ teaspoon pepper
½ pound Velveeta cheese, sliced
1 quart milk

Melt butter in 3-quart baking dish. Pour macaroni into melted butter; stir until coated. Add salt, pepper, cheese and milk to macaroni. Bake uncovered at 325° for 1½ hours. Do not stir while baking.

5 to 6 servings

Mary Weary, Retired
—Wooster

QUICK TUNA CASSEROLE

1 8-ounce package potato chips
4½-ounce can tuna
1 10-ounce can cream of chicken soup
1 15-ounce can green peas with liquid

Preheat oven to 350°. Grease 2-quart baking dish with butter or margarine. Crush 2 cups potato chips and spread in bottom of baking dish. In mixing bowl, combine tuna, soup and peas. Pour half mixture over potato chips; add a layer of uncrushed chips. Then add remainder of tuna mixture. Top with a few uncrushed chips. Bake 35 to 45 minutes. Serve with a salad and warm, homemade bread.

4 servings

Dennis Wieberdink, Creative Services
—Kewaskum

TUNA CASSEROLE

1 7- or 8-ounce package noodles
¾ cup chopped onion
2 cups sliced celery
¼ cup butter
2 10-ounce cans cream of celery soup
1 12-ounce can evaporated milk
½ teaspoon Worchershire sauce
2 7-ounce cans tuna, drained

Prepare noodles according to package directions. In fry pan, saute onion and celery in butter until transparent. Add soup, milk, Worcestershire sauce and tuna; mix well. Spread noodles in bottom of 9 x 13" pan; pour tuna mixture over top. Cover with foil and bake at 375° for 40 minutes.

8 to 10 servings

Cheri Baird, Finance
—Kewaskum

CHICKEN CASSEROLE

½ cup green pepper, chopped
½ cup celery chopped
¼ cup onion, chopped
1 tablespoon butter or margarine
2 large cans boneless chicken
¾ teaspoon salt
¼ teaspoon pepper
½ cup mayonnaise
12 slices bread, divided
2 eggs
1½ cups milk
1 10.75-ounce can cream of mushroom
    soup
¼ cup Parmesan cheese

Cook green pepper, celery and onion in butter 3 minutes; add chicken, salt, pepper and mayonnaise. Trim crusts from bread. Grease 10 x 13″ baking dish and line with 6 bread slices. Spread chicken mixture on bread and top with remaining bread. Beat eggs and add milk. Pour over casserole and cover with waxed paper. Let stand overnight. Before baking, spread soup evenly over top. Bake at 325° for 1 hour. Sprinkle top with cheese and bake an additional 15 minutes.

8 to 10 servings

Anita Cassidy, Dept. 8400
—Jacksonville

CHICKEN TORTILLA CASSEROLE

2 small onions, diced
1 4-ounce can chopped Ortega green
    chiles
½ cup margarine
1 10-ounce can cream of chicken soup
1 10-ounce can cream of mushroom soup
1 5-ounce can evaporated milk
1 stewed or baked chicken, deboned and
    cut into bite-size pieces
1 pound grated sharp Cheddar cheese
1 4-ounce can sliced olives, drained
1 cup chicken broth
12 corn tortillas, torn into bite-size
    pieces

Brown onions and chiles in margarine. Add soups and milk. Stir and simmer 10 minutes. Transfer to 4-quart casserole or baking dish. Add remaining ingredients; mix well. Bake at 350° for 45 minutes, until hot and bubbly.

8 to 10 servings

Barbara Hanson, Retired
—California Sales Office

CHICKEN CASSEROLE

2 cups cooked chicken chunks
2 cups cooked rice
1 4-ounce can mushrooms, drained,
    chopped
1 8-ounce can water chestnuts, drained,
    chopped
2 teaspoons onion powder
¼ cup Parmesan cheese
1 cup whipping cream
1 14½-ounce can vegetable broth
Salt and pepper to taste
1 10-ounce can Pillsbury biscuits

Mix together all ingredients, except biscuits. Put in 2-quart ungreased casserole dish and bake at 350° for 30 minutes. Arrange biscuits on top; bake at 375° for an additional 15 minutes.

4 to 6 servings

Janet Backhaus, M.I.S. Dept.
—Kewaskum

MEXICAN CHICKEN CASSEROLE

Sauce:
1 10-ounce can cream of mushroom soup
1 10-ounce can cream of chicken soup
1 15-ounce can Rotel tomatoes with
    green chiles
1 14.5-ounce can chicken broth
2 tablespoons chili powder
Salt and pepper to taste

1 chicken, cooked, deboned and cut into
    bite-size pieces
12 corn tortillas, thawed and torn into
    pieces
2 onions, chopped
1 bell pepper, chopped
2 cups grated American cheese

Using a blender, combine all sauce ingredients. In buttered 9 x 13" casserole dish, put in a layer ½ chicken and ½ tortilla pieces; then ½ onion, bell pepper and cheese. Cover with sauce. Repeat with another layer of each, saving some cheese to sprinkle on top. Bake at 350° for 1 hour.

12 servings

Shirley Ann Smith, Retired
—Jacksonville

CHICKEN SPECTACULAR

3 cups cooked chicken
1 5 to 6-ounce box Uncle Ben's Wild and White rice, cooked
1 10-ounce can cream of celery soup
1 4-ounce jar sliced pimiento
1 medium onion, chopped
2 cups French-style green beans
1 cup mayonnaise
Salt and pepper to taste
1½ cups coarsely crushed potato chips

Mix all ingredients together, except chips; spoon into 3-quart casserole. Bake at 350° for 25 to 30 minutes. Top with crushed potato chips.

Verna Robinson, Retired
—Wooster

CHICKEN STRATA

1 8-ounce package stuffing mix
1 cup chicken broth
½ cup butter or margarine, melted
2½ cups diced, cooked chicken
½ cup chopped celery
½ cup chopped onion
½ cup mayonnaise
¾ teaspoon salt
2 eggs, beaten
1½ cups milk
1 10-ounce can cream of mushroom soup
½ cup grated Cheddar cheese

Combine stuffing mix, broth and butter; spoon into 2-quart casserole. Mix together chicken, celery, onion, mayonnaise and salt; spread over stuffing mixture. Blend eggs and milk well; pour over casserole, cover and refrigerate overnight.

Before baking, spread soup over top and bake at 350° for 30 minutes. Remove from oven and top with grated cheese. Return to oven until cheese melts.

6 to 8 servings

Carol Oberle, Production Scheduling
—Jacksonville

CHICKEN CASSEROLE

2 cups cooked turkey or chicken
2 cups cooked broccoli or broccoli/cauliflower mix
1 8-ounce can mushrooms, drained
1 10¾-ounce can cream of chicken soup
1 10¾-ounce can cream of mushroom soup
1 soup can milk
8 to 10 slices American processed cheese
1 6-ounce package chicken flavor Stove Top stuffing

Layer in greased 9 x 13" pan poultry, vegetables and mushrooms. Combine soups with milk and pour over meat and vegetables. Lay cheese slices over soup mixture. Prepare stuffing according to package directions. Spread stuffing mixture on cheese layer. Bake at 350° for 60 minutes.

8 to 10 servings

Barb Ebert, Sales Administrator
—Kewaskum

ARIZONA CHICKEN CASSEROLE

2 10-ounce cans cream of chicken soup
3 cups diced, cooked chicken
3 cups Chinese noodles

Preheat oven to 350°. Grease large casserole dish. Combine all ingredients in dish; stir well. Cover and bake for 30 minutes.

(I usually serve broccoli on the side.)

4 to 6 servings

Rayne Bryla, Production Expeditor Asst.
—Canada

CHICKEN CASSEROLE

2 cups cubed, cooked chicken breasts
1 8-ounce package noodles, cooked and drained
1 10-ounce can cream of chicken soup
1 5-ounce can Carnation evaporated milk
1 teaspoon salt
1½ cups shredded Cheddar cheese
1 cup finely chopped celery
½ cup finely chopped mango, or bell pepper
Buttered bread crumbs

Mix all ingredients together, except crumbs; spoon into casserole dish. Top with bread crumbs. Bake at 325° for 45 minutes.

4 to 6 servings

Edna M. Oster, Retired
—Kewaskum

CHICKEN CASSEROLE

1 7-ounce box elbow macaroni, cooked
1 10-ounce can mushroom soup
2 cups cubed, cooked chicken
1 small onion, chopped
2 cups milk or chicken broth
1 10-ounce can cream of celery soup
1 cup cubed Colby or Cheddar cheese
1 8-ounce can whole water chestnuts, drained, optional
1 cup chopped celery, optional
1 cup bread crumbs

Mix all ingredients except bread crumbs together; refrigerate overnight.

Remove from refrigerator, pour into greased 9 x 13" baking dish and let stand at room temperature for 1 hour. Top with bread crumbs. Bake at 350° for 1½ hours.

12 to 15 servings

Ernie Haegler, Retired
—Kewaskum

CHICKEN AND BROCCOLI CASSEROLE

2 10-ounce packages frozen broccoli or equivalent fresh broccoli
6 boneless, skinless chicken breasts
2 10-ounce cans cream of mushroom soup
1 cup Hellman's mayonnaise
½ teaspoon curry powder
1 tablespoon lemon juice
6 to 8 slices bacon, cooked and crumbled, optional
1 cup grated sharp Cheddar cheese
¾ cup bread crumbs

Cook broccoli until tender; drain. Place in bottom of 9 x 13" pan. Partially cook chicken in microwave approximately 2 minutes. Place chicken on top of broccoli. Mix soup, mayonnaise, curry powder and lemon juice; spread over chicken. Sprinkle bacon, cheese and then bread crumbs over top. Bake uncovered at 350° for 30 minutes.

6 servings

Laura Wollerman, Direct Sales

CHICKEN/BROCCOLI CASSEROLE

4 chicken thighs, breasts or combination
2 10-ounce packages frozen broccoli spears
2 10-ounce cans cream of chicken soup
½ cup Miracle Whip
6 to 8 slices American cheese
½ cup soft bread crumbs
Butter

Cook chicken and broccoli separately. Do not overcook! Place broccoli on bottom of casserole dish (no bigger than 9 x 13"). Place chicken on top of broccoli. Mix together soup and Miracle Whip; pour over chicken. Lay cheese slices over chicken; sprinkle bread crumbs on top and dot with butter. Bake at 350° for 40 to 45 minutes or until cheese begins to turn brown. Let stand 5 to 10 minutes before serving.

3 to 4 servings

Chris Hohner, M.I.S.
—Kewaskum

CHICKEN CASSEROLE

1 10-ounce can cream of mushroom soup
1 10-ounce can cream of celery soup
1⅓ cups milk
1 cup uncooked rice
1 chicken, cut up
1 envelope Lipton onion dry soup mix

Mix together soups, milk and rice; pour into greased casserole dish. Place chicken pieces on top of rice mixture. Top with onion soup mix; cover and bake at 375° for 2½ hours.

Luanne Berghammer, 1600 Drip CDT
—Kewaskum

POOR MAN'S TURKEY CASSEROLE

2 turkey drum sticks or 1 thigh
1 10-ounce can cream of mushroom soup
1½ to 2 cups cooked rice
2 cups frozen green beans, cooked
1 heaping tablespoon butter
½ cup diced onions

Cover drum sticks with water and cook in 6-quart kettle for 1½ hours or until tender. Cool; remove skin and cut turkey off bone into small pieces. Mix turkey, soup, rice and

beans together in 2- or 3-quart kettle. Melt butter in small saucepan; add onion and saute until glossy. Add onions to meat mixture; mix well. Cook over medium heat until hot.

4 to 6 servings

Denise Braatz, Oil Core
—Kewaskum

SIX BEAN CASSEROLE

2 pounds pork sausage, cut in chunks
1 onion, chopped
1 green pepper, chopped
1 16-ounce can Campbells baked beans (barbecue)
1 16-ounce can lima beans, drained
1 16-ounce can wax beans, drained
1 20-ounce can Brooks hot chili beans
1 16-ounce can red kidney beans, drained
1 16-ounce can French green beans, drained
1 6-ounce can tomato paste
1 10-ounce can tomato soup
1 cup packed brown sugar
3 teaspoons Worcestershire sauce

Saute sausage with onion and green pepper; drain well. Transfer to Dutch oven; add remaining ingredients. Bake at 350° for 1 hour.

18 to 20 servings

Phyllis Stroh, Wife of Fred Stroh, Deceased
—Wooster

PENNSY SUPPER

6 wieners, sliced into coins, divided
4 medium-to-large potatoes, cooked and
   diced
2 tablespoons minced onion
¼ cup butter, softened
1 cup cooked peas
Salt and pepper to taste
1 tablespoon prepared mustard
1 10-ounce can cream of mushroom soup

In 2½-quart casserole, combine 5 of the
sliced hot dogs with potatoes, onion and
butter. In bowl, combine peas, salt, pepper,
mustard and soup. Pour over hot dog
mixture and toss to mix. Dot with reserved
hot dog. Cover. Bake at 350° for 25 to 30
minutes.

4 to 6 servings

Janice Thill, Sales
—Kewaskum

CALIFORNIA TAMALE CASSEROLE

¾ cup yellow cornmeal
1½ cups milk
1 egg, beaten
1 pound lean ground beef
1 package chili seasoning mix
2 teaspoons seasoned salt
1 16-ounce can tomatoes
1 17-ounce can whole kernel corn,
   drained
1 7½-ounce can pitted black olives,
   drained
1 cup shredded Cheddar cheese

Mix cornmeal, milk and egg in 2½-quart
casserole. Brown meat in skillet, stirring to
keep crumbly. Add chili seasoning, salt,
tomatoes, corn and olives; mix well. Stir
into cornmeal mixture. Bake at 350° for 1
hour 15 minutes. Sprinkle cheese on top
and bake until cheese melts, about 5
minutes.

6 to 8 servings

Skip Hillary, Sales
—Texas

PORK CHOPS AND BEANS CASSEROLE

8 pork chops
Salt and pepper to taste
1 28- to 32-ounce can baked beans
½ cup catsup
2 tablespoons molasses or brown sugar

Brown pork chops in frying pan; drain
grease. Season with salt and pepper. Place
pork chops in baking dish. Combine baked
beans, catsup and molasses; pour over pork
chops. Bake at 375° for 1 hour or until
chops are tender.

8 servings

Michael Hendricks, Dept. 900
—Kewaskum

MEXICAN CASSEROLE

1½ pounds ground beef
1 medium onion, chopped
1 10-ounce can cream of chicken soup (or
   celery or mushroom)
1 10-ounce can tomatoes, chopped and
   drained
1 10-ounce can enchilada sauce
1 4-ounce can green chilies, chopped
½ teaspoon oregano
⅛ teaspoon cumin
8 to 10 flour tortillas, torn into pieces to
   fit pan
3 cups shredded Cheddar cheese
2 cups shredded Monterey Jack cheese
½ cup sliced black olives

Crumble and cook beef and onion until beef
is browned; drain. Add soup, tomatoes,
sauce, chilies and seasonings. Heat thoroughly over medium heat, letting simmer gently
for 10 minutes. Place ⅓ torn tortillas in
bottom of 9 x 13" pan. Add Cheddar cheese
to meat mixture, stir until blended. Put 1/3
meat sauce on top of tortillas, another layer
of tortillas and more meat sauce (3 layers).
Top with Jack cheese and spread black
olives over top. Bake at 350° for 30
minutes.

10 to 12 servings

Linda Ertl, Q.C. Dept.
—Kewaskum

BEEF AND RICE CASSEROLE

1 cup rice
2 cups water
1 teaspoon salt
1 teaspoon shortening
½ pound ground beef
1 10-ounce can cream of mushroom soup
Cheese slices

Place rice, water, salt and shortening in saucepan. Bring to boil, turn heat to low and cover. Let stand until rice is cooked. Brown meat and drain. Combine meat, rice and soup in casserole dish. Bake at 350° for 30 to 45 minutes. Place cheese slices on top to melt.

4 servings

Shari Bickell, Dept. 2000
—Jacksonville

BAKED CHOP SUEY

2 pounds ground beef
8 stalks celery, finely chopped
1 small onion, diced
1½ cups uncooked rice
1 4-ounce can mushrooms
1 15-ounce can bean sprouts
1 8-ounce can water chestnuts, sliced, optional
1 10.75-ounce can chicken rice soup
1 10.75-ounce can mushroom soup
2 tablespoons soy sauce
2 soup cans water
Chow Mein noodles

Brown meat in frying pan; drain off grease and cool. In mixing bowl, combine all ingredients except noodles; mix well. Pour into large casserole dish. Bake at 350° for 1½ hours. Serve with Chow Mein noodles.

8 to 10 servings

Ruth Raether, Retired
—Kewaskum

CHOP SUEY CASSEROLE

1½ pounds ground beef
1 large onion
1 cup diced celery
¾ cup rice, uncooked
2 tablespoons soy sauce
1½ cups hot water
1 10-ounce can cream of chicken soup
1 10-ounce can cream of mushroom soup
¼ to ½ cup Chinese noodles

In fry pan, brown meat; drain off grease. Add onion and celery. Pour into 2-quart casserole. Add remaining ingredients except noodles. Bake uncovered at 350° for 1 hour. Top with noodles and bake ½ hour more.

6 to 8 servings

Laura Hammes, Retired
—Kewaskum

CHINESE HAMBURGER CASSEROLE

1 4-ounce can sliced mushrooms
1 can water chestnuts, sliced
1 pound ground beef
1 10-ounce can cream of chicken soup
1 10-ounce can cream of mushroom soup
2 tablespoons soy sauce
1½ cups thick sliced celery
2 medium onions, sliced thick
½ cup uncooked rice
1 can crisp Chinese noodles

Drain liquid from mushrooms and water chestnuts and add enough water to make 1 cup liquid; set aside. Brown meat in 12" fry pan; add remaining ingredients, except noodles. Pour into 2-quart baking dish. Bake covered at 350° for 30 minutes. Uncover and bake an additional 30 minutes. Sprinkle top with noodles and return to oven for 15 minutes.

6 to 8 servings

Barbara Hanson, Retired
—California Sales Office

THREE CHEESE CASSEROLE

1 pound ground beef
½ cup chopped onion
2 8-ounce cans tomato sauce
1 teaspoon sugar
¼ teaspoon salt
¼ teaspoon garlic salt
¼ teaspoon pepper
4 cups noodles (approx. 12-ounce package)
1 cup cream-style cottage cheese
1 8-ounce container soft cream cheese
¼ cup sour cream
⅓ cup chopped green pepper
¼ cup grated Parmesan cheese

In large skillet, cook ground beef and onion until meat is lightly browned and onion is tender. Stir in tomato sauce, sugar, salt, garlic salt and pepper. Remove from heat.

Prepare noodles as label directs; drain. Combine cottage cheese, cream cheese, sour cream and green pepper. Spread half of noodles in 7 x 11" baking dish. Top with small amount of meat sauce. Cover with cheese mixture. Layer remaining noodles, then meat sauce. Top with Parmesan cheese. Bake at 350° for 30 minutes.

8 servings

Marianne Wondra, Retired
—Kewaskum

HAMBURGER CASSEROLE

1 pound ground beef
¼ cup chopped onion
¼ cup chopped green pepper
1 tablespoon chili powder
1½ cups noodles, cooked
4 ounces Velveeta cheese, cubed
1 4-ounce can mushrooms
1 10-ounce can tomato soup
1 6-ounce can peas or corn, drained

In skillet brown meat, onion and green pepper; drain grease and add chili powder. In large casserole dish, mix meat, noodles, cheese, mushrooms, tomato soup and peas

or corn; mix well. Bake covered at 350° for 45 minutes to 1 hour.

6 to 8 servings

Bonnie Clapper, Dept. 15EE
—Kewaskum

HAMBURGER, CORN AND NOODLES

1 pound ground beef
½ cup chopped onions
2 tablespoons shortening
1½ tablespoons flour
2 cups tomato juice
1½ teaspoons salt
¼ teaspoon pepper
¼ teaspoon paprika
¼ cup sugar
¼ pound, about 2 cups, noodles, uncooked
1½ cups kernel corn
2 ounces sharp cheese

In large fry pan, cook meat and onions in shortening until golden brown. Add flour and blend well. Add tomato juice, seasonings, noodles and corn; mix well. Place in greased casserole dish; sprinkle top with cheese. Bake at 350° for 1 hour.

6 to 8 servings

W.F. Fickert, Retired
—Kewaskum

CRUNCHY BEEF BAKE CASSEROLE

1 7-ounce package elbow macaroni (2 cups, uncooked)
1 pound ground beef
1 10-ounce can cream of mushroom soup
¾ cup shredded Cheddar cheese
1 14½-ounce can whole tomatoes, cut up
¼ cup chopped green pepper
¾ teaspoon seasoned salt
1 3-ounce can Durkee French fried onions

Prepare macaroni as directed on package, drain. Brown ground beef; drain grease. Combine all ingredients except onions. Pour half mixture into 2-quart casserole. Add ½ can onions. Pour remaining mixture over onions. Cover, bake at 350° for 30 minutes. Top with remaining onions and bake uncovered 5 minutes longer.

4 to 6 servings

Cele Schmidt, Administrative
—Kewaskum

DAD'S SPECIAL CASSEROLE

4 ounces medium noodles (½ of 8-ounce package)
1 pound ground beef
½ cup finely chopped onion
1 10-ounce can cream of celery soup
½ cup milk
½ teaspoon salt
¼ teaspoon pepper
¼ teaspoon thyme, optional
1 8-ounce package shredded American cheese

Cook noodles until tender; drain and rinse in cold water. Cook meat and onion until onion is transparent and meat has lost its color. Add soup, milk and seasonings.

Arrange half the noodles in buttered 1½-quart baking dish. Add meat and half the cheese. Repeat, using cheese for the top layer. Bake at 350° for 20 to 25 minutes.

4 to 6 servings

Randy Gartman
—Kewaskum

VIRGIE'S CASSEROLE

3 cups shell macaroni
2 pounds ground beef
1 14½-ounce can tomato wedges
¼ cup sliced black olives
½ cup water
Sugar to taste

Preheat oven to 350°. In 2-quart saucepan, cook macaroni to desired doneness; drain and rinse with hot water and set aside.

Brown ground beef in fry pan over medium heat; drain grease. Combine macaroni, ground beef, tomato wedges, black olives and water. Add sugar to taste. Spoon into 9 x 13″ (glass) casserole. Bake for 20 minutes or until bubbly.

6 to 8 servings

Roger D. Thompson, Dept. 20
—Jacksonville

HAMBURGER CHEESE CASSEROLE

2 pounds ground round
1 teaspoon garlic powder
2 teaspoons salt, or to taste
2 teaspoons sugar
Pepper to taste
4 8-ounce cans tomato sauce
1 8-ounce package cream cheese, softened
1 pint sour cream
5 green onions with tops, thinly sliced
1 12-ounce package medium-size noodles
2 cups grated Cheddar cheese

Brown ground round and pour off fat. Add garlic powder, salt, sugar and pepper. Cook until well blended; add tomato sauce. Simmer 15 minutes. Combine cream cheese, sour cream and green onions. Cook noodles as directed on package and drain.

In buttered 4-quart casserole, layer ingredients: noodles, meat sauce, cheese mixture and grated cheese. Repeat layers.

Refrigerate for 24 hours. Bake at 350° for 30 minutes.

8 servings

Shirley Ann Smith, Retired
—Jacksonville

PIZZA HOT DISH

1 pound ground beef
1 medium onion, chopped
2 10-ounce cans tomato soup
½ teaspoon garlic salt
½ teaspoon oregano
½ teaspoon onion salt
¼ teaspoon pepper
1 6-ounce package medium-wide noodles
¼ pound grated Cheddar cheese
¼ cup Parmesan cheese

Preheat oven to 350°. Brown meat and add onions; saute with meat. Add soup and spices; simmer 15 minutes over low heat. Cook noodles to desired doneness; drain. Grease 9 x 13" pan. Place noodles on bottom of pan. Pour meat over noodles. Sprinkle Cheddar cheese and Parmesan cheese on top. Cover with foil and bake 35 minutes. Remove foil and bake another 10 minutes. Cut into squares to serve.

6 to 8 servings

Margie Beck, Retired
—Kewaskum

ZESTY ITALIAN CASSEROLE

1½ pounds ground beef
¼ medium onion, chopped
1 4-ounce can mushroom pieces and stems, drained
1 12-ounce package wide egg noodles
1 15-ounce can tomato sauce
1 6-ounce can tomato paste
1 10-ounce can tomato soup
½ soup can water
1 tablespoon basil
1¼ tablespoons oregano
½ teaspoon ground bay leaves
2 teaspoons parsley, optional
1 tablespoon Italian seasoning
1 teaspoon garlic powder

Brown meat and onions together in large fry pan. Add mushrooms when meat is almost done. While meat is browning, prepare noodles according to package directions; drain and return to pot. When beef is browned, add tomato sauce, paste, soup and water; mix well. Add spices mixing well after each. Let simmer for 5 to 8 minutes. Add meat and sauce mixture to noodles; stir. Let stand for 3 to 5 minutes for noodles to absorb sauce.

8 to 10 servings

Chris Hohner, M.I.S.
—Kewaskum

FISH CREOLE

1 pound fresh or frozen fish fillets
½ cup chopped onion
½ cup chopped green pepper
1 clove garlic, minced
¼ cup butter or margarine
1 16-ounce can tomatoes, cut up, with liquid
1 tablespoon dried parsley flakes
1 tablespoon instant chicken bouillon granules
¼ teaspoon bottled hot pepper sauce
1 tablespoon cornstarch
1 tablespoon cold water
Hot cooked rice

Thaw fish, if frozen. In 10" skillet, cook onion, green pepper and garlic in butter or margarine until tender but not brown. Add undrained tomatoes, parsley flakes, bouillon granules and hot pepper sauce. Simmer covered for 10 minutes. Stir together cornstarch and cold water. Stir into tomato mixture. Cook and stir until thickened and bubbly. Cut fish into 1" pieces. Add fish to tomato mixture, stirring to coat. Return to boiling; reduce heat. Simmer covered for 5 to 7 minutes or until fish flakes easily when tested with a fork. Serve fish mixture over rice.

4 servings

Tamara Dickerson, Dept. 20
—Jacksonville

RAJUN CAJUN JAMBALAYA

12 servings brown rice
1 smoked sausage ring
2 16-ounce cans red beans
2 16-ounce cans black beans
3 cups frozen corn
1 16-ounce can diced tomatoes
2 8-ounce cans tomato sauce
1 6-ounce can sliced mushrooms
2 diced peppers (any combination of red, yellow or green)
1 diced medium bayou bulb (onion)
1 tablespoon garlic powder
1 tablespoon salt
1 teaspoon onion powder
1½ tablespoons celery powder
1 tablespoon black pepper
½ tablespoon dried red pepper
1½ tablespoons white pepper
1 tablespoon cayenne pepper, or to taste
1 pound frozen medium or large size thaw-and-serve shrimp

Prepare rice as directed on package. Slice and lightly brown sausage. Combine rice and sausage and all remaining ingredients except spices and shrimp in large Dutch oven. Cover and cook at simmer level. After dish begins to bubble, add spices and shrimp. Continue to simmer for 30 to 45 minutes stirring occasionally (allow enough time for spices to act and react with the ingredients, or the end of your spoon disappears).

If you wish to make your dinner even more Cajun elegant, add oysters and crab meat to the pot when there is only about 10 minutes of cooking time remaining. Caution: Do not use high heat; scorched Jambalaya is gator chow.

12 to 16 servings

Tom Kvasnicka, Finance
—Kewaskum

SEAFOOD STUFFED EGGPLANT

2 large eggplants
Boiling water
1 cup raw shrimp
2 tablespoons green onions
2 cloves garlic, minced
3 teaspoons parsley
½ cup butter
Salt and pepper to taste
1 cup crabmeat
¼ cup French bread crumbs
4 tablespoons Romano cheese

Cut eggplants in half lengthwise. Cook in boiling water to cover. When cool, scoop out and chop or mash pulp.

Preheat oven to 350°. In skillet, saute shrimp, onions, garlic and parsley in butter. Season with salt and pepper. Cook about 10 minutes; add eggplant pulp and crabmeat. Stir together and cook 5 minutes. Sprinkle with bread crumbs and cheese. Bake for 10 to 20 minutes.

Bill (and Eleanor) Hofheinz
Retired Sales Representative
—Louisiana

TUNA LOAF

1 cup canned (drained) or fresh peas
¼ teaspoon pepper
1 6-ounce, or larger, can tuna
1½ cups milk
2 tablespoons chopped onion
1 teaspoon lemon juice
2 eggs, beaten
¼ cup uncooked cream of wheat
½ teaspoon salt
Crushed soda crackers

Mix all ingredients, except crackers, together. Put in loaf pan; cover with crushed soda crackers. Bake at 350° for 1 hour.

4 to 6 servings

Anna Kumrow, Retired
—Kewaskum

COD
with Crabmeat Stuffing

2 slices whole wheat bread
½ medium onion
2 stalks celery with leaves
3 to 4 sprigs fresh parsley
1 tablespoon canola oil
12 ounces imitation crabmeat
3 tablespoons dry white wine, or chicken stock
½ teaspoon salt
Dash white pepper
1½ pounds cod fillets
2 teaspoons lemon juice
2 teaspoons butter, melted
1 teaspoon dill weed
Paprika

In food processor, using S-blade, shred bread to coarse crumbs; set aside. In same workbowl, finely chop onion, celery and parsley. In 10" fry pan, over medium heat, saute vegetables in oil, 3 to 4 minutes, stirring frequently. In same processor workbowl, coarsely shred crab. Stir crab and wine into vegetables; mix well. Remove from heat; stir bread crumbs into crab mixture. Add seasonings; mix well. Spoon into greased 7 x 11" pan. Arrange fish on top of stuffing in single layer. Drizzle lemon juice and butter over fish. Sprinkle with dill weed and paprika. Bake at 325° for 20 to 25 minutes until fish flakes with a fork.

4 to 6 servings

Adeline Halfmann, Retired
—Kewaskum

SALMON PATTIES

½ cup crushed saltine crackers
2 eggs
Scant ⅛ cup milk
1 15-ounce can salmon, drained and flaked*
1 teaspoon lemon juice
¼ cup chopped onion
¼ teaspoon salt
⅛ teaspoon pepper
½ teaspoon sage
¼ teaspoon celery salt
1 tablespoon butter or margarine, melted

Spray 10 or 12" fry pan with non-stick cooking spray. Combine ingredients in order given. Shape mixture into patties and fry until browned on both sides.

* Tuna may be substituted for the salmon, but decrease lemon juice to ½ teaspoon.

Variation: Double entire recipe, except for milk which should be increased to ½ cup, spoon mixture in a greased loaf pan. Bake at 350° for 30 to 40 minutes. Top of loaf should be golden brown and all liquid absorbed.

4 to 6 servings

Elizabeth Stafford, Dept. 2000
—Jacksonville

GRILLED SWORDFISH STEAKS

¼ cup oil
½ cup soy sauce
¼ cup red wine vinegar
2 tablespoons lemon juice
2 tablespoons brown sugar
Dash Worcestershire sauce
1 clove garlic, crushed
4 swordfish steaks, skinned

Combine first seven ingredients; blend well. Pour marinade into heavy storage bag with swordfish steaks; marinate in refrigerator for six hours or more. Grill steaks for 10 minutes on each side.

4 servings

Monica Janzen, Creative Services
—Kewaskum

CHICKEN DIVAN

1 pound fresh broccoli, cut into spears, cooked and drained
2 5-ounce cans chunk white chicken, drained
1 10-ounce can condensed broccoli-cheese soup
⅓ cup milk
½ cup shredded Cheddar cheese
2 tablespoons dry bread crumbs
1 tablespoon butter or margarine, melted

In 9 x 13" baking dish or 9" pie pan arrange broccoli and chicken. Combine soup and milk; pour over broccoli and chicken. Sprinkle cheese over soup mixture. Combine bread crumbs and margarine; sprinkle over cheese. Bake at 450° for 20 minutes until hot and bubbling.

4 servings

Anna Schaeffer, Dept. 15WW
—Kewaskum

CHICKEN POT PIE

4 boneless chicken breasts
½ bag (16 ounces) frozen mixed
 vegetables
1 10-ounce can cream of chicken soup
1 10-ounce can chicken broth
½ cup margarine
1 cup flour
1 cup milk

Boil and dice chicken breasts and put on bottom of 9 x 13" pan. Add mixed vegetables. Pour soup and broth over chicken and vegetables. Melt margarine; mix with flour and milk. Pour over chicken and vegetables. Bake at 350° for 45 minutes.

4 servings

Jewell Zielieke, Sales
—Kewaskum

CHICKEN ENCHILADA

½ cup chopped onions
1 clove garlic, minced
½ cup sliced black olives
4 ounces chopped green chilies, drained
½ cup sour cream
1 10¾-ounce can cream of chicken soup,
 divided
½ cup cubed, cooked chicken
½ cup shredded Cheddar cheese, divided
6 flour tortillas

Mix together onions, garlic, olives, chilies, sour cream and ½ cup chicken soup. Add chicken and ¼ cup cheese. Put 1/6 mixture in each tortilla and roll up. Place in greased

9 x 13" baking pan. Spread remaining soup and cheese over top. Bake at 350° for 30 minutes.

6 servings

Dick (and Jean) Myers, Retired
—Kewaskum

CHICKEN FAJITAS

Marinade:
¾ cup Robusto Italian dressing (or other
 brand, but add 2 cloves garlic, chopped)
4 to 5 teaspoons soy sauce
½ teaspoon ground cumin
Juice of ½ lime, plus slices of remaining
 half
1 small onion, sliced

3 whole chicken breasts
3 sweet bell peppers; red, green and
 yellow, cut in strips
1 medium onion, sliced and halved
2 tablespoons olive oil
8 to 10 medium flour tortillas
Sour cream
Salsa
12 black olives, sliced

Place chicken in marinade in 9 x 13" glass pan or in heavy duty storage bag. Marinate 4 hours in refrigerator; turn occasionally.

Saute peppers and onion in olive oil until crisp-tender. Keep warm. Using indirect method and medium-hot coals, grill chicken 4 to 5 minutes per side until done, but not dry. Slice across grain in ¼" strips.

Warm tortillas in microwave according to package directions. Place chicken, sweet peppers and onions on tortillas. Add sour cream, salsa and black olives to taste. Fold bottom up first, then left and right sides to middle. Flip over and serve.

8 to 10 servings

Bob Branston, Creative Services
—Kewaskum

CHICKEN BREASTS

3 whole chicken breasts, split
1 10-ounce can cream of mushroom soup
1 10-ounce can cream of chicken soup
¼ cup wine
1 8-ounce can mushrooms
2 cups crushed croutons
½ cup butter, melted

Place chicken in 9 x 13" baking dish. Mix soups, wine and mushrooms; spread over chicken. Top with croutons and butter. Bake at 350° for 1 hour.

6 servings

Ruth Raether, Retired
—Kewaskum

BAKED CHICKEN AND RICE

1 10.75-ounce can cream of chicken or celery soup
1 soup can water
1 cup uncooked rice
4 chicken breasts
1 tablespoon butter or margarine

Pour soup, water and rice in baking dish; mix well. Layer chicken on rice; dot with butter. Bake at 350° for 40 minutes.

4 servings

Kathy Smith, Manager, Regal Outlet Store
—Jacksonville

SOUR CREAM CHICKEN BREASTS

3 chicken breasts, split
1 cup sour cream
1 10-ounce can cream of mushroom soup
½ soup can cream sherry wine
1 small can sliced mushrooms
Paprika

Place chicken breasts in 9 x 13" baking dish without overlapping. Mix remaining ingredients together and spoon over each chicken breast and to corners of pan. Sprinkle with paprika. Bake covered at 350° for 1 hour; uncover and bake for 30 minutes.

Variation: Substitute 1 whole cut up chicken and 1 can cream of chicken soup for cream of mushroom soup.

6 servings

Pat Buechel, 16PR-CDT
—Kewaskum

CHICKEN NORMANDY

2 chicken breasts, skinned, halved
¼ teaspoon pepper
Flour
2 tart cooking apples, quartered, cored, sliced
1½ tablespoons butter or margarine
2 teaspoons oil
¼ cup minced onion
½ cup chicken broth or bouillon
½ cup evaporated skim milk

Sprinkle chicken with pepper. If desired, dip in flour and pat briskly to remove excess. In large skillet, saute apple slices in butter or margarine until tender. Remove and keep warm.

Add oil to skillet and when warm, add chicken. Cook, turning once, over moderate heat 8 to 10 minutes, or until golden brown. Add onion to skillet and saute until tender. Drain remaining fat from skillet. Add chicken broth or bouillon and simmer gently 30 minutes. Broth will be reduced by about half and chicken nearly done. Add evaporated milk and apples; cook until apples are warmed through and sauce is slightly thickened.

4 servings

Skip Hillary, Sales
—Texas

CHICKEN SALTIMBOCCA

3 large chicken breasts
6 thin slices boiled ham
3 slices Mozzarella cheese, halved
1 medium tomato, seeded and chopped
½ teaspoon dried sage, crushed
⅓ cup fine, dry bread crumbs
2 tablespoons grated Parmesan cheese
2 tablespoons snipped parsley
4 tablespoons butter or margarine,
   melted

Remove skin and bones from chicken. Cut each in half lengthwise. Place chicken, boned side up, on cutting board. Place a piece of clear plastic wrap over meat. Working from center out, pound each piece lightly with a meat mallet to 5 x 5" size. Remove wrap. Place a ham slice and half a cheese slice on each cutlet, cutting to fit. Top with chopped tomato and dash of sage. Tuck in sides; roll up, jelly roll style, pressing to seal well. Combine bread crumbs, Parmesan cheese and parsley. Dip chicken in melted butter; than roll in crumb mixture. Place in shallow baking pan, seam side down. Bake at 350° for 30 to 40 minutes.

6 servings

L.N. (and Pat) Peterson
Founder Chairman of the Board

CHICKEN AND DRESSING

1 whole chicken
1 large onion, diced
1 teaspoon salt
1 teaspoon black pepper
2 tablespoons ground sage
3 medium green onions, chopped

Dressing:
3 6-ounce packages Martha White
   Cotton Pickin Cornbread
1 5-ounce can evaporated milk
1 cup water

Boil chicken, without liver, gizzard and heart. Debone and cut into small pieces; reserve broth. Combine meat with next 5 ingredients; mix well. Place in roasting pan

and bake at 350° until brown and firm; stir occasionally and season to taste.

While chicken is cooking, combine dressing ingredients; stir well. Grease a 12" steel skillet with Crisco; dust with flour. Pour cornbread mixture into hot skillet; cook at 350° until brown and firm.

When both are done, crumble cornbread into chicken and stir well. Adjust seasonings if necessary.

6 to 8 servings

George Robinson
(for Mrs. H.B. Robinson), Dept. 2000
—Jacksonville

CHICKEN AND DUMPLINGS

1 whole chicken
Water

Dumplings:
2 cups flour
4 teaspoons baking powder
1 teaspoon sugar
½ teaspoon salt
Cold water or milk to make a stiff drop
   batter

Place chicken in soup pot; cover with water and simmer until tender, 2 or 3 hours. When done, remove chicken and debone. Return chicken to stock and bring to boil.

Sift flour, baking powder, sugar and salt together. Add water or milk a little at a time until mixture is stiff. Drop by spoonfuls into boiling stock, cover and cook for 12 minutes. Do not lift cover until dumplings are done.

6 to 8 servings

Deborah Young, Outlet Store Manager
—Pigeon Forge, TN

CHICKEN WITH RICE

1 cup uncooked rice
10 pieces chicken, skinned
1 10-ounce can golden mushroom soup
1 package dry onion soup mix
1 soup can water
Poultry seasoning, salt and pepper to taste

Layer ingredients in order listed in ungreased 9 x 13" pan. Cover with aluminum foil. Bake at 350° for 2 hours.

4 to 6 servings

Linda Gehring, Dept. 2000
—Kewaskum

CHICKEN CONTINENTAL

¾ cup flour
Salt and pepper
3 pounds chicken, cut up, skin removed
¼ cup butter or margarine
1 teaspoon poultry seasoning
¼ teaspoon salt
¼ teaspoon pepper
½ tablespoon dried parsley
2 10-ounce cans mushroom soup
2 cups water
2 cups Minute Rice

Mix flour with salt and pepper in plastic bag; add chicken pieces and shake to coat. Brown chicken in butter on all sides. Remove and set aside. To drippings add poultry seasoning, salt, pepper, parsley, soup and water; simmer until hot and bubbly.

Spread rice evenly in bottom of 9 x 13" pan or small roaster. Pour soup mixture over rice and stir. Place chicken on top. Bake, covered, at 350° for 45 minutes, or until chicken is done.

4 to 6 servings

Leah Hartmann, International Division
—Kewaskum

CHICKEN WITH PEACHES AND WALNUTS

1 2½- to 3-pound broiler/fryer chicken, cut up and skinned
½ cup whole grain flour
1 1-pound/13-ounce can peach halves or slices in light syrup
¾ cup margarine
⅓ cup orange juice
⅓ cup walnuts

Wash chicken and pat dry. Coat with flour, shaking off excess. Place in shallow, medium baking dish. Drain peaches, saving ¾ of syrup. Melt margarine in small saucepan; stir in orange juice and peach syrup. Pour over chicken. Bake at 375° for 1 hour; basting several times. Add peaches and walnuts. Continue baking, basting once, for 15 minutes or until chicken is tender and glazed.

4 servings

Linda Hodges, Outlet Store
—Pigeon Forge, TN

ROASTED DUCK

2 duck breasts, skinned and deboned
1 can pineapple cubes, juice reserved
Lemon pepper to taste

Sauce:
6 tablespoons duck sauce liqueur*
1 tablespoon orange liqueur or freshly squeezed orange juice
2 tablespoons honey
1 green pepper, cut in strips
½ teaspoon nutmeg

* Available in Chinese section of grocery store.

Marinate duck in pineapple and juice for 6 to 8 hours. Cover both sides of duck with lemon pepper. Preheat gas grill or broiler to high. In mixing bowl, combine sauce ingredients.

Cook duck on grill for 6 minutes; turn over. Reduce heat, cover with sauce and finish cooking, 4 to 6 minutes.

2 servings

Ken Layden, Sales Representative
—Charlotte

TURKEY KABOBS

1 whole turkey breast, deboned and cut into 2" cubes
1 to 3 teaspoons freshly grated ginger-root
½ teaspoon dry mustard
1 tablespoon molasses (or sugar)
½ cup soy sauce
1 large clove garlic, minced
Pineapple, onion, cherry tomatoes and green pepper

Combine all ingredients and marinate overnight. Put meat on skewers with pineapple, onion, cherry tomatoes and green pepper, as desired. Cook on hot grill until well browned.

12 to 14 servings

Tom Hoffman, Purchasing
—Kewaskum

SAUERKRAUT BAKE DISH

1½ pounds pork, cut in cubes
1 32-ounce can sauerkraut
1 12-ounce package Kluski noodles
1 10-ounce can cream of mushroom soup
1 to 2 cups potato chips

In fry pan, brown meat until done. Drain grease and set aside. Mix remaining ingredients together; add meat and mix well. Pour into buttered casserole dish. Sprinkle with lightly crushed potato chips. Bake at 350° for 1½ hours.

6 to 8 servings

Kathleen Remus, Dept. 15WW
—Kewaskum

SKILLET DINNER

1½ to 2 pounds bulk seasoned pork sausage
1 cup chopped onions
1 cup chopped green pepper
1 clove garlic, minced
8 ounces tri-color rotini pasta
1 28-ounce can stewed tomatoes with liquid
1 8-ounce can tomato sauce
½ cup water
1 4-ounce can sliced mushrooms, drained
2 tablespoons chili powder
1 teaspoon cumin
1 teaspoon salt
½ cup sliced black olives
1 cup sour half-and-half
1½ cups shredded Co-Jack cheese

In large non-stick fry pan over medium-high heat, brown sausage, breaking into bite-size pieces. Drain in colander; discard fat. Return to fry pan with onions, peppers and garlic. Cook and stir 5 to 7 minutes until onions are glossy. Add remaining ingredients, except olives, sour half-and-half and cheese. Bring to boil, stirring occasionally. Cover; reduce heat to low and simmer 30 to 40 minutes, until pasta is al dente. Stir in sour half-and-half and olives; heat through. Sprinkle cheese evenly over top. Cover for 5 minutes to melt cheese.

Variation: Add 1 15-ounce can whole kernel corn, drained with mushrooms.

6 to 8 servings

Adeline Halfmann, Retired
—Kewaskum

RIO RANCHO DELIGHT

This recipe won first place in the Spam contest at the State Fair in Little Rock, AR in October, 1993.

½ cup margarine
½ cup flour
¼ teaspoon garlic powder
2 teaspoons cumin powder
3 tablespoons chili powder
¼ teaspoon black pepper
1 heaping teaspoon paprika
1 large jalapeno pepper, minced
1 teaspoon jalapeno juice
3 cups water
1 cup rice, cooked and fluffed
1 12-ounce can regular Spam, cut into ¼" strips
3 cups grated American cheese
½ cup thinly sliced green onions

In heavy saucepan, melt margarine; add flour and mix well. Add spices, jalapenos, juice and water; cook until thick. Simmer 5 minutes.

In baking dish, layer rice and Spam; pour sauce over rice and Spam. Sprinkle cheese on top. Bake at 400° until cheese melts; garnish with green onions.

4 to 6 servings

Jack Steivers, Purchasing Agent
—Jacksonville

PASTA/PANCETTA

1 medium onion, chopped
2 tablespoons butter
3 tablespoons olive oil
1 slice pancetta cut ¼" thick or Canadian bacon
1 14½-ounce can Italian tomatoes
Salt to taste
½ to 1 teaspoon red pepper (½ teaspoon dried)
1 pound pasta, any shape, uncooked
3 tablespoons shredded Parmesan cheese
1 tablespoon shredded Romano cheese

Saute onions in butter and oil until pale gold. Add pancetta and cook 1 minute. Add tomatoes, salt, pepper and cook over medium heat 25 minutes.

Cook pasta. Combine pasta and sauce with cheeses and serve.

6 servings

Dick (and Jean) Myers, Retired
—Kewaskum

HAM 'N BROCCOLI ROLLS

6 thin slices boiled ham
6 slices Swiss cheese
1 10-ounce package frozen broccoli spears, cooked and drained
2 tablespoons margarine
2 tablespoons flour
½ teaspoon salt
¼ teaspoon sweet basil
Dash black pepper
1½ cups milk
1 2.8-ounce can Durkee French fried onions

Top ham slices with cheese. Place broccoli spears on each slice and roll. Secure with toothpicks. Place in shallow baking dish. In saucepan, melt margarine; blend in flour and seasonings. Gradually add milk; cook and stir until thick. Stir in ⅔ can fried onions. Pour over ham; cover and bake at 350° for 25 minutes. Top with remaining onions and bake, uncovered 5 minutes longer.

6 servings

Linda Gehring, Dept. 2000-Set Pack
—Kewaskum

HAM LOGS

1½ pounds ground ham
¾ pound ground pork
2 eggs
1½ cups bread crumbs

Sauce:
¾ cup brown sugar
2¼ teaspoons dry mustard
¼ cup + 2 tablespoons vinegar
¾ cup hot water

Combine ham, pork, eggs and bread crumbs. Form into small logs and place in 9 x 13" pan. Combine all sauce ingredients and pour over logs. Bake at 350° for 1 hour.

6 to 8 servings

Rita Spoerl, Retired
—Kewaskum

OUR FAVORITE HAM LOAF

2 pounds lean ground pork
1 pound ground cured ham
1 egg, beaten
½ cup milk
1 cup crushed cornflakes or oatmeal
1 teaspoon salt
½ 10-ounce can tomato soup

Combine all ingredients; press into loaf pan. Bake at 350° for 2 hours.

10 servings

Karen Sparks, Accounts Payable
—Kewaskum

SWEDISH HAM BALLS

1 pound ground smoked ham
1 pound ground pork
1¾ cups bread crumbs
1 cup milk
2 eggs
1½ cups packed brown sugar
½ cup cider vinegar
½ cup water
1½ teaspoons dry mustard

In medium mixing bowl, combine ham, pork, crumbs, milk and eggs. Mix until completely blended. Shape mixture into 1½" balls. Place in 9 x 13" pan; set aside. Preheat oven to 350°. In medium saucepan, combine remaining ingredients. Bring to boil over medium-high heat, stirring occasionally. Boil 1 minute and pour over meat balls. Bake uncovered for 2 hours, basting occasionally.

6 to 8 servings

Susan Portmann-Anderson, Marketing
—Kewaskum

ORANGE RICE PORK CHOPS

6 ¾" pork chops
Salt and pepper to taste
1⅓ cups cooked rice
1 cup orange juice
1 can condensed chicken soup (not cream)

In fry pan, brown chops and season. Spread rice in 12 x 7" baking dish. Pour orange juice over top and mix. Place chops on top and pour soup over all. Cover and bake at 350° for 45 minutes. Uncover and bake 10 minutes more.

6 servings

Bill (and Lucy) McCarty, Retired
—Kewaskum

PORK CHOPS WITH GRAVY

Lawrys seasoning salt and pepper to taste
6 to 8 medium-thick pork chops, fat trimmed
1 large onion, sliced
1 10-ounce can cream of mushroom soup
½ to ¾ soup can water
Kitchen Bouquet

Sprinkle seasoning salt and pepper on pork chops as desired. Brown pork chops on both sides in cast aluminum pan. Remove from pan. Put small amount of water in pan; add onions and cook to transparent. Return pork chops to pan.

In medium mixing bowl, blend soup and ½ to ¾ can of water. Stir in Kitchen Bouquet until light brown color. Pour over pork chops and onions; turn heat to low; cover and simmer for 1 to 1½ hours.

6 to 8 servings

Lester (and LaVerne) Schaub, Retired
—Kewaskum

SCALLOPED POTATOES AND PORK CHOPS

5 cups thinly sliced potatoes
1 cup chopped onions
Salt and pepper to taste
1 10-ounce can mushroom soup, undiluted
½ cup sour cream
6 pork chops, 1" thick

In greased 9 x 13" pan, layer ½ potatoes, onions, salt and pepper. Repeat layers. Combine soup and sour cream; pour over potatoes mixture. Bake at 375° for 35 minutes.

While potatoes are baking, brown chops. Place chops on top of potatoes, cover and return to oven for 45 minutes or until chops are tender. Uncover last 15 minutes of baking.

6 servings

Marianne Wondra, Retired
—Kewaskum

PORK TENDERLOIN WITH CREAM AND CAPERS

1¼ pounds pork tenderloin
2 shallots
1½ tablespoons butter
Salt and ground pepper to taste
½ cup chicken stock
½ cup heavy cream
2 tablespoons capers

Cut tenderloin in ¾" thick slices. Mince shallots. Melt butter in large fry pan. Season pork with salt and pepper; saute over medium heat, turning once, until done but still springy to touch, about 6 minutes. Transfer to plate.

Add stock to pan and deglaze pan. Add shallots and cook over high heat, stirring often, until liquid is thickened, about 10 minutes. Stir in cream and return meat to pan along with any juices. Cook over low

heat just to warm, about 5 minutes. Add capers and season to taste.

4 servings

Kim Peterson
—Kewaskum

SCHWEINEHAXE

6 large pork hocks
3 medium onions, chopped
4 cloves garlic
Salt and freshly ground pepper to taste
½ teaspoon nutmeg
½ teaspoon cloves
½ teaspoon allspice

Preheat oven to 450°. Clean hocks and place on end in shallow roasting pan. Roast for 15 minutes or until skin has turned a light brown.

Saute onion and garlic in Dutch oven large enough to hold the hocks. Add hocks, cover with water. Add spices and boil over high heat. Reduce heat to simmer, partially cover and cook for 1½ to 2 hours.

Remove from liquid, place hocks in shallow roasting pan and broil each side approximately 15 minutes to crisp skin. Keep warm until ready to serve.

Serve with red cabbage with apples.

6 servings

Kim Peterson
—Kewaskum

PICKLED PIGS FEET

8 pigs feet with uppers
1 quart vinegar
1 tablespoon whole cloves
4 bay leaves
1 stick cinnamon
¼ cup salt
1 teaspoon pepper
¼ cup brown sugar
1 small onion, sliced

Place pigs feet in soup pot with water to cover; bring to boil. Reduce heat to low. Simmer 2½ to 3 hours or until meat is tender. Remove pigs feet to large bowl; reserve liquid. Combine vinegar, cloves, bay leaves, cinnamon, salt, pepper, brown sugar and onion in small saucepan; simmer 1 hour. Strain liquid to remove spices and add to 2 to 4 cups of reserved liquid. Pour over pigs feet and chill for 2 days or longer.

4 servings

Francis (and Jeane) Gilboy, Retired
—Kewaskum

RAZORBACK SQUIRREL MULLIGAN

2 squirrels, serving-size pieces
4 pork chops, or small pork roast
1 cut up chicken
2 large onions, chopped
10 large potatoes, peeled and cut up
½ cup catsup
2 hot peppers, chopped
1 quart tomatoes
1 15-ounce can English peas
1 15-ounce can creamed corn
1 tablespoon flour

Boil squirrels, pork chops and chicken in water to cover until tender; remove bones. Return meat to broth; add onions and potatoes. Cook until almost tender. Add catsup, peppers, tomatoes, peas and corn. Cook 15 to 20 minutes, stirring frequently. Mix flour with 1 cup hot liquid; stir until all lumps are gone. Add to mulligan to thicken.

Bill Garlington, Sr. Industrial Engineer
—Jacksonville

FILET OF LAMB WITH BASIL AND GARLIC FLAN

10 cloves garlic, divided
2 cups chicken stock
2 eggs
1 egg yolk
8 ounces heavy cream
3 medium zucchini
6 plum tomatoes
Salt and pepper to taste
½ to 1 teaspoon dry thyme
1 tablespoon olive oil
½ tomato
10 basil leaves
2 pounds (½ loin) lamb*
2 cups lamb stock

For garlic flan, preheat oven to 300°. Peel 9 garlic cloves, cut in half and take out the germ. Blanch three times in water, then cook with chicken stock and reduce to glaze. Pour into blender and process until smooth. Beat eggs, add cream and garlic mixture. Cook in 2-ounce cups surrounded by boiling water for 35 minutes.

Increase oven temperature to 350°. Wash zucchini and plum tomatoes under cold water. Cut in half lengthwise and slice very thin. In a small flat sheet pan, alternate slices of tomatoes and zucchini, season with salt and pepper, dry thyme and olive oil. Bake for 10 minutes.

Peel the ½ tomato and keep only the meat. Make paste with tomato pulp, basil, last garlic clove and olive oil in blender.

Increase oven temperature to 400°. Place loins of lamb in hot pan, give nice color on both sides and cook them in hot oven for 5 minutes for medium-rare, rest for at least 5 minutes before serving.

Deglaze pan with lamb stock, reduce to ⅓ and add tomato paste to give a good consistency, then strain sauce, check seasoning.

Put garlic flan in center of plate, then sauce, four noisettes cut from loin around the flan and zucchini and tomatoes on the edge.

* ½ loin = approximately ¾ pound meat and ¼ pound tenderloin.

6 servings

Kim Peterson
—Kewaskum

KIELBASA AND CABBAGE

6 slices bacon
1 medium head cabbage, cut into small
  wedges
1 medium onion, chopped
¼ cup water
1 teaspoon minced garlic
1 teaspoon salt
2 tablespoons sugar
2 teaspoons caraway seed
1 pound kielbasa

In large skillet, fry bacon until crisp; remove from pan and set aside. To drippings,
add cabbage, onion, water, garlic, salt,
sugar and caraway. Cook covered over
medium heat for 10 minutes. Add kielbasa;
cover and cook for another 10 minutes or
until kielbasa is heated through. Top with
crumbled bacon.

4 to 6 servings

Marilyn Loomis, 15 East Line
—Kewaskum

MEAT POT

3 to 4 quarts sauerkraut
1 to 2 cups water
1 2-quart jar cooked white pinto navy
  beans
2 to 3 16-ounce cans small whole
  potatoes, drained
1 apple, sliced with peel
1 bay leaf
1 clove garlic
7 Italian sausages
7 brats
7 hot dogs
1 large ring bologna, skinned
7 thin, lean pork chops

In large cooking pot, blend sauerkraut with
juice, water, beans, potatoes with juice,
apple, bay leaf and garlic. Heat to boil. At
same time, brown all meat individually,
pouring off grease into sauerkraut mixture. Cut bologna in 6 to 8 pieces.

Add browned meats to sauerkraut mixture
placing pork chops on top last. Simmer 2
hours, stirring occasionally by putting a
spatula down the sides of pot so as not to
disturb pork chops. You can brown all

meats the day before, refrigerate and then
assemble and cook the next day.

12 to 18 servings

Linda Gehring, Dept. 2000-Set Pack
—Kewaskum

SMOKED SAUSAGE ROAST

2 pounds smoked sausage (Eckridge)
2 cups water
2 16-ounce cans green beans
6 to 8 medium-size potatoes, peeled
1 large onion, diced
1 medium-size head cabbage, sliced

Brown sausage in 10" fry pan; transfer to
5-quart Dutch oven. Add 2 cups water,
green beans, potatoes, onion and cabbage.
Cook over medium heat, uncovered, for 1
hour or until all water has evaporated.
Potatoes should have light brown color to
have good flavor.

6 to 8 servings

Anita Cassidy, Dept. 8400
—Jacksonville

HAM-BURGER ROLL-UPS

1 cup fresh bread crumbs
½ cup milk
1½ pounds ground round beef
2 tablespoons minced onion
2 teaspoons Worcestershire sauce
2 teaspoons seasoned salt
¼ teaspoon seasoned pepper
6 slices boiled ham, ⅛" thick
18 whole cloves
3 tablespoons butter or margarine
⅔ cup light brown sugar
½ cup fresh orange juice
2 teaspoons prepared mustard
1 16-ounce can apricot halves, drained
1 8-ounce can sliced cling peaches,
  drained
½ cup pineapple chunks, drained
½ cup green grapes, optional

Start about 1½ hours before dinner, or
prepare the night before and refrigerate.

Soak bread crumbs in milk a few minutes. In medium bowl, combine bread mixture with ground round, onion, Worcestershire, salt and pepper. Mix well. Preheat oven to 350°. Divide meat mixture into 6 portions; spread a portion on each ham slice. Roll jelly roll-fashion; place side by side, seam-side down in 9 x 13" pan. Stud each roll with 3 cloves.

Melt butter in small saucepan. Stir in brown sugar and orange juice. Cook until sugar is melted; then stir in mustard. Pour sauce over ham rolls. Bake 45 minutes, basting occasionally. Add apricots, peaches, pineapple chunks and grapes. Bake an additional 10 minutes, or until fruit is heated through.

6 servings

L.N. (and Pat) Peterson
Founder Chairman of the Board

MANICOTTI

1 pound ground beef
½ pound ground pork or 3 pork
   sausages, skinned
1 onion, chopped
1 32-ounce jar spaghetti sauce
1 15-ounce can stewed tomatoes
Italian seasoning
Dash red pepper
Garlic powder to taste
1 teaspoon oregano
½ pound grated Mozzarella cheese
1 8-ounce package manicotti noodles,
   partially cooked and drained

In frying pan, brown meat and onion. Drain off grease and let cool. In medium saucepan, combine spaghetti sauce, tomatoes and seasonings. Simmer for 20 minutes. Add ½ grated cheese and some sauce to make thick consistency; stuff noodles and place in baking dish. Pour remaining sauce on top of noodles and sprinkle with remaining cheese. Bake at 350° for 40 minutes.

6 to 8 servings

Heather Werner, 1600 DCT Drip
—Kewaskum

ZUCCHINI LASAGNA

5 strips bacon, cut up
1 pound ground beef
1 large onion, diced
2 cups tomatoes
5 cups diced, unpeeled zucchini
½ teaspoon garlic powder
½ teaspoon celery salt
½ teaspoon Italian seasoning
2 teaspoons salt
⅛ teaspoon pepper
½ teaspoon ground oregano
½ cup grated Cheddar cheese
8 ounces shredded Mozzarella cheese
½ cup dry bread crumbs

In large skillet, brown bacon and beef. Drain off grease and set aside. Add all ingredients except cheeses and bread crumbs. Simmer uncovered 20 minutes, stirring occasionally. Mix meat and zucchini mixture together and put into 9 x 13" baking dish. Top with cheeses and bread crumbs.

Bake uncovered at 350° for 1 hour.

6 to 8 servings

Bill (and Lucy) McCarty, Retired
—Kewaskum

BAKED PIZZA

1 8-ounce package lasagna noodles
1½ pounds ground beef
1 10.75-ounce can cream of mushroom
   soup
2 soup cans water
Favorite pizza toppings - onions,
   mushrooms, green peppers, olives, etc.
1 14-ounce jar Ragu pizza sauce
Shredded Mozzarella cheese

Place uncooked noodles on bottom of 9 x 13" pan. Put raw meat on noodles. Mix soup and water and pour over meat. Add any other ingredients. Pour pizza sauce over top; sprinkle with cheese. Bake at 350° for 1 hour.

Cheese may also be put on top during last 15 minutes of baking.

12 to 18 servings

Bonnie Will, Personnel Dept.
—Kewaskum

MEXICAN GOULASH

1½ pounds ground beef
1 package dry taco seasoning
1 15-ounce can tomato sauce
1 15-ounce can whole kernel corn, drained
1 15-ounce can ranch-style beans
1 16-ounce bag Doritos
8 ounces grated Cheddar cheese
Picante sauce
Sour cream

Brown meat in 11" skillet and drain. Add taco seasoning and tomato sauce; stir. Pour in corn and beans; stir. Let simmer 15 minutes. Put Doritos on individual plates and spoon meat mixture on top. Sprinkle grated cheese, picante sauce or sour cream on top to taste.

4 to 6 servings

Gail Smart, Data Processing Dept.
Saladmaster, Inc.
—Arlington, TX

CABBAGE ROLLS

8 cabbage leaves
1 pound ground beef
¾ cup cooked rice
1 teaspoon salt
⅛ teaspoon pepper
1 egg
¼ cup chopped onion
1 10-ounce can tomato soup
1 soup can water

Pour boiling water over cabbage leaves. Let stand in water for 5 minutes so that leaves are soft enough to roll. Combine meat, rice, salt, pepper, egg and onion; mix well. Put small amount (⅛) of mixture in cabbage leaf and roll; fasten with toothpick.

Place rolls in baking dish. Combine soup and water; mix well. Pour over cabbage rolls and bake 1 hour. If juice gets too thick, add more water.

8 servings

Helene Benzing, Retired
—Kewaskum

CABBAGE ROLLS

1 large head cabbage, cored
2 pounds ground chuck
½ cup uncooked rice
1 large onion, diced
2 eggs
Salt, pepper and garlic salt to taste
1 16-ounce can sauerkraut
½ to 1 pound kielbasa, thickly sliced
1 15-ounce can tomato sauce
1 10-ounce can tomato soup

Parboil cabbage; cool. Mix meat, rice, onions, eggs, salt, pepper and garlic salt. Place 1 tablespoon meat combination on cabbage leaf. Roll and tuck in ends. Place in roasting pan with kielbasa and sauerkraut. Mix together tomato sauce and soup; pour over cabbage rolls. Bake at 375° for 1½ hours.

12 to 16 servings

Tom Hoffman, Purchasing
—Kewaskum

STUFFED PEPPERS

1 pound ground beef
1 medium onion, chopped
1 egg
¼ teaspoon pepper
1 small can Spanish Rice
¼ cup catsup
1 teaspoon salt
½ cup uncooked Minute rice
5 or 6 large peppers
2 or 3 medium-size potatoes, peeled and quartered
1 10-ounce can tomato soup
½ soup can water

Combine all ingredients except peppers, potatoes, soup and water; mix well. Cut peppers in half and remove seeds; place in baking dish, cut side up. Fill each pepper with rice/meat mixture. Place potato chunks on top of peppers.

Mix soup and water; pour over peppers. Bake at 350° for 1½ hours.

10 to 12 servings

Catherine Schickert
—Kewaskum

MEAT PIES

Filling:
1 teaspoon shortening
1 pound ground beef
1 pound ground pork
1 bunch green onions, chopped
1 bell pepper, chopped
1 clove garlic, minced
Salt, black pepper and red pepper to taste
1 tablespoon flour

Crust:
4 cups flour
2 teaspoons salt
1 teaspoon baking powder
½ cup shortening
1 egg
1 cup milk

For filling, melt shortening in heavy fry pan. Cook meat, vegetables and seasonings. Stir often. When meat is done remove from heat. Stir in flour.

For crust, sift dry ingredients; cut in shortening. Combine egg and milk, blend well. Work liquid mixture gradually into dry ingredients until proper consistency to roll. Break into small pieces and roll very thin. Cut into rounds using a saucer as guide.

Place a large tablespoon of meat filling along edge and halfway to center of round dough. Fold in half; seal edges with fork. Drop in deep fat and cook until golden brown. Drain and serve hot.

Approximately 18 pies

Emogene Brundige, Dept. 2000
—Jacksonville

NEW COUNTRY PIE

Crust:
½ cup bread crumbs
1 pound ground beef
¼ cup chopped onions
Salt and pepper
½ cup tomato sauce

Filling:
1⅓ cups rice
1½ cups tomato sauce
1 cup water

Combine crust ingredients and pat on bottom and up sides of 9 x 9" pan. Combine filling ingredients and fill crust. Bake at 350° covered for 25 minutes, and uncovered for 15 minutes.

8 to 9 servings

Jill Brennan, Sales Dept.
—Kewaskum

GERMAN MEATBALLS

2 slices white bread, cubed
1 12-ounce can beer, divided
1 pound lean ground round
½ cup shredded American process cheese
1 teaspoon salt
Dash pepper
2 tablespoons butter
½ cup chopped onion
1 tablespoon brown sugar
1 tablespoon vinegar
1 teaspoon beef stock
1 12-ounce package egg noodles, cooked to package directions
1 teaspoon caraway seed

Soak bread in ½ cup beer. Combine beef, cheese, salt, pepper and bread mixture; mix well. Shape into 16 meatballs. Brown on high in butter in heavy 10" skillet. Remove meatballs. Cook onion on medium in drippings. Stir in sugar, vinegar, beef stock and remaining beer. Return meatballs to sauce. Cover. Cook over low heat 20 minutes. Thicken gravy if desired. Serve over hot buttered noodles sprinkled with caraway seeds.

4 servings

Kay Fuller, Daughter of Adrienne Evans
(deceased)
—Club Aluminum

BIRDSNEST MEATBALLS

1½ pounds ground beef
1 pound pork sausage
1 small package crushed saltine crackers
6 to 8 slices bread, ripped into bite-size
   pieces
1 large onion, chopped
½ teaspoon salt
½ teaspoon pepper
1 6-ounce package Stove Top stuffing
2 10.75-ounce cans cream of mushroom
   soup
1 cup water

Combine first 7 ingredients; mix well. Form meatballs into birdsnest shape, leaving center partially open. Bake at 350° in 9 x 13" baking dish for 30 minutes. Remove from oven. Make stuffing according to package directions. Add to center of meatballs. Mix soup with water and pour over meatballs. Bake for additional 1 hour.

6 to 8 servings

Anita Cassidy, Dept. 8400
—Jacksonville

BRIDE'S MEATLOAF

1 cup fine cracker crumbs
1 cup milk
1½ pounds hamburger
1 teaspoon salt
½ teaspoon Accent
Pepper to taste
2 eggs, beaten
2 tablespoons chopped celery
2 tablespoons chopped parsley
½ cup chopped onion
½ cup chili sauce or 1 10-ounce can
   tomato soup

Soak cracker crumbs in milk. Add hamburger, salt, Accent, pepper, eggs, celery, parsley and onion; mix well. Put in buttered shallow loaf pan. Spread with chili sauce or tomato soup. Bake at 350° for 1 hour.

6 to 8 servings

Darlene Pesch, Retired
—Kewaskum

MEATLOAF

1 pound lean ground beef
1 egg, beaten
½ cup finely chopped onion
1½ teaspoons salt
⅔ cup tomato paste
⅔ cup evaporated milk (5-ounce can)
¼ to ½ cup catsup

Mix all ingredients except catsup together well. Grease loaf pan with Crisco and heat in oven until warm. Spread meatloaf in pan. Bake at 350° until brown and firm. Spread catsup over meatloaf; let stand 5 to 10 minutes before serving.

6 to 8 servings

George Robinson
(for Mrs. H.B. Robinson), Dept. 2000
—Jacksonville

ITALIAN MEATLOAF

1 pound ground beef
1 egg
1 teaspoon oregano
1 teaspoon Italian seasoning
⅛ teaspoon basil
Ritz crackers
1 pound Mozzarella cheese
2 4-ounce cans mushrooms, drained, or 8
   ounces fresh mushrooms

Mix first 5 ingredients. Crush enough crackers into meatloaf mixture to hold mixture together. Separate mixture into two parts. Form one part into u-shape and place in glass loaf pan to form sides. Grate or slice cheese. Put ½ cheese in hollow of meatloaf; add mushrooms and then remaining cheese. Take second part of meatloaf mixture, make same shape and form on top of other. Pinch the two parts together. Bake at 350° for 45 to 55 minutes. Let cool 10 minutes before serving.

6 to 8 servings

Heide Ewerdt, Dept. 1400
—Kewaskum

SICILIAN MEATLOAF

2 eggs, beaten
½ cup tomato juice or paste
1½ cups soft bread crumbs
2 tablespoons parsley
½ teaspoon salt
½ teaspoon mixed Italian spices
½ teaspoon pepper
1 clove garlic, minced
2 pounds ground beef
4 to 6 slices ham
1½ cups shredded Mozzarella cheese

In bowl, combine eggs and tomato juice. Stir in bread crumbs, parsley, spices and garlic. Add ground beef and mix well.

Shape meat mixture into 8 x 10" rectangle on foil or waxed paper. Arrange ham slices on top of meat leaving small margin around edges. Sprinkle cheese over ham. Starting from short end, carefully roll up meat using foil or waxed paper to lift. Seal edges and ends. Place seam side down in bread pan.

Bake at 350° for approximately 1½ hours. Remove from oven and let stand 10 to 20 minutes before removing to serve.

8 to 10 servings

Laura Wollerman, Direct Sales
—Kewaskum

SWEET AND SOUR MEATLOAF

1 8-ounce can tomato sauce
1 teaspoon prepared mustard
¼ cup brown sugar
¼ cup vinegar
2 pounds ground round
1 small onion, minced
¼ cup crushed crackers
1½ teaspoons salt
¼ teaspoon pepper
1 egg, beaten

Combine first four ingredients; stir until sugar dissolves. Combine meat with remaining ingredients plus ½ cup of tomato sauce mixture. Shape into oval loaf and turn into shallow baking dish. Pour remaining sauce over meat loaf. Bake at 400°

for 45 minutes; baste while baking. For extra sauce to serve over sliced meatloaf, double sauce ingredients.

8 to 10 servings

Jim Portmann, Retired Sales Representative
—Minneapolis

OVEN BARBECUED BRISKET

Marinade:
2 tablespoons liquid smoke
4 tablespoons Worcestershire sauce
1 teaspoon onion powder
1 teaspoon garlic powder

6 to 8 pounds beef brisket, all fat trimmed

Barbecue Sauce:
1 cup catsup
⅓ cup margarine
¼ cup brewed coffee
3 tablespoons Worcestershire sauce
1 tablespoon sugar
¼ teaspoon salt
¼ teaspoon pepper

Mix marinade ingredients; pour over meat in glass dish. Cover and marinate 6 to 8 hours; turning occasionally. Place meat in heavy duty aluminum foil. Pour marinade over top of meat. Seal edges of foil; bake at 250° for 5 to 6 hours.

In saucepan, combine sauce ingredients; simmer 10 minutes. Open foil and add barbecue sauce. Cook 2 to 3 additional hours with foil open.

12 to 14 servings

Kathy Roquemore, Nationwide Accceptance
—Arlington, TX

BEEF BRISKET

4 to 6 pounds brisket of beef
3 cans beer
1 envelope dry onion soup mix
1 4-ounce can chopped green chilies,
   undrained
½ cup chopped celery

Marinate brisket in beer in covered glass dish overnight, turning several times. Drain; discard beer. Place brisket in foil-lined baking dish. Top with onion soup mix, green chilies and chopped celery. Seal foil tightly. Bake at 250° for 8 hours.

10 to 12 servings

Skip Hillary, Sales
—Texas

BEEF WELLINGTON

2½ to 3 pounds beef tenderloin, well
   trimmed
2 cups flour
¼ teaspoon salt
½ cup solid shortening
1 egg yolk, beaten
3 to 4 tablespoons ice water
⅔ cup liver pate (deli, canned or
   homemade)
1 egg white, slightly beaten

Heat oven to 425°. Tie tenderloin crosswise in 3 or 4 places and along center lengthwise to hold meat in shape. Fold narrow ends under so you have a fairly even round roast about 8 x 3½".

Place meat on rack in shallow baking pan. Roast for 35 minutes. Remove from oven; refrigerate to cool outside surface, about 10 minutes. Remove strings.

Meanwhile prepare pastry. In medium bowl, mix flour and salt. With a table fork or pastry blender, cut shortening into flour until coarse crumbs form. Mix egg yolk and water; stir into flour mixture until all flour is moistened, adding more water if needed. Form into ball. On lightly floured surface, roll into 16 x 13" rectangle; reserve trimmings. Spread liver pate on pastry to within 2" from edges and

the same length as meat. Center meat on pastry, bottom side up. Wrap pastry around meat, overlapping at center. Brush edges with beaten egg white and seal. Trim ends if necessary; fold up. Place seam side down in greased shallow baking pan. Make decorative cutouts or strips from leftover pastry; arrange on top of pastry-covered meat. Brush remaining egg white over all. Pierce pastry with toothpick in several places to allow moisture to escape. Bake at 425° 25 to 35 minutes, until pastry is lightly browned; 140° on meat thermometer.

8 to 10 servings

Adeline Halfmann, Retired
—Kewaskum

BARBECUED SPARERIBS

5 tablespoons sugar
1 cup chicken stock
3 tablespoons honey
3 tablespoons catsup
1 teaspoon salt
3 tablespoons soy sauce
4 pounds spareribs

Mix all ingredients together except ribs. Place ribs in glass container or heavy plastic storage bag and pour sauce over to coat. Marinate for 2 hours. Bake at 325° for 2 to 3 hours.

2 to 4 servings

Anna Kumrow, Retired
—Kewaskum

BARBECUED RIBS

1 8-ounce bottle Sweet and Spicy Salad
   Dressing
½ cup peach preserves
1 tablespoon soy sauce

Combine ingredients in small saucepan; heat on low until preserves melt. Dip ribs in sauce and place in smoker for 3 to 4 hours. Mesquite chips or hickory chips may be placed on coals to provide a smoky flavor. If using conventional charcoal grill, apply sauce to ribs during last 30 minutes of cooking to prevent burning.

Tip: Buy 1 pound spareribs for each female and 2 pounds for each male. This sauce is good for chicken also.

Makes 1½ cups sauce

> Albert (and Ann) Oak
> Executive VP of Manufacturing
> —Kewaskum

SWISS STEAK SUPREME

¾ cup flour
2 pounds round steak, cut in 1" slices
2 tablespoons fat
2 cups sliced onions
1 teaspoon dry mustard
2 teaspoons salt
¼ teaspoon pepper
1 clove garlic, minced
½ cup water
1 16-ounce can tomatoes
1 tablespoon crushed red pepper

Pound flour into steak; pan fry in fat in skillet until brown on both sides. Cover with onions, mustard, salt, pepper, garlic, water, tomatoes and red pepper. Cover and cook over low heat or bake at 350° for 30 minutes.

8 to 10 servings

> Donnie McCallister, Dept. 2000
> —Jacksonville

EASY DOES IT SWISS STEAK

3 tablespoons oil
2 pounds round steak
¼ cup flour, divided
1 envelope dry onion soup mix
1 8-ounce can tomato sauce
½ cup water

Pour oil into baking dish; place in oven and preheat at 400°. Trim steak and pound 2 tablespoons flour into each side. Place in heated baking dish; turn to coat both sides. Sprinkle soup mix on top. Combine tomato sauce and water; pour over meat. Reduce oven temperature to 325°, cover tightly and bake 2½ to 3 hours or until fork tender.

6 to 8 servings

> Judy Knudson, Dept. 2000
> —Kewaskum

PEPPER STEAK

1 pound round steak
1 cup sliced green pepper
1 cup sliced onion
⅔ cup sliced celery
2 tablespoons oil
1 cup beef broth
3 tablespoons soy sauce
1 teaspoon sugar
4 teaspoons cornstarch
2 tablespoons cold water
2 medium tomatoes, peeled and cut into
   wedges

Cut steak in ¼" wide strips; set aside. In large skillet, quickly cook in hot oil green pepper, onion and celery until crisp-tender. Remove from pan; set aside. Cook steak in hot oil until brown. Add beef broth and soy sauce. Cover and simmer until tender (1 to 1½ hours). Combine sugar, cornstarch and water; add to steak. Cook until thick. Add celery, green pepper, onion and tomatoes. Heat through. Serve over rice.

6 servings

> Bonnie Clapper, Dept. 15EE
> —Kewaskum

ROUND STEAK

1 envelope Lipton onion soup mix
1 10-ounce can cream of chicken or
  mushroom soup
1 soup can water
1½ to 2 pounds steak, cut into ½ to 1"
  cubes

Combine first 3 ingredients in slow cooker; mix well. Add round steak; stir well to coat meat. Cook on #2 or #3 setting for 5 to 6 hours. Serve over rice, noodles or mashed potatoes.

4 to 6 servings

Cynthia Braun, Dept. 1300
—Kewaskum

BARBIE'S BAKED STEAK

4 or 5 serving-size pieces round steak
Salt and pepper to taste
1 small onion, chopped
4 tablespoons butter or margarine
1 4-ounce can Dawn's Mushroom Sauce
1½ sauce cans water

Season round steak with salt and pepper; brown in butter or margarine. In small bowl, combine mushroom sauce and water; blend well and pour over meat. Place meat, onions and sauce in baking dish; cover. Bake at 250° to 275° for 2 to 3 hours. Serve over rice.

4 to 5 servings

Howard (and Esther) Manteufel
Retired Sales Rep.
—Texas

MARINATED FLANK

¾ cup oil
¼ cup soy sauce
3 tablespoons honey
2 tablespoons cider vinegar
1½ teaspoons garlic powder
1½ teaspoons ground ginger
1 minced green onion with tops
1 to 1½ pounds beef flank steak

Combine all ingredients except flank in a jar or shaker jar. Shake vigorously until well blended. In large plastic storage bag, pour marinade over flank. Squeeze excess air out of bag and seal. Place bag in bowl or container; refrigerate overnight or up to 24 hours. Grill over hot coals. Marinade also excellent for sirloin chunks for shish kabobs.

4 to 6 servings

Susan Portmann-Anderson, Marketing
—Kewaskum

KOREAN BARBECUED BEEF

1 pound beef, boneless top loin or sirloin
  steak
¼ cup soy sauce
3 tablespoons sugar
2 tablespoons oil
¼ teaspoon pepper
3 green onions, finely chopped
2 cloves garlic, chopped

Trim fat from beef and cut into ⅛" slices. Mix all ingredients until beef is well coated. Cover and refrigerate for 1½ hours. Drain beef. Stir-fry in wok over medium heat until light brown, 2 to 3 minutes. Serve over rice.

4 to 6 servings

Carol Jokinen, Dept. 2000
—Jacksonville

DESSERTS

Stove-top aluminum drip coffeemaker

OVERNIGHT CARAMEL ROLLS

18 Rhodes frozen dinner rolls
1 3-ounce package butterscotch pudding (not instant)
1 cup chopped pecans
½ cup butter
½ cup packed brown sugar

Lightly grease 9 x 13" pan or 12-cup bundt pan. Arrange frozen rolls in pan and sprinkle with dry pudding mix and nuts. In small saucepan, bring butter and brown sugar to a boil over medium heat, stir constantly. Remove from heat and pour over rolls. Cover with waxed paper and a clean towel. Let rise overnight.

Preheat oven to 350°. Bake 30 to 35 minutes until golden brown. Invert pan on serving platter while warm.

Hint: During warm, humid weather let rise overnight in refrigerator. Remove and let stand on counter about 1 hour before baking.

Makes 18 rolls

Susan Portmann-Anderson, Marketing
—Kewaskum

MONKEY BREAD

3 10-ounce packages refrigerated buttermilk biscuits
¾ cup sugar
1 teaspoon cinnamon
2½ ounces coarsely chopped walnuts
¾ cup margarine (1½ sticks)
1 cup sugar
1 teaspoon cinnamon

Cut each biscuit into 4 pieces. Put ¾ cup sugar and 1 teaspoon cinnamon in plastic bag; mix well. Add biscuits; shake to coat. Butter bundt pan and spread walnuts in bottom. Arrange coated biscuits on top of walnuts.

In small saucepan, bring margarine, 1 cup sugar and 1 teaspoon cinnamon to rolling boil. Pour over dough and bake at 350° for

30 minutes. Let cool 2 minutes. Turn out onto plate and serve warm.

12 to 16 servings

Jean Prost, Sales
—Kewaskum

HARVEST TIME APPLE ROLLS

This recipe was a prize winner in the Rolling Pin Contest in Little Rock, AR in October, 1993.

¼ cup warm water
1 package fast-rising yeast
½ cup warm milk
⅓ cup oil
1 egg
1 teaspoon salt
¼ cup sugar
½ teaspoon mace
3 cups flour
1 tablespoon oil
1 tablespoon butter or margarine, melted

Filling:
4 red or yellow Delicious apples, peeled, cored and sliced
½ cup sugar
3 tablespoons margarine
½ teaspoon cardamom
¼ teaspoon cinnamon
⅛ teaspoon cloves

Glaze:
1 cup powdered sugar
2 tablespoons milk
¼ teaspoon vanilla
Pinch of salt
1 teaspoon grated orange rind

In small bowl, combine warm water and yeast; let stand for 5 minutes. In large bowl, combine warm milk, ⅓ cup oil and egg; whisk until blended. Add yeast mixture, salt, sugar, and mace. Slowly stir in flour to make soft dough. Warm oil and pour into large bowl. Transfer dough to oiled bowl, turn to fully coat dough. Put in warm place and let rise until double in size.

Combine all filling ingredients in 2-quart saucepan and cook until tender. Liquid should be thick, not runny and should yield approximately 1½ cups. Let cool completely. This can be made a day or two beforehand.

Transfer dough to floured surface, knead 4 to 5 minutes. Roll into rectangle about 14 x 12". Spread apple mixture over dough leaving 1" border. Roll dough; moisten and pinch edges together. Cut into 1½" pieces and place on sprayed or greased pizza pan or similar size baking pan. Let rise until double in size. Bake at 350° for 25 to 30 minutes. Remove from oven and brush with melted butter or margarine.

In small bowl, mix together glaze ingredients, except orange rind. Drizzle on warm rolls. Sprinkle with orange rind.

Makes 10 to 12 rolls

Jack (and Betty) Stivers, Purchasing Agent
—Jacksonville

HORNS

2 8-ounce packages cream cheese,
softened
1 pound (2 cups) butter, softened
5½ cups flour

Filling:
2 8-ounce packages cream cheese
2 egg yolks
¼ to ½ cup sugar, or to taste
1 teaspoon lemon juice
¼ teaspoon vanilla
Powdered sugar

Combine first three ingredients; mix by hand until doughy. Shape into baseball-size balls. Wrap individually in waxed paper and refrigerate overnight. Set out at room temperature while making filling.

Beat all filling ingredients until creamy; set aside. Roll out dough balls one at a time on powdered sugar-covered surface into 10" circles. Cut dough into 8 wedges. Place

1 teaspoonful filling on dough. Roll up from wide side to tip. Place on ungreased cookie sheets with narrow side down. Bake at 350° for 20 minutes or until light brown. Cool completely. Roll in powdered sugar.

Makes 32 to 40

Heide Ewerdt, Dept. 1400
—Kewaskum

BUTTERHORNS

Crust:
2 cups flour
1 cup butter
1 12-ounce carton small curd cottage
cheese
1 teaspoon vanilla
½ teaspoon salt

Filling:
1 egg white, beaten
½ cup sugar
½ teaspoon cinnamon
½ cup finely chopped nuts

Mix crust ingredients together. Divide into 3 balls; cover and refrigerate overnight.

Flour working area and roll each ball into circle. Whisk filling ingredients together. Spread ⅓ filling onto dough. Cut into 8 pieces. Moisten ends with butter before rolling up. Place cut side down on greased baking sheet. Bake at 350° for 18 to 20 minutes. Frost if desired.

Makes 24 butterhorns

Doris Wesenberg, Retired
—Kewaskum

APPLE WALNUT MUFFINS

2 cups unbleached flour
2 teaspoons cinnamon
½ teaspoon salt
1½ teaspoons baking soda
2 large eggs, lightly beaten
1 cup vegetable oil
1 cup sugar
1 teaspoon vanilla
4 cups chopped, tart apples (peeled or unpeeled)
1 cup chopped walnuts

Sift flour, cinnamon, salt and baking soda together in mixing bowl; set aside. In another mixing bowl; stir together eggs, oil, sugar, vanilla and apples. Add apple mixture and nuts to dry ingredients; stir only until dry ingredients are moistened. Fill greased or paper-lined muffin tins ⅔ full. Bake at 350° for 20 minutes. Cool in tins for 5 minutes before removing muffins to wire rack to cool completely.

Note: Muffins freeze well.

Makes 24

Marion Erdmann, Retired, Cost Accounting
—Kewaskum

BLUEBERRY MUFFINS

½ cup margarine, softened
1 cup sugar
2 eggs
2 cups flour
½ teaspoon salt
2 teaspoons baking powder
½ cup milk
1 teaspoon vanilla
2½ cups blueberries
Sugar for topping

Line muffin pans with papers. Preheat oven to 375°. Cream margarine and sugar until fluffy and light. Add eggs one at a time, beating after each addition. Combine dry ingredients and add alternately with milk and vanilla. Fold blueberries into batter and spoon into muffin papers. Sprinkle sugar on top of each. Bake for 20

minutes or until toothpick comes out clean.

Makes 18 to 24 muffins

Bonny Murphy, Retired
—Wooster

BLUEBERRY (OR CHERRY) MUFFINS

1 cup oatmeal, uncooked
1 cup orange juice
3 cups flour
4 teaspoons baking powder
½ teaspoon baking soda
1 cup sugar
1 cup Crisco oil
3 eggs, beaten
3 cups blueberries or cherries

Topping:
1 teaspoon cinnamon
¼ cup sugar
¼ cup chopped walnuts

Mix oatmeal and orange juice. Stir in flour, baking powder and soda. Add sugar, oil and eggs. Beat until well blended. Stir in berries. Spoon into 24 muffin cups.

Mix together all topping ingredients. Sprinkle evenly over batter. Bake at 400° for 15 minutes.

Makes 24 muffins

Bethana Herriges, Outlet Store
—Kewaskum

MICROWAVE BRAN MUFFINS

4 eggs
1 quart (4 cups) buttermilk
5 cups flour
3 cups sugar
1 tablespoon pumpkin pie spice
5 teaspoons baking soda
2 teaspoons salt
1 cup vegetable oil
15 ounces Raisin Bran cereal

Beat eggs and blend with buttermilk. Add dry ingredients; mix in oil and bran flakes. Refrigerate for 24 hours. Line microwave muffin pan with paper cups; fill muffin cups ¾ full. Microwave on medium power 2 to 2½ minutes for 2 muffins; 2½ to 3½ minutes for 4 muffins and 3½ to 4½ minutes for 6 muffins.

Note: Dough will keep in refrigerator for 3 to 4 weeks.

Makes about 48 muffins

Rick Yahr, Purchasing
—Kewaskum

APPLESAUCE RAISIN BREAD

2½ cups flour
1¼ cups sugar
1 tablespoon baking powder
1 teaspoon salt
1½ teaspoons baking soda
1 teaspoon cinnamon
1 cup raisins
1 cup chopped walnuts
2 eggs
1 cup applesauce
½ cup oil

Mix all dry ingredients in bowl. Stir in raisins and nuts. Set aside. Combine eggs, applesauce and oil. Gradually add dry ingredients. Pour into loaf pan. Bake at 350° for 50 minutes.

Makes 1 loaf, about 18 slices

Carol Jokinen, Department 2000
—Jacksonville

BANANA APPLE BREAD

4 bananas, mashed
1 cup sugar
½ cup applesauce
2 eggs or ½ cup egg substitute
2 cups flour
1 tablespoon baking powder
1 teaspoon baking soda
1 teaspoon vanilla
1 teaspoon salt

Preheat oven to 350°. Spray two medium loaf pans with Pam. Mix all ingredients in a large bowl. Pour into prepared pans. Bake for 35 to 40 minutes or until toothpick comes out clean.

Makes 2 loaves, about 30 slices

Albert (and Ann) Oak
Executive Vice President of Manufacturing
—Kewaskum

BANANA NUT BREAD

2 cups flour
½ teaspoon baking powder
½ teaspoon baking soda
½ teaspoon salt
½ cup butter or margarine
1 cup sugar
2 eggs
3 bananas, mashed
½ cup chopped nuts

Sift together flour, baking powder, baking soda and salt. Set aside. Cream butter while gradually adding sugar. Add eggs one at a time; beating well after each. Add bananas to flour mixture and mix well. Stir this into creamed mixture, add nuts. Pour into greased loaf pan. Bake at 350° for 1 hour.

Makes 1 loaf, about 18 slices

Anita Cassidy, Department 8400 Supervisor
—Jacksonville

BANANA NUT BREAD

1 teaspoon baking soda
½ cup buttermilk
½ cup margarine, softened
1½ cups sugar
2 eggs
1½ cups flour
½ teaspoon salt
1 cup mashed, very ripe bananas
1 cup pecans

Mix baking soda and buttermilk together; set aside. Cream together margarine and sugar; add eggs, flour, salt, bananas and nuts. Add buttermilk mixture. Stir well. Pour into greased and floured loaf pan. Bake at 350° for 1 hour.

Makes 1 loaf

> *Goldia Wilkins, Department 21*
> *—Jacksonville*

BANANA BREAD

⅓ cup butter, softened
1 cup sugar
2 eggs
3 tablespoons sour milk (1 tablespoon vinegar and 2 tablespoons milk)
1 teaspoon baking soda
1 teaspoon baking powder
½ teaspoon salt
2 cups flour
3 ripe bananas, mashed
½ cup chopped nuts, optional

In large mixing bowl, cream butter, sugar and eggs. Mix in remaining ingredients. Pour into greased loaf pan. Bake at 350° for 1 hour. Cool before serving.

Makes 1 loaf, about 18 slices

> *Heather Werner, 1600 CDT Drip*
> *—Kewaskum*

CARROT BREAD

1 cup sugar
¾ cup oil
2 eggs
1½ cups sifted flour
1 teaspoon baking soda
½ teaspoon salt
½ cup chopped nuts
1 cup grated carrots

Preheat oven to 350°. Mix all ingredients together. Bake in greased and floured bread pan for 1 hour.

Makes 12 to 18 slices

> *Fritz (and Alice) Raether, Retired*
> *—Kewaskum*

ZUCCHINI BREAD

3 eggs, beaten
½ cup oil
2 cups sugar
1 tablespoon vanilla
2¼ cups grated zucchini
3 cups flour
1 teaspoon salt
1 teaspoon baking soda
1 tablespoon cinnamon
¼ teaspoon baking powder
¼ cup honey
1 cup chopped nuts

Frosting:
1 8-ounce cream cheese, softened
½ cup butter or margarine, softened
1 pound (about 4¼ cups) powdered sugar
½ cup milk
1 teaspoon vanilla
1 cup chopped nuts

Mix eggs, oil, sugar and vanilla. Add grated zucchini. Sift dry ingredients and add to egg mixture. Add honey and nuts. Pour into two greased and floured loaf pans. Bake at 350° for 1 hour. Cool.

Cream together cream cheese and butter. Add sugar and milk; beat well. Stir in vanilla. Spread on cooled loaves. Sprinkle frosting with nuts.

Makes 2 loaves, about 30 slices

> *Anita Cassidy, Department 8400 Supervisor*
> *—Jacksonville*

ZUCCHINI BREAD

1 cup oil
3 eggs
2 cups sugar
2 cups grated raw zucchini
2 teaspoons vanilla
3 cups flour
1 teaspoon soda
¼ teaspoon baking powder
¼ teaspoon salt
3 teaspoons cinnamon
1 cup chopped pecans

Grease and flour two large loaf pans. Combine oil, eggs, sugar, zucchini and vanilla. Blend well. Stir in (do not beat) flour, soda, baking powder, salt, cinnamon and pecans. Fill pans and bake 1½ hours at 325°.

Makes 2 loaves, about 36 slices

Verna Robinson, Retired
—Wooster

ZUCCHINI BREAD

3 eggs
1 cup vegetable oil
1½ cups sugar
1 cup grated, packed zucchini (skin on)
3 teaspoons vanilla
3 cups flour
1 teaspoon salt
1 teaspoon baking soda
1 teaspoon cinnamon
¼ teaspoon baking powder
1 cup chopped walnuts, optional
½ cup raisins

Beat eggs until fluffy. Add oil, sugar, zucchini and vanilla. Mix well. Add dry ingredients and mix well. Add nuts and raisins. Spoon into two large greased loaf pans. Bake at 350° for 1 hour.

Makes 2 loaves, about 36 slices

Rayne Bryla
Production Expeditor Assistant
—Orangeville

SUPER ZUCCHINI BREAD

2¼ cups sugar
1 cup cooking oil
3 eggs, beaten
1 teaspoon vanilla
3 cups flour
1 teaspoon salt
1 teaspoon cinnamon
1½ teaspoons baking soda
¼ teaspoon baking powder
2 to 3 cups grated zucchini
1 cup raisins, optional
1 8-ounce can crushed pineapple, drained
½ to 1 cup chopped nuts

Grease and flour two loaf pans. Cream together sugar, oil, eggs and vanilla. Sift together flour, salt, cinnamon, soda and baking powder; blend with creamed mixture. Fold in zucchini, raisins, pineapple and nuts. Bake at 325° to 350° for 1 hour or until tests done.

Makes 2 loaves, about 36 slices

Rita M. Felton, Retired
—Wooster

BREAD PUDDING

9 slices white bread
2 13-ounce cans evaporated milk
1 cup milk
4 eggs
½ cup butter, melted
1 cup sugar
2 teaspoons vanilla

In large bowl, tear bread into small pieces. Add remaining ingredients. Pour into a buttered 9 x 13" baking dish. Bake at 350° for 30 minutes.

12 to 18 servings

Nancy White, Nationwide Acceptance
—Arlington, TX

NEW ORLEANS STYLE BREAD PUDDING

6 eggs
2½ cups sugar
1 tablespoon cinnamon
1 tablespoon nutmeg
1 tablespoon vanilla
½ cup margarine, melted
1 quart milk
6 cups bread crumbs (1 loaf French bread pinched into crumbs)
1 cup chopped pecans
1 cup raisins

Rum Sauce:
2 cups powdered sugar
2 tablespoons milk
2 tablespoons rum

Whip eggs until frothy. Add sugar, spices, vanilla and margarine. Mix well. Add milk and bread crumbs. Mix and let soak 15 minutes. Add pecans and raisins. Pour into greased 9 x 13" pan. Bake at 350° for 45 minutes.

In small bowl, blend together sauce ingredients. Mix well; serve over hot Bread Pudding.

12 to 18 servings

Barbara Nelson, Nationwide Acceptance
—Arlington, TX

BANANA OATMEAL COOKIES

1½ cups sifted flour
½ teaspoon baking soda
¼ teaspoon nutmeg
¾ teaspoon cinnamon
1 teaspoon salt
1 cup sugar
¾ cup shortening
1 egg
2 teaspoons vanilla
1 cup mashed bananas
1¾ cups quick oats
½ cup chopped nuts

Sift all dry ingredients together in large mixing bowl. Beat sugar, shortening and egg until light and fluffy. Add flour mixture and remaining ingredients. Mix well.

Drop by teaspoonful onto ungreased cookie sheet. Bake at 400° for 12 to 15 minutes, or until edges are brown.

Makes about 60 cookies

Carolyn Lessley
Saladmaster, Inc.

FESTIVE FRUIT COOKIES

½ cup shortening
½ cup brown sugar
¾ cup sugar
1 teaspoon vanilla
1 egg, slightly beaten
1 6-ounce can frozen orange juice concentrate, thawed (undiluted) divided in half
2½ cups flour
1 teaspoon baking soda
½ teaspoon baking powder
½ teaspoon salt
2¾ cups coconut
¾ cup chopped pecans

Icing:
2 cups powdered sugar
½ cup margarine, softened

Cream shortening and sugars until light and fluffy. Add vanilla, egg and half the orange juice. Beat well. Combine flour, baking soda, baking powder and salt. Add to sugar mixture, stirring to moisten. Stir in coconut and pecans. Drop by teaspoon onto greased cookie sheet. Bake at 350° for 9 to 10 minutes. Remove to wire racks for cooling. Spread with icing while warm.

To make icing, mix powdered sugar, margarine and remaining half of orange juice. Ice cookies while warm.

Makes 50 to 60 cookies

Carolyn Lessley
Saladmaster, Inc.

MONSTER CHOCOLATE CHIP COOKIES

1 pound (about 3½ cups) unbleached flour
1 teaspoon salt
1 teaspoon baking soda
1/16 teaspoon cinnamon
1 tablespoon vanilla
1 pound (2 cups) margarine, softened
9 ounces (1¼ cups) sugar
9 ounces (1¼ cups packed) dark brown sugar
3 eggs
1 pound (2⅔ cups) semi-sweet chocolate chips
10 ounces (2½ cups) pecan pieces

Mix together all ingredients. Use ice cream scoop to place on ungreased cookie sheet, six scoops per sheet. Bake at 350° for 15 minutes.

Makes 36 to 45 cookies

Rick Zugel, Sales
—Atlanta

OATMEAL GINGERSNAPS

1½ cups flour
1 cup sugar
1 teaspoon baking soda
1 teaspoon ginger
¼ teaspoon cloves
¾ cup quick-cooking oatmeal
½ cup shortening
¼ cup molasses
1 egg
½ teaspoon salt
Sugar for coating

Sift together flour, sugar, baking soda, ginger and cloves. Add oatmeal, shortening, molasses, egg and salt. Beat for 2 minutes. Form into 1" balls. Roll in sugar. Bake on ungreased cookie sheet at 375° for 8 to 10 minutes. Let stand for 1 minute before removing from pan.

Makes 24 to 36 cookies

Jean Dippel, Retired
—Kewaskum

GINGER CRINKLE COOKIES

⅔ cup salad oil
1 cup sugar
1 egg
4 tablespoons molasses
2 cups flour
2 teaspoons baking soda
½ teaspoon salt
1 teaspoon cinnamon
1 teaspoon ginger
Sugar for coating

Mix all ingredients together. Form into balls and roll in sugar. Place on ungreased cookie sheet and bake at 350° for 15 minutes.

Makes 36 cookies

Kitty Krueger, Retired
—Kewaskum

PEANUT BUTTER COOKIES

1 cup Crisco (do not use margarine)
1 cup peanut butter
2 cups sugar
3 cups flour
1 teaspoon baking soda
1 teaspoon salt
3 tablespoons plus 2 teaspoons boiling water
1 teaspoon vanilla

Cream Crisco, peanut butter and sugar. Sift flour, baking soda and salt; add to creamed mixture. Add boiling water and vanilla. Mix well. Roll into balls, place on ungreased cookie sheet about 1" apart and flatten with fork. Bake at 350° for 14 minutes.

Makes 50 cookies

Carolyn Jackson, Retired
—Wooster

PEANUT BUTTER COOKIES

1 cup peanut butter
1 cup sugar
1 egg

Mix all ingredients together. Shape into balls and place on ungreased cookie sheet. Criss-cross with fork dipped in flour. Bake at 350° for 10 minutes.

Note: This recipe does not call for any flour. It does work and they are very good cookies.

Makes about 24 cookies

Kitty Krueger, Retired
—Kewaskum

RICE DATE BALLS

8 ounces chopped dates
½ cup margarine
1 to 2 tablespoons water
1 cup flaked coconut
½ cup chopped pecans
1 tablespoon vanilla
2 cups Rice Krispies cereal

In 3-quart saucepan, boil dates, margarine and water until mushy. Add coconut, pecans, vanilla and cereal. Form into 1" balls and refrigerate.

Makes about 36

Donna Lindesmith, Dept. 8400
—Jacksonville

SALLY ANNE COOKIES

1 cup butter, softened
½ cup shortening
1 cup sugar
1 cup brown sugar
3 eggs
1 teaspoon baking soda
1 teaspoon baking powder
2 teaspoons cinnamon
¼ teaspoon cloves
3¾ cups flour
1 cup chopped nuts

In large mixing bowl, cream together butter, shortening and sugars. Add eggs. Stir in baking soda, baking powder, cinnamon and cloves. Add flour and mix well. Stir in nuts. Divide dough into thirds. Form 3 logs and wrap in waxed paper. Refrigerate 24 hours. Slice dough about ¼" thick and place on cookie sheets. Bake at 350° for 8 to 10 minutes.

Makes 36 to 48 cookies

Anne Quackenboss, MIS
—Kewaskum

SUGAR COOKIES

1 cup margarine, softened
1 cup white sugar
1 cup powdered sugar
1 cup cooking oil
2 eggs
1 teaspoon vanilla
4 cups all-purpose flour
1 teaspoon cream of tartar
1 teaspoon baking soda
½ teaspoon salt

Cream together margarine and sugars. Add oil, eggs and vanilla; mix well. Combine flour, cream of tartar, baking soda and salt. Gradually mix into creamed mixture. Store covered in refrigerator overnight. Form into small balls and place on ungreased cookie sheet. Flatten with bottom of small glass dipped in sugar. Bake at 350° for 10 to 12 minutes.

Makes approximately 5 dozen

Theresa Rohlinger, Consumer Service
—Kewaskum

KART-WHEELS

1½ cups flour
½ cup margarine or butter, softened
¼ cup powdered sugar
½ teaspoon baking powder
2 tablespoons milk
1 cup pie filling or jam (any flavor)

Mix flour, margarine, powdered sugar, baking powder and just enough milk until dough forms. If dough seems dry, mix in more milk 1 teaspoon at a time. Divide dough into 6 equal parts. Shape each part into ball. Place on ungreased cookie sheet; flatten slightly. Make indentation 1¾" in diameter and about ¾" deep in center of each flattened ball. Fill each indentation with about 2 tablespoons of pie filling or jam. Bake at 375° for 20 to 25 minutes or until edges begin to brown.

Makes 6

Diane Piwoni
—Kewaskum

FRUIT-FILLED COOKIES

4½ **cups flour**
¾ **teaspoon baking soda**
¾ **teaspoon salt**
1½ **cups butter or margarine, softened**
¾ **cup sugar**
¾ **cup brown sugar**
1 **egg**
¼ **cup milk**
1¼ **cup ready-to-use mincemeat**
¼ **cup orange marmalade**

Sift together flour, baking soda and salt; set aside. Cream butter and sugars until slightly fluffy. Beat in egg and milk; mix well. Gradually add flour mixture, mixing well after each addition. Wrap dough in waxed paper and chill ½ hour. Combine mincemeat and marmalade; set aside. Preheat oven to 375°.

On floured surface, roll half the dough to ⅛" thickness. (Leave remaining half of dough in refrigerator until ready to use.) Cut dough with a 2½" round cookie cutter. Cut a small hole in the center of half the rounds. (A floured thimble will work, or use a doughnut cutter with a removable center.) Place 12 plain rounds on an ungreased cookie sheet. Place 1 teaspoon of

mincemeat mixture on center of each round. Top with a cut-out round and press edges with a lightly floured fork to seal. Bake at 375° for 10 to 12 minutes. Cool on pan for 1 minute before removing them to rack to cool thoroughly. Repeat procedure with remaining half of dough.

Note: These cookies can be cooled and frozen in a tightly sealed container for up to 1 month.

Makes 6 dozen cookies

Elizabeth Stafford, Dept. 2000
—Jacksonville

THIMBLE COOKIES

½ **cup butter**
¼ **cup sugar**
1 **egg yolk**
1 **teaspoon vanilla**
1 **cup flour**
1 **egg white, lightly beaten**
Chopped nuts or crushed cornflakes
Red jelly or jam

Cream butter and sugar. Beat in egg yolk and vanilla. Blend in flour. Shape into small balls; dip in egg white and roll in nuts or cornflakes. Place on lightly greased baking sheet. Make a depression in center of each using thimble or end of wooden spoon. Bake at 325° for 12 to 15 minutes. Fill centers with jelly or jam.

Makes about 2½ dozen

Fern Vanin, Purchasing
—Orangeville

INDIAN FEAST DAY COOKIES

1½ cups sugar
1 cup shortening
¼ cup milk
1 egg, beaten
1 teaspoon vanilla
3 cups flour
1 teaspoon baking soda
¼ teaspoon salt

Cream together sugar and shortening until light and fluffy. Combine milk, egg and vanilla. Stir together dry ingredients, add alternately with liquid to shortening mixture, beating well after each addition. Divide in half. On lightly floured surface, roll half the dough at a time to a rectangle, ⅛" thick, trimmed to 12 x 6". Cut into 18 2" squares. With a sharp knife, make cuts in dough gently shaping with fingers to make designs. Repeat rolling, cutting and shaping with remainder or use your favorite cookie cutters. Bake on ungreased cookie sheet at 350° for 15 to 16 minutes.

Makes 3 dozen

Goldia Wilkins, Dept. 21
—Jacksonville

MOLASSES COOKIES

1 cup shortening
1 cup sugar
1 cup dark molasses
1 cup boiling water
2 teaspoons baking soda
1 teaspoon salt
1 teaspoon cinnamon
1 egg
5¼ cups flour

Mix all ingredients together and refrigerate overnight. Roll out on lightly floured surface; cut into desired shapes. Bake at 350° for 8 to 12 minutes, depending on thickness.

Makes 36 to 60

Carol Wiskerchen
—Kewaskum

APPLE PIE BARS

Crust:
2 cups flour
½ cup sugar (optional)
½ teaspoon baking powder
½ teaspoon salt
1 cup butter or margarine, softened
2 egg yolks, beaten

Filling:
¼ cup flour
½ cup sugar
1 teaspoon cinnamon
¼ teaspoon nutmeg
6 cups apples, peeled, cored and sliced (⅛")
2 egg whites, slightly beaten

Glaze:
2 tablespoons butter or margarine, melted
2 tablespoons milk
1¼ cups powdered sugar
Few drops vanilla extract

Combine flour, sugar, baking powder and salt. Cut in butter as for pie crust. Mix in egg yolks (mixture will be crumbly). Press half onto bottom of 10 x 15" jelly roll pan or 9 x 13" cake pan. Set aside remaining mixture.

Combine all dry filling ingredients and mix with apples. Arrange over crust. Crumble remaining crust mixture over filling. Brush egg whites over all. Bake at 350° for 30 minutes in jelly roll pan or 40 minutes in cake pan. Cool. Mix glaze ingredients; drizzle over top crust.

18 to 36 bars

Kathleen Remus, Dept. 15WW
—Kewaskum

CARROT BARS

2 cups sugar
1¼ cups salad oil
3 eggs
2 teaspoons cinnamon
1 teaspoon salt
1 3¾-ounce jar each baby food carrots, applesauce and apricots
1 cup chopped nuts
2 cups flour
2 teaspoons baking soda

Frosting:
1 8-ounce package cream cheese
1 pound (about 4¼ cups) powdered sugar
½ cup butter or margarine, softened
1 teaspoon vanilla

In large bowl, combine all ingredients and mix well. Spread in greased and floured 11 x 15" jelly roll pan. Bake at 350° for 25 to 30 minutes. Cool and frost.

To make frosting, in medium bowl combine all frosting ingredients and mix well. Spread evenly on cooled bars.

Makes 24 to 30 bars

Helen Guenther, Retired
—Kewaskum

CHERRY DESSERT

1 cup sugar
1 heaping tablespoon butter, softened
1 egg
1 19-ounce can sour pie cherries, drained reserving liquid, divided
1 cup flour
1 teaspoon baking soda

Sauce:
1 tablespoon butter
1 tablespoon flour
½ cup sugar
Whipped cream, optional

Mix sugar, butter, egg, 1 cup drained cherries, flour and baking soda. Pour into greased 7 x 11" pan. Bake at 375° for 30 minutes.

In small saucepan, combine butter, flour and sugar mixing well. Add reserved cherry juice and remaining cherries. Cook until hot and bubbly, and slightly thickened, stirring frequently. Cut cake in serving pieces and top with hot sauce. Top with unsweetened whipped cream if desired.

12 to 15 servings

Jo (and Ray) McDaniels
Retired Sales Representative
—Missouri

COCONUT BARS

3 cups flour
1½ cups butter or margarine, softened
3 tablespoons powdered sugar
2 cups chopped nuts
3 cups brown sugar
4 eggs
2 teaspoons vanilla
1 package (15 or 16 ounces) coconut

Combine flour, butter and powdered sugar. Pat into 9 x 13" pan. Bake at 350° for 20 minutes. Mix remaining ingredients together and spread over baked crust. Bake at 325° for 35 to 40 minutes or until golden brown.

18 to 24 bars

Carolyn Jackson, Retired
—Wooster

LEMON SQUARES

Crust:
2 cups flour
½ cup powdered sugar
½ teaspoon salt
1 cup butter, softened

Filling:
4 large eggs
2 cups sugar
⅓ cup lemon juice
¼ cup flour
½ teaspoon baking powder
Powdered sugar for topping

Mix together 2 cups flour, powdered sugar and salt. Cream in butter until mixture forms a pliable dough. Pat evenly into bottom of buttered 9 x 13" pan. Bake at 350° for 15 minutes. Let stand at room temperature for 5 minutes.

Beat together all filling ingredients until smooth. Pour over slightly cooled crust. Return to oven immediately and bake for 20 to 25 minutes or until pale golden. Remove from oven and sprinkle generously with powdered sugar. Let cool completely. Cut into squares and store in air-tight container.

Makes 24 squares

Rayne Bryla
—Canada

PUMPKIN SQUARES

2 cups sugar
1 cup oil
4 eggs
2 cups flour
2 teaspoons baking powder
1 teaspoon baking soda
1 teaspoon pumpkin pie spice
¼ teaspoon cloves
½ teaspoon cinnamon
¼ teaspoon nutmeg
½ teaspoon salt
1 16-ounce can pumpkin
1 cup chopped nuts

Frosting:

1 8-ounce package cream cheese
1 pound (about 4¼ cups) powdered sugar
½ cup margarine, softened
2 teaspoons vanilla

Mix together sugar, oil and eggs. Sift all dry ingredients together and add to egg mixture. Mix well. Add pumpkin and nuts. Spread in greased 11 x 17" jelly roll pan; bake at 350° for 20 to 25 minutes. Cool.

Mix all frosting ingredients; beat well. Frost cooled pumpkin squares.

36 to 40 squares

Carolyn Lessley, Saladmaster, Inc.
—Arlington, TX

PUMPKIN BARS

4 eggs
1 cup salad oil
2 cups sugar
1 15-ounce can pumpkin (2 cups)
2 cups flour
2 teaspoons baking powder
1 teaspoon baking soda
½ teaspoon salt
2 teaspoons cinnamon
½ teaspoon ginger
½ teaspoon cloves
½ teaspoon nutmeg
1 cup raisins
1 cup chopped nuts

Frosting:
1 8-ounce package cream cheese, softened
½ cup butter, softened
1 pound (about 4¼ cups) powdered sugar
1 teaspoon vanilla
Chopped nuts, optional

Combine eggs, salad oil, sugar and pumpkin. Add remaining ingredients and mix well. Pour into greased jelly roll pan. Bake at 350° for 25 to 30 minutes. Cool.

Mix together all frosting ingredients except nuts. Beat until fluffy. Spread on bars. Top with more chopped nuts, if desired.

36 to 40 bars

Diane Schraufnagel, Dept. 8300-1
—Kewaskum

PUMPKIN BARS

1 16-ounce can pumpkin (2 cups)
2 cups sugar
4 eggs
¾ cup margarine, melted
2 cups flour
2 teaspoons baking powder
1 teaspoon baking soda
½ teaspoon cinnamon

Frosting:
½ cup margarine, softened
1 8-ounce package cream cheese, softened
3½ cups powdered sugar
1½ teaspoons vanilla

In large bowl, mix together all ingredients in order listed. Spread in greased and floured 10 x 15" jelly roll pan. Bake at 325° for 25 to 30 minutes. Cool and frost.

In medium bowl, cream together margarine and cream cheese. Add powdered sugar gradually and beat well. Add vanilla. Frost cooled bars.

Makes 24 to 36 bars

Lucy Horton, Drips, CDT
—Kewaskum

CREAM CHEESE BARS

2 8-ounce packages refrigerated crescent rolls
2 8-ounce packages cream cheese, softened
1½ cups sugar, divided
1 egg, separated
2 teaspoons vanilla, divided
½ cup chopped nuts

Separate and press 1 package of crescent roll dough into bottoms and ½" up sides of 9 x 13" pan. In medium bowl, cream together cream cheese, 1 cup sugar, egg yolk and 1 teaspoon vanilla. Spread evenly onto crust. Lay remaining crescent roll dough on top of cheese mixture. Beat egg white with remaining vanilla; spread on top of dough. Mix ½ cup sugar and nuts and sprinkle on top of egg white mixture. Bake at 350° for 30 minutes.

Makes 24 to 32 bars

Kitty Krueger, Retired
—Kewaskum

JUSTIN'S SQUARES

2 cups butterscotch chips
1 cup peanut butter
½ cup butter
2 cups colored mini-marshmallows

Place chips, peanut butter and butter in large microwave-safe bowl. Microwave 3 minutes. Stir to mix. Add marshmallows. Pour into greased 9 x 13" pan. Refrigerate for 1 to 2 hours. Cut into squares.

Makes 24 squares

Rayne Bryla, Production Expeditor Assistant
—Orangeville

GOODY BARS

Crust:
1 cup flour
½ cup brown sugar
½ cup butter

Filling:
2 tablespoons flour
½ teaspoon salt
½ teaspoon baking powder
¾ cup coconut
½ cup nuts
2 eggs, beaten
1 cup brown sugar
1 teaspoon vanilla

To make crust, mix ingredients together. Press into 9 x 13" pan. Bake at 350° for 15 to 20 minutes.

Combine filling ingredients and spread over crust. Bake at 350° for 15 to 20 minutes. Cut into squares.

Makes 24 to 32 bars

Viola Fritz, Retired
—Kewaskum

SPONGE BARS

4 eggs
2 cups sugar
2 cups flour
2 teaspoons baking powder
½ teaspoon salt
1 teaspoon vanilla
1 cup water

Frosting:
1 egg
½ cup butter
1 teaspoon vanilla
2 cups powdered sugar
1 cup chopped peanuts

Beat 4 eggs until thick; add sugar and beat 6 minutes. Add flour, baking powder, salt, vanilla and water. Beat 1 minute or until well mixed. Bake in 11½ x 18" jelly roll pan at 350° for 20 minutes or until done.

Beat egg, butter, vanilla and powdered sugar well. Spread on bars. Sprinkle peanuts on top. These bars freeze well.

Makes about 50 bars

Lloyd Teeselink, Retired
—Kewaskum

SEVEN LAYER DELIGHT

½ cup margarine, softened
1 cup flour
½ cup chopped pecans
1 8-pounce package cream cheese
1 cup powdered sugar
3 cups coconut, divided
1 3.4-ounce package vanilla pudding
1 8-ounce container Cool Whip
Maraschino cherries, optional

Mix together margarine, flour and pecans. Spread into bottom of 9 x 13" glass baking dish. Bake until lightly browned. Cool.

Combine cream cheese and powdered sugar. Mix well. Spread evenly on crust. Prepare pudding as directed on package. Layer in order: 1 cup coconut, pudding, 1 cup coconut, Cool Whip and 1 cup coconut. Garnish with cherries, if desired. Chill before serving.

18 to 24 servings

Catherine Speer, Dept. 9500
—Jacksonville

MIXED NUT BARS

½ cup margarine
¾ cup brown sugar
1½ cups flour
1 12-ounce can mixed nuts
1 6-ounce package butterscotch chips
½ cup white corn syrup
2½ teaspoons margarine

Mix together first three ingredients. Press into 9 x 13" ungreased pan and bake in a preheated 350° oven for 10 minutes. Spread mixed nuts over baked crust.

In saucepan, melt butterscotch chips, corn syrup and 2½ teaspoons margarine. Pour over nuts; bake at 350° for 10 minutes.

24 to 32 bars

Barb Ebert, Sales Administrator
—Kewaskum

CRUNCHY BARS

1 cup whipping cream
1 cup sugar
1 cup white corn syrup
5 cups Corn Flakes
2 cups Rice Krispies
2 cups peanuts

Combine whipping cream, sugar and syrup in 3-quart saucepan; boil to soft ball stage. In large bowl, combine cereal and peanuts. Pour hot mixture over dry ingredients and mix well. Press into well greased 9 x 13" pan. Cool and cut into bars.

Makes about 32 bars

Rita Spoerl, Retired
—Kewaskum

FILLED WALNUT BARS

Crust:
½ cup butter or margarine, softened
½ cup brown sugar
1 cup flour

Filling:
2 large eggs
1 cup brown sugar
1 teaspoon vanilla
1 tablespoon flour
¼ teaspoon salt
¼ teaspoon baking powder
1½ cups coarsely chopped walnuts

Cream butter and ½ cup brown sugar until fluffy. Slowly add 1 cup flour. Beat until smooth. Press firmly into bottom of 9 x 9" pan. Bake at 350° for 10 to 18 minutes until lightly browned. Cool.

On medium speed, beat eggs until light. Slowly add brown sugar, while continuing to beat. Add vanilla, flour, salt and baking powder, beating just until combined. Stir in walnuts. Spread over cooled crust. Bake at 375° for 25 minutes until brown and fairly firm. Cool and cut into bars.

Makes 24 bars

Lester (and LaVerne) Schaub, Retired
—Kewaskum

O'HENRY BARS

6 cups Kelloggs Special K cereal
1 cup sugar
1 cup Karo syrup
1 tablespoon butter or margarine
1⅓ cups peanut butter
1 6-ounces package chocolate chips,
  melted (optional)

Place cereal in greased bowl. Boil sugar and syrup ½ minute. Add butter and peanut butter. Pour over cereal and mix well. Spread into greased 9 x 13" pan. Frost with melted chocolate chips if desired. Cut into squares.

Makes 24 to 32 bars

Henrietta Gremminger, Retired
—Kewaskum

OATMEAL CHIPPERS

1 cup flour
1 cup quick-cooking oatmeal
½ cup brown sugar
½ cup sugar
¾ cup butter, softened
1 teaspoon salt
1 teaspoon vanilla
½ teaspoon baking soda
2 eggs
1 cup chocolate chips
½ cup chopped nuts

Combine all ingredients except chocolate chips and nuts in mixing bowl. Blend at low speed about 1 minute. Stir in chocolate chips and nuts. Spread in greased 9 x 13" pan. Bake at 350° for 25 to 30 minutes or until golden brown.

Makes 24 to 32 bars

Viola Fritz, Retired
—Kewaskum

CHOCOLATE MARSHMALLOW BARS

1 package graham crackers, (20 to 22
  squares)
1 cup margarine (2 sticks)
1 12-ounce package chocolate chips
2 eggs
2 cups powdered sugar
4 cups miniature marshmallows

Line 9 x 13" pan with whole graham cracker squares. Set aside. Melt margarine and chocolate chips together in double boiler. Beat eggs and powdered sugar together, and add to chocolate mixture. Remove from heat and mix well. Add marshmallows and spread over top of crackers. Refrigerate. When cool, cut into squares.

Makes 24 to 32 bars

Michael Hendricks, Dept. 900
—Kewaskum

CHOCOLATE CARAMEL BARS

These taste like Snickers Bars!

1 11½-ounce package milk chocolate
  morsels
2 tablespoons vegetable shortening
1 14-ounce package Kraft caramels
5 tablespoons butter or margarine
2 tablespoons water
1 cup coarsely chopped peanuts

Over hot water, melt chocolate morsels and shortening. Stir until melted and smooth. Spread half of chocolate in 8" square pan lined with aluminum foil. Refrigerate until firm, about 15 minutes.

Return remaining chocolate to low heat. Combine caramels, butter and water in top of double boiler. Cook and stir over hot water until melted. Stir in nuts. Pour into chocolate lined pan. Refrigerate about 15 minutes until firm. Spread remainder of chocolate on top. Refrigerate about 1 hour before cutting into 1 x 2" rectangles.

Makes 32 bars

Delores Liegl
—Kewaskum

GERMAN CHOCOLATE CARAMEL BARS

1 German Chocolate cake mix
1 5-ounce can evaporated milk, divided
¾ cup butter, melted
1 14-ounce package caramels
1 12-ounce package chocolate chips

In mixing bowl, combine cake mix, ⅓ cup evaporated milk and butter. Pat half of this mixture into 9 x 13" buttered pan. Bake at 375° for 10 minutes. Melt caramels with remaining ⅓ cup evaporated milk over low heat in double boiler. Spread over hot crust. Sprinkle chocolate chips over caramel. Crumble remaining batter into small pieces with your hands and drop onto chocolate chips. Bake at 350° for 20 minutes.

Makes 24 to 32 bars

Bonnie Clapper, Dept. 15EE
—Kewaskum

CHOCOLATE REVEL BARS

1 cup butter or margarine, softened
2½ cups flour, divided
2 cups brown sugar, packed
2 eggs
4 teaspoons vanilla, divided
1 teaspoon baking soda
3 cups quick-cooking rolled oats
1½ cups semi-sweet chocolate chips
1 14-ounce can sweetened condensed milk
2 tablespoons butter
½ cup chopped walnuts

In large mixing bowl, beat butter or margarine with electric mixer on medium speed for 30 seconds. Add half of the flour, all the brown sugar, eggs, 2 teaspoons vanilla and baking soda. Beat on low speed until thoroughly combined. Beat in remaining flour. Stir in oats.

In medium saucepan, cook chocolate chips, sweetened condensed milk and 2 table-spoons butter over low heat until chocolate is melted, stirring occasionally. Remove from heat and stir in remaining vanilla and nuts. (Microwave works well also.)

Pat ⅔ of oat mixture (about 3½ cups) into bottom of ungreased 15 x 10 x 1" pan. Spread chocolate mixture over oat mixture. Dot with remaining oat mixture. Bake at 350° for 25 minutes or until top is lightly golden. Chocolate mixture will still look moist. Cool on wire rack. Cut into bars.

Makes 60 bars

Anne Quackenboss, MIS
—Kewaskum

MOCK BABY RUTH BARS

4 cups oatmeal
1 cup brown sugar
¼ cup corn syrup
⅔ cup margarine, melted
¼ cup plus ⅔ cup creamy peanut butter
1 teaspoon vanilla
1 6-ounce package chocolate chips
1 6-ounce package butterscotch chips

Mix together oatmeal, brown sugar and corn syrup. Pour melted margarine over mixture and stir. Add ¼ cup peanut butter and vanilla. Mix well. Spread in greased 9 x 13" pan. Bake at 400° for 12 minutes. Melt chocolate and butterscotch chips over hot water or in microwave. Add ⅔ cup peanut butter; mix well. Spread on top of bars. Cool and cut.

24 to 32 bars

Karen Sparks, Accounts Payable
—Kewaskum

TRI-LEVEL BROWNIES

Crust:
2 cups oatmeal
1 cup flour
1 cup brown sugar
¾ cup butter, melted
½ teaspoon baking soda
½ teaspoon salt

Second layer:
2 ounces unsweetened baking chocolate
½ cup butter
1½ cups sugar
2 eggs
½ cup milk
1 teaspoon vanilla
½ teaspoon baking powder
½ teaspoon salt
1⅓ cups flour
1 cup chopped nuts

Frosting:
2 ounces unsweetened baking chocolate
½ cup butter
3 cups powdered sugar
2 teaspoons vanilla
¼ cup hot water

In large bowl, combine all crust ingredients and press into greased 9 x 13″ pan. Bake at 350° for 10 minutes.

Melt chocolate and butter together in microwave until smooth; cool. Add remaining ingredients. Combine well and spread over crust. Bake at 350° for 30 to 40 minutes.

To make frosting, melt chocolate and butter together in microwave until smooth. Let cool. Stir in powdered sugar and vanilla. Gradually add hot water. Beat ingredients with mixer until slightly thick and well mixed. Frost bars.

24 to 32 bars

Laura Wollerman, Direct Sales
—Kewaskum

BROWNIES

4 cups sugar
2 teaspoons salt
1 teaspoon vanilla
1 pound (2 cups) margarine, softened
8 eggs
1⅓ cups cocoa
3 cups flour
1 cup chopped nuts, optional

Combine sugar, salt, vanilla, margarine and eggs. Cream together well. Add cocoa, flour and nuts. Mix well. Pour into two greased jelly roll pans. Bake at 350° for 25 to 30 minutes. Frost with chocolate frosting.

72 brownies

Mary Ann Miller, Dept. 15WW
—Kewaskum

HERSHEY SYRUP BROWNIES

1 cup sugar
½ cup margarine, softened
1 16-ounce can Hershey syrup
4 eggs
1 cup flour

Frosting:
1 cup sugar
6 tablespoons milk
6 tablespoons butter
1 cup chocolate chips

Mix all ingredients until smooth. Pour into floured and greased 9 x 13″ pan. Bake at 350° for 20 to 25 minutes. Do not over bake.

Bring sugar, milk and butter to boil in medium saucepan. Remove from heat, stir in chocolate chips. When chips are completely melted, pour over brownies and serve. No need to cool.

Makes 24 to 32 brownies

Rich Yahr, Purchasing
—Kewaskum

CHEWY BROWNIES

½ cup vegetable oil
1 cup sugar
1 teaspoon vanilla
2 eggs
¼ teaspoon baking powder
¼ teaspoon salt
⅓ cup cocoa
½ cup flour
½ cup chopped nuts

Creamy brownie frosting:
3 tablespoons margarine
3 tablespoons cocoa
1 tablespoon light corn syrup
½ teaspoon vanilla
1 cup powdered sugar
1 to 2 tablespoons milk

Blend oil, sugar and vanilla in mixing bowl. Add eggs. Mix well. Add baking powder, salt and cocoa. Add flour gradually. Add nuts. Spread into greased 9" square pan. Bake at 350° for 20 to 25 minutes or until brownie pulls away from sides of pan. Cool on rack. Frost.

To make frosting, cream margarine, cocoa, corn syrup and vanilla in small bowl with hand mixer until light and fluffy. Add powdered sugar and milk. Beat until thick. Spread evenly over cooled brownies.

9 to 12 servings

Carol Darmody
—Kewaskum

NEVER FAIL FUDGE

¼ cup cocoa
1½ cups sugar
⅛ teaspoon salt
½ cup evaporated milk
2 tablespoons white syrup
½ teaspoon vanilla
1 tablespoon butter
1 cup chopped nuts

Mix cocoa, sugar and salt in 3-quart saucepan; add milk and syrup. Cook until mixture forms a soft ball when dropped in cold water. Add vanilla and butter; beat until creamy. Stir in nuts. Pour into buttered 9 x 13" pan. Refrigerate until firm.

Makes 117 pieces

Bill Garlington, Sr. Industrial Engineer
—Jacksonville

FIVE MINUTE FUDGE

¾ cup evaporated milk
2 cups sugar
1¾ cups marshmallows
¾ cup chopped nuts
1¾ cups milk chocolate chips
1 teaspoon vanilla
Nut halves for garnish

Combine milk and sugar in 3-quart saucepan. Heat to boiling. Cook 5 minutes, stirring constantly. Remove from heat; add marshmallows, chopped nuts, chocolate chips and vanilla. Stir until marshmallows are melted. Pour into buttered 9" square pan. Garnish with nut halves. Cut into squares.

Makes 81 pieces

Rebecca Scott, Department 2400
—Jacksonville

GRANDMA'S WHITE FUDGE

2¼ cups sugar
½ cup sour cream
¼ cup milk
2 tablespoons butter
1 tablespoon light corn syrup
¼ teaspoon salt
2 teaspoons vanilla
1 cup chopped walnuts
½ cup chopped candied cherries

Combine sugar, sour cream, milk, butter, corn syrup and salt in saucepan; cook and stir until soft ball stage. Cool. Add vanilla and beat until mixture loses its gloss and holds shape. Add nuts and cherries. Pour into greased pan. Let stand until firm.

Makes 1½ pounds

Kitty Krueger, Retired
—Kewaskum

HEAVENLY FOOD

4 eggs
1 cup sugar
1 cup dry bread or graham cracker
   crumbs
1 teaspoon baking powder
2 cups dates, cut up
1 cup chopped walnuts
3 to 4 bananas, sliced
1 20-ounce can pineapple tidbits, drained
1 11-ounce can mandarin oranges,
   drained
2 pints whipping cream, whipped
Maraschino cherries

Beat eggs thoroughly. Slowly add sugar, crumbs and baking powder. Stir in dates and walnuts. Bake in 9" pan at 350° for 30 to 35 minutes. Cool. Break cake into pieces. On large serving plate, layer cake, bananas, pineapple, oranges and whipped cream. Make as many layers as you can in the form of a hill or mountain. Cover with remaining whipped cream. Decorate with sliced maraschino cherries.

10 to 12 servings

Linda Gehring, Set Pack
—Kewaskum

MILE HIGH DESSERT

½ cup brown sugar
½ cup margarine, softened
1 cup flour
¾ cup chopped nuts
1 10-ounce package frozen strawberries
   or raspberries, partially thawed
2 egg whites
¾ cup sugar
2 teaspoons lemon juice
1 8-ounce container whipped topping

Mix together brown sugar, margarine, flour and chopped nuts. Pat into 9 x 13" pan. Bake in preheated 350° oven for 15 minutes; crumbling with fork as it bakes. Cool and reserve ¼ to ⅓ cup for top.

In large bowl, mix together fruit, egg whites, sugar and lemon juice; beat until peaks form, 15 to 20 minutes. Fold in whipped topping. Spread filling over crumbled crust and sprinkle balance of crumbs on top of dessert. Set in refrigerator or freezer.

12 to 18 servings

Diane Schneider, Sales Department
—Kewaskum

PINEAPPLE BAKED DISH

1 20-ounce can pineapple chunks, reserve
   juice
1 cup sugar
3 tablespoons flour
1 cup grated Cheddar cheese
⅔ stack Ritz crackers, crushed
½ cup margarine, melted

Drain pineapple, reserving juice. Place pineapple in bottom of 8" square pan. Combine sugar, flour, cheese and reserved juice. Pour over pineapple chunks. Combine crackers and margarine and spoon over fruit. Bake at 350° for 25 to 30 minutes. Serve hot or warm.

(Use a 9 x 13" pan when doubling this recipe.)

12 to 16 servings

Barb Liegl
—Kewaskum

APPLE CRISP

Topping:
1 cup oats, uncooked
¼ cup brown sugar, firmly packed
¼ teaspoon ground cinnamon
¼ cup margarine, melted

Filling:
¼ cup brown sugar, firmly packed
2 tablespoons flour
½ teaspoon cinnamon
¼ cup water
6 cups apples, peeled and sliced

Combine oats with brown sugar and cinnamon. Add margarine and mix well. Set aside.

Combine brown sugar with flour and cinnamon. Stir in water. Add fruit; tossing until coated. Spoon apple mixture into 8" square baking pan. Top with oat mixture. Bake at 350° for 40 to 45 minutes or until fruit is tender.

Variations: Use pears or peaches in place of apples.

9 to 12 servings

Naoma P. Butts, Retired
—Wooster

APPLE SLICES

Crust:
2 cups flour
¾ cup margarine
½ teaspoon salt
2 egg yolks
½ cup milk
1 tablespoon lemon juice

Filling:
3 tablespoons flour
¾ cup sugar
½ teaspoon cinnamon
4 cups thinly sliced apples, about 8
2 tablespoons butter

Mix crust ingredients and chill 2 hours. Divide in half; reserving half for top. Roll out dough to fit 12 x 18" sheet pan. Pat dough on bottom and up sides of pan.

Combine dry ingredients. Mix with apples. Arrange on crust and dot with butter. Roll out reserved dough and place on top. Cut slits in dough to allow steam to escape. Bake at 400° for 30 minutes. When slightly cool, frost with thin powdered sugar icing if desired.

36 servings

Merlin (and Gen) Luedtke, Retired
—Kewaskum

CHERRY DELIGHT

2 cups milk
1 6-ounce package instant vanilla pudding
1 16-ounce container Cool Whip
1 pound graham crackers, about 66 squares
1 20-ounce can cherry pie filling

Mix milk and pudding. Allow pudding to start setting then mix with Cool Whip. Line 8 x 10" cake pan with one layer of graham crackers. Cover with half the pudding mixture. Add another layer of graham crackers. Top with remaining pudding. Cover with third layer of graham crackers and spread pie filling over top. Refrigerate overnight. Serve cold.

12 servings

Kenny Fariss, Dept. 2000
—Jacksonville

PEACH COBBLER

1 29-ounce can sliced peaches
1 cup sugar
½ cup margarine
1 teaspoon vanilla
1 cup flour
¾ cup sugar
2½ teaspoons baking powder
Pinch of salt
Cinnamon to taste
½ cup milk

In saucepan, combine peaches, 1 cup sugar, margarine, vanilla and bring to boil. Cook and stir until margarine is melted. In 9 x 13" baking dish, combine flour, ¾ cup sugar, baking powder, salt and cinnamon. Add milk and stir until well blended. Pour fruit mixture over dough in baking dish. Bake at 400° until browned.

12 to 18 servings

> *Bill Garlington, Sr. Industrial Engineer*
> *—Jacksonville*

PEACH COBBLER

½ cup butter
1 cup sugar
1 cup flour
1 cup milk
½ teaspoon baking powder
2 cups fresh or frozen sliced peaches

Melt butter in 9 x 13" pan. Combine sugar, flour, milk and baking powder. Pour into pan over butter. Top with fruit. Bake at 350° for 45 minutes to 1 hour.

12 to 18 servings

> *Donnie McCallister, Dept. 2000*
> *Jacksonville*

PEACH COBBLER

½ cup butter
1 30 to 32-ounce can sliced peaches, undrained
1 cup flour
1 teaspoon baking powder
1 teaspoon vanilla
1 cup sugar
½ teaspoon salt
½ cup milk

Melt butter in 9 x 13" pan. Pour peaches in pan. Combine remaining ingredients; pour over peaches. Bake at 425° for 10 minutes. Reduce heat to 375° and bake 20 minutes. Serve hot.

12 to 18 servings

> *Rebecca Scott, Dept. 2400*
> *—Jacksonville*

SCANDINAVIAN KRINGLER

Crust:
1 cup flour
½ cup margarine or butter
2 tablespoons water

Puff topping:
1 cup water
½ cup margarine or butter
1 cup flour
3 eggs
½ teaspoon almond extract

Frosting:
1 cup powdered sugar
1 tablespoon margarine or butter, softened
½ teaspoon almond extract
2 to 3 tablespoons milk or cream
Sliced almonds

In small bowl, mix flour and margarine with pastry blender. Sprinkle with water, 1 tablespoon at a time. Stir with fork just until soft dough forms. (I use my food processor to mix the crust!) Divide dough in half. On ungreased cookie sheet, press each half into a 3 x 12" strip.

In medium saucepan, heat water and margarine to boiling. Remove from heat and immediately stir in flour until smooth. Add eggs one at a time, beating until smooth after each addition. Stir in almond extract. Spoon half the batter over each crust, spreading to ¾" from edges. Bake at 350° for 50 to 60 minutes or until golden brown and puffy. Immediately remove from pan; cool. Topping will shrink and fall.

In small bowl, blend all frosting ingredients except nuts, until smooth. Spread on cooled kringler. Sprinkle with nuts. Cut each into 8-10 slices.

16 to 20 servings

> *Tom Hoffman, Purchasing*
> *—Kewaskum*

RHUBARB DELIGHT

Crust:
1½ cups flour
½ cup powdered sugar
1 cup butter, softened

Topping:
4 eggs
2½ cups sugar
½ cup flour
4 cups rhubarb

In large bowl, mix together all crust ingredients. Pat into 9 x 13" pan. Bake at 350° for 15 minutes. Cool.

Mix together all topping ingredients and spread over crust. Sprinkle cinnamon on top. Bake at 350° for 25 minutes or until golden brown.

12 to 18 servings

Kitty Krueger, Retired
—Kewaskum

YOGURT COFFEE CAKE

1 cup whole wheat flour
½ cup all-purpose flour
1 cup sugar
½ teaspoon salt
2 teaspoons baking powder
½ cup canola oil
2 eggs
1 8-ounce carton yogurt, plain or with fruit

Topping:
½ 16-ounce can fruit pie filling, optional
⅓ cup sugar
1 teaspoon cinnamon
⅓ cup chopped nuts

Blend all cake ingredients together and spread into greased and floured 9 x 9" pan. Spread fruit filling over batter if desired. Mix sugar, cinnamon and nuts in small bowl. Sprinkle on top of cake. Bake at 350° for 45 minutes.

10 servings

Marty Polzean, Retired
—Kewaskum

SUNDAY MORNING COFFEE CAKE

¼ cup butter
2 egg yolks
1 cup sugar
1 teaspoon salt
2 teaspoons baking powder
1¼ cups cake flour
½ cup milk
2 egg whites, beaten

Topping:
¼ cup sugar
½ teaspoon cinnamon

Cream butter, egg yolks and 1 cup sugar. Mix salt and baking powder with flour. Add alternately with milk. Fold in beaten whites last. Spoon into greased 7 x 11" coffee cake pan. Mix together sugar and cinnamon for topping; sprinkle on top of batter. Bake at 350° for 25 to 30 minutes.

10 to 15 servings

Viola Fritz, Retired
—Kewaskum

FRUIT CRUMB COFFEE CAKE

1 18 to 19-ounce package deluxe white cake mix
1 cup flour
1 package dry yeast
⅔ cup warm water
2 eggs
1 18-ounce jar red raspberry or strawberry preserves
¼ cup sugar
1 teaspoon cinnamon
6 tablespoons butter, softened
1 cup powdered sugar
1 tablespoon milk

Preheat oven to 375°. Reserve 2½ cups dry cake mix. In large mixing bowl, combine remaining cake mix, flour, yeast, water and eggs. Mix by hand until well blended. Spread batter evenly in greased 9 x 13" pan. Spoon preserves evenly over dough. In medium bowl, combine reserved cake mix, sugar, cinnamon and butter with fork until mixture is consistency of fine crumbs. Sprinkle on top of preserves. Bake 30 to 35 minutes. Cool.

In small mixing bowl, combine powdered sugar and milk. Drizzle over cooled cake.

12 to 18 servings

Marilyn Loomis, 15 East Line
—Kewaskum

KRUMMEL KUCHEN (Crumb Cake)

2 cups flour
1½ cups sugar
2 teaspoons baking powder
¼ teaspoon salt
½ cup margarine, softened
2 eggs, beaten
½ cup milk
1 teaspoon vanilla
Cinnamon
Chopped pecans

Mix dry ingredients together; cut in margarine. Reserve 1 cup of mixture. To remaining mixture, add eggs, milk and vanilla; beat well. Pour into greased 7 x 11" pan. Cover top with reserved mixture. Sprinkle with cinnamon and chopped pecans. Bake at 350° for 35 to 45 minutes.

Variation: Chocolate chips may be sprinkled on top with pecans before baking.

12 to 15 servings

Rick (and Kathy) Zugel, Sales
—Atlanta

CRUMB CAKE

2 cups brown sugar
2 cups flour
½ cup shortening
1 cup sour milk (2 teaspoons vinegar added to 1 cup milk)
2 teaspoons baking soda
Pinch of salt
1 teaspoon vanilla
1 medium egg

Combine brown sugar, flour and shortening; mix well. Reserve ¾ cup for topping. To remaining mixture add sour milk, baking soda, salt, vanilla and egg. Mix well. Pour into greased and floured 9 x 13" pan. Sprinkle top with reserved crumb mixture. Bake at 350° for 30 minutes.

12 to 18 servings

Cynthia Braun, Dept. 1300
—Kewaskum

BROWN CAKE

1½ cups flour
1 cup sugar
½ teaspoon salt
½ teaspoon cinnamon
1 teaspoon baking soda
½ teaspoon cloves
2 tablespoons cocoa
¼ teaspoon nutmeg
1 cup sour milk
1 egg
½ cup shortening
½ cup chopped nuts
½ cup dates and coconut, optional

Sift together dry ingredients; add milk, egg and shortening. Mix well. Stir in nuts, dates and coconut. Pour into 9 x 13" pan. Bake at 350° for 40 minutes.

12 to 18 servings

Merlin (and Gen) Luedtke, Retired
—Kewaskum

FRUIT KUCHEN

Crust:
1½ cups flour
¾ cup butter, softened
½ teaspoon salt
1 egg, beaten
2 tablespoons milk

Filling:
3 cups fruit (apples, berries, rhubarb or peaches may be used)
3 eggs, beaten
1½ cups sugar
2 tablespoons flour
¾ cup milk

Topping:
½ cup sugar
½ cup flour
2 tablespoons butter, softened

Combine flour, butter, salt, egg, and milk and pat into bottom and up sides of a greased 9 x 13" pan. Spread fruit over top. Combine eggs, sugar, flour and milk. Mix well and pour over top of fruit. Mix topping ingredients until crumbly; spread over filling. Bake at 350° for 40 minutes.

12 to 18 servings

Kathy Mielkie, 15EE
—Kewaskum

MEXICAN FRUITCAKE

2 cups sugar
2 cups flour
2 eggs
2 teaspoons baking soda
1 20-ounce can crushed pineapple with juice
1 cup chopped nuts

Frosting:
1 4-ounce package cream cheese, softened
½ teaspoon vanilla
½ stick margarine, softened
1 cup powdered sugar

Mix first six ingredients together by hand. Pour into greased 9 x 13" pan. Bake at 350°

for 45 minutes. Cool. Mix frosting ingredients and spread on cake.

12 to 18 servings

Arlene Herriges, Dept. 15EE
—Kewaskum

ROMAN APPLE CAKE

¾ cup shortening
1 cup sugar
½ cup brown sugar
2 eggs
1 cup buttermilk with 1 teaspoon baking soda
2 cups flour
1 teaspoon cinnamon
1 teaspoon baking powder
2 cups peeled, cubed, raw apples

Topping:
¼ cup sugar
¼ cup brown sugar
½ teaspoon cinnamon
½ cup chopped nuts

Mix cake ingredients in order given. Pour into greased 9 x 13" pan.

Combine topping ingredients and sprinkle on top of batter. Bake at 325° for 1 hour.

12 to 18 servings

Judy Knudson, Dept. 2000
—Kewaskum

FRESH APPLE CAKE

½ cup butter
1 cup sugar
1 egg
1½ cups all-purpose flour
1 teaspoon baking soda
1 teaspoon cinnamon
1 teaspoon nutmeg
½ teaspoon salt
2½ cups chopped, tart apples, about 1 pound
½ cup coarsely chopped walnuts

Preheat oven to 350°. In mixing bowl, cream butter and sugar; add egg. Beat until light and fluffy; about 1 minute. Thoroughly stir together flour, baking soda, cinnamon, nutmeg and salt. Stir into creamed mixture. Add apples; turn into greased 9 x 9 x 2" pan. Sprinkle with chopped nuts and bake for 40 to 45 minutes or until cake tests done. Serve warm or cool with whipped cream or ice cream.

8 to 9 servings

Philip Zingsheim, Retired
—Kewaskum

APPLE WALNUT CAKE

4 cups coarsely chopped apples
2 cups sugar
2 eggs
½ cup oil
2 teaspoons vanilla
2 cups flour
2 teaspoons baking soda
1 teaspoon salt
2 teaspoons cinnamon
½ cup chopped walnuts or pecans

Lemon glaze:
1 cup powdered sugar
1½ tablespoons lemon juice
½ teaspoon vanilla
1 teaspoon corn syrup

Preheat oven to 350°. Grease and flour 9 x 13" pan. Combine apples and sugar; set aside. In large mixing bowl, beat eggs slightly, add oil and vanilla. Beat 1 minute at medium speed. Combine dry ingredients and add alternately with apple mixture. Stir in walnuts. Pour batter in pan. Bake for 45 to 50 minutes or until cake tests done with toothpick. When cool, top with lemon glaze or powdered sugar.

To make lemon glaze, blend all ingredients in bowl until smooth. Drizzle over cooled cake.

12 to 18 servings

Ruby J. Morrison, Dept. 2000
—Jacksonville

APPLE CAKE

2 cups sugar
1½ cups oil
3 eggs
3 cups flour
1 teaspoon cinnamon
1 teaspoon baking soda
¾ teaspoon salt
2 teaspoons vanilla
3 or 4 cups chopped apples
½ cup chopped nuts

Preheat oven to 325°. Grease and flour tube pan. Mix together sugar, oil and eggs. Add flour, cinnamon, baking soda, salt, vanilla, apples and nuts. Mix well. Pour in tube pan. Bake for 1½ hours.

8 to 12 servings

Mary Belcher, Dept. 2000
—Jacksonville

BEET CAKE

½ cup cocoa
1⅛ cups oil
1 teaspoon vanilla
1¾ cups flour
1½ cups sugar
1½ teaspoons baking soda
½ teaspoon salt
3 eggs, beaten
1¼ cups cooked, mashed beets
½ cup chopped nuts

In mixing bowl, combine cocoa, oil and vanilla; mix well. In another bowl, combine flour, sugar, baking soda and salt. Mix and add to cocoa mixture. Blend in eggs and beets.

With electric mixer, beat at medium speed for 2 minutes. Stir in nuts. Pour into greased 9 x 13" pan. Bake at 350° for 25 to 30 minutes. Frost with favorite chocolate frosting if desired.

12 to 18 servings

Kathy Mielke, Dept. 15EE
and
Jean Dippel, Retired
—Kewaskum

CARROT CAKE

1½ cups flour
1 teaspoon baking powder
1 teaspoon baking soda
1 teaspoon cinnamon
¼ teaspoon salt
1 cup sugar
½ cup oil
2 eggs
¼ cup milk
1 cup grated carrots or 2 small jars
   strained carrots baby food

Preheat oven to 350°. Grease and flour tube pan. Sift flour, baking powder, baking soda, cinnamon and salt; set aside. Mix sugar and oil; add sifted ingredients. Add eggs one at a time. Add milk and carrots. Blend well. Pour into tube pan and bake for 1 hour.

8 to 12 servings

Mary Belcher, Dept. 2000
—Jacksonville

WESTHAVEN CAKE

1 cup dates, cut into pieces
1 cup hot water
1 teaspoon baking soda
½ cup shortening
1 cup sugar
2 eggs
½ teaspoon salt
1 teaspoon baking powder
1¾ cups flour
1 tablespoon cocoa
1 cup chocolate chips
½ cup chopped nuts
Powdered sugar

Combine dates, hot water and baking soda in small bowl. Set aside and cool. Cream shortening, sugar, eggs and salt. Add baking powder, flour and cocoa. Mix well. Add date mixture. Pour into greased and floured 9 x 13" pan. Scatter chocolate chips and nuts on top of batter. Bake at 350° for 30 to 45 minutes. Cool and sprinkle with powdered sugar.

12 to 18 servings

Ruth Raether, Retired
—Kewaskum

CHOCOLATE CHIP DATE CAKE

1 cup dates, cut up
1 cup hot water
1 teaspoon baking soda
1 cup sugar
2 eggs
1 cup shortening
½ teaspoon salt
1 teaspoon vanilla
1¾ cups flour
2 tablespoons cocoa
1 cup chocolate chips
½ cup chopped nuts
¼ cup brown sugar

In small bowl, mix dates, hot water and baking soda. Set aside to cool. In mixing bowl, combine sugar, eggs, shortening, salt and vanilla. Add date mixture and mix well. Add flour and cocoa. Mix well and pour into greased and floured 9 x 13" pan. Scatter chocolate chips and nuts over batter; sprinkle brown sugar over chips and nuts. Bake at 350° for 30 to 40 minutes.

12 to 18 servings

Kitty Krueger, Retired
—Kewaskum

CHOCOLATE CHIP DATE CAKE

1 cup chopped dates
1½ cups water
1¾ teaspoons baking soda, divided
½ cup shortening
1 cup sugar
2 eggs
1½ cups flour
¼ teaspoon salt
¾ cup brown sugar
¾ cup chocolate chips

Boil dates and water 2 to 3 minutes. Let cool. Combine 1 teaspoon baking soda, shortening, sugar and eggs; add dates. Combine flour, ¾ teaspoon baking soda and salt; mix with date mixture. Pour into greased and floured 9 x 13" pan.

Sprinkle brown sugar and chocolate chips over top. Bake at 350° for 30 minutes.

12 to 18 servings

Bob Heller, Dept. 1100
—Kewaskum

ORANGE CHIFFON CAKE

2¼ cups sifted cake flour
1½ cups sugar
3 teaspoons baking powder
1 teaspoon salt
½ cup oil
5 egg yolks, unbeaten
2 tablespoons grated orange rind
Juice of 2 medium oranges plus water to make ¾ cup
1 cup egg whites (7 to 8 eggs)
½ teaspoon cream of tartar

Measure and sift into mixing bowl cake flour, sugar, baking powder and salt. Make a well and add oil, egg yolks, orange rind and orange juice/water. Beat with spoon until smooth and set aside. Measure egg whites and cream of tartar into large mixing bowl and beat until very stiff. Do not underbeat. Pour egg yolk mixture gradually over whipped egg whites gently folding with rubber spatula just until blended. Do not stir.

Pour into ungreased 10" tube pan and bake at 325° for 65 minutes. Immediately turn pan upside down, placing tube part over neck of funnel or bottle. Cool completely. Loosen cake from sides; turn over and hit sharply on table to loosen.

12 to 16 servings

Rose Peter (my mother's recipe)
—Kewaskum

PEACH DELIGHT CAKE

1 16-ounce can sliced peaches in light syrup, reserve juice
Water
1 18 to 19-ounce package yellow cake mix
1 6-ounce container peach yogurt or ⅔ cup plain yogurt
1 4-ounce container Cool Whip

Grease and flour two 9" round cake pans. Preheat oven to 350°. Drain peaches, reserving juice. Add water to juice to make 1¼ cups liquid. Prepare cake mix as directed on box using peach juice mixture. Pour batter into pans. Bake as directed on package; cool. Cut peaches into bite-size pieces. Mix yogurt and Cool Whip. Fold in peaches. Fill layers with half peach mixture. Spoon remaining mixture over top of cake. Refrigerate approximately 2 hours before serving.

12 servings

Kitty Krueger, Retired
—Kewaskum

RED PLUM SPICE CAKE

2 cups sugar
1 cup cooking oil
3 eggs
2 cups flour
½ teaspoon baking soda
¼ teaspoon salt
1 teaspoon cinnamon
1 teaspoon cloves
2 small jars red plum baby food
1½ teaspoons red food coloring

In medium bowl, combine ingredients in order given, mixing well after each addition. Pour into greased and floured bundt pan. Bake at 350° for 30 minutes. Cool.

12 to 16 servings

Goldia Wilkins, Dept. 21
—Jacksonville

CHOCOLATE POTATO CAKE

1 cup butter or margarine, softened
2 cups sugar
1 cup cocoa
½ cup milk
4 eggs, beaten
2 cups flour
2 teaspoons baking powder
½ teaspoon salt
1 teaspoon cinnamon
1 teaspoon cloves
1 teaspoon allspice
1 cup mashed potatoes
1 teaspoon vanilla
1 cup chopped nuts

Cream butter and sugar together until fluffy. Add cocoa, milk and eggs. Beat until smooth. Sift together flour, baking powder, salt and spices. Add to creamed mixture alternately with potatoes. Add vanilla and nuts.

Bake in well greased and floured pans at 350°.

Two 9" round cake pans - 30 minutes
9 x 13" pan - 40 minutes
12-cup bundt pan - 50 minutes or until toothpick comes out clean.

Top with sifted powdered sugar or your favorite frosting. (We prefer Philly cream cheese frosting.)

Jim Myre, Sales
—California

SWEET POTATO CAKE

2 cups sugar
1½ cups oil
4 eggs, beaten
2 cups flour
2 teaspoons baking soda
2 teaspoons baking powder
1 teaspoon salt
1 teaspoon cinnamon
1 teaspoon nutmeg
1 teaspoon cloves
3 cups cooked, mashed sweet potatoes
1 teaspoon vanilla

Mix sugar and oil together. Add eggs; mix well. Combine all dry ingredients and stir into sugar and egg mixture. Bake in greased and floured 9 x 13" pan at 325° for 35 to 40 minutes.

Variations: Substitute pureed pumpkin, carrots or zucchini for sweet potatoes.

12 to 18 servings

Nancy White, Nationwide Acceptance
—Arlington, TX

RHUBARB SLAB CAKE

2½ cups flour
1 cup Crisco
1 tablespoon sugar
1 egg yolk; add milk to make ⅔ cup
½ teaspoon salt
4 cups rhubarb, thinly sliced
1½ cups sugar
1 cup crushed cornflakes

Mix together flour, Crisco, 1 tablespoon sugar, egg mixture and salt. Cut mixture in half and roll out to fit 10 x 15" jelly roll pan. Combine rhubarb and sugar and spread over crust. Sprinkle with cornflakes. Cover with last half of dough. Bake at 350° for 1 hour. When cool, ice with thin powdered sugar frosting.

24 to 30 servings

John Pearson, Retired
—Kewaskum

RHUBARB CAKE

2 cups chopped rhubarb
½ cup sugar
1 cup milk
1 tablespoon vinegar
½ cup shortening
1 egg
2 cups flour
1 teaspoon baking soda
1 teaspoon cinnamon
Pinch salt
1½ cups sugar
1 teaspoon vanilla

Frosting:
6 tablespoons butter
1½ cups brown sugar
½ cup milk
1 cup coconut
½ cup chopped nuts

Combine rhubarb and sugar; let stand for 1 hour. Combine milk and vinegar; let stand for 1 hour. Cream together shortening and egg. Beat well and add flour, baking soda, cinnamon, salt, sugar, milk mixture and vanilla. Beat for 2 minutes. Stir in rhubarb mixture and pour into greased and floured 9 x 13" pan. Bake at 350° for 1 hour.

Mix together frosting ingredients. Spread on warm cake. Place under broiler 3 to 4 minutes, until frosting bubbles.

12 to 18 servings

Diane Schraufnagel, Dept. 8300
—Kewaskum

QUICK RHUBARB DESSERT

4 cups diced rhubarb
½ to ¾ cup sugar
1 3-ounce package sugar-free strawberry gelatin
1 18 or 19-ounce package white or yellow cake mix (dry)
1 cup cold water
½ cup butter, melted

Pour or sprinkle all ingredients in 9 x 13" pan, one layer at a time. Do not stir. Bake at 350° for 1 hour.

12 to 18 servings

Kathy Mielkie, Dept. 15EE
—Kewaskum

BEST RHUBARB KUCHEN

Crust:
¾ cup butter
1 tablespoon sugar
Pinch of salt
1 egg
2 cups flour
6 cups rhubarb, cut-up

Custard:
4 eggs, beaten
Pinch of salt
1¾ cups sugar
4 tablespoons butter, melted

Topping:
1 cup sugar
1 cup flour
Pinch of salt
½ cup butter, softened

Combine first five ingredients and pat into bottom and ⅔" up sides of 9 x 13" pan. Spread rhubarb over crust.

In medium bowl, combine custard ingredients. Mix well and spread over rhubarb.

In small bowl, mix dry topping ingredients. Cut in butter; mix to crumbly stage. Crumble over rhubarb and custard. Bake at 350° for 50 minutes.

12 to 18 servings

Merlin (and Gen) Luedtke, Retired
—Kewaskum

RHUBARB KUCHEN

1 cup flour
1 teaspoon baking powder
¼ teaspoon salt
2 tablespoons shortening
1 egg, slightly beaten
2 tablespoons milk
2 cups chopped rhubarb
1 cup whole raspberries
½ tablespoon unflavored gelatin

Topping:
1 cup sugar
½ cup flour
¼ cup butter, melted

Sift together flour, baking powder and salt. Cut in shortening; add egg and milk to form a crumbly mixture. Press into bottom and up sides of 8 x 8" pan. Add chopped rhubarb and raspberries. Sprinkle gelatin over rhubarb and raspberries.

Blend topping and sprinkle over rhubarb mixture. Bake at 375° for 25 to 30 minutes.

9 to 12 servings

Philip Zingsheim, Retired
—Kewaskum

ZUCCHINI CAKE

½ cup margarine, softened
½ cup oil
1¾ cups sugar
2 eggs
1 teaspoon vanilla
½ cup sour cream
2½ cups flour
1 teaspoon baking soda
¼ cup cocoa
½ teaspoon cinnamon
½ teaspoon cloves
½ teaspoon salt
2 cups grated zucchini
½ cup chocolate chips
¼ cup nuts

Cream margarine, oil and sugar. Add eggs, vanilla and sour cream; beat well. Add dry ingredients and zucchini. Mix lightly. Pour into greased and floured 9 x 13" pan. Sprinkle chocolate chips and nuts on top. Bake at 325° for 40 minutes.

12 to 18 servings

Joe (and Kris) Swanson
—Kewaskum

CHOCOLATE ZUCCHINI CAKE

½ cup butter, softened
1¾ cups sugar
½ cup oil
2 eggs
2 cups grated zucchini
1 teaspoon vanilla
½ cup sour milk
2½ cups sifted flour
1 teaspoon salt
¼ cup cocoa
½ teaspoon baking powder
½ teaspoon cinnamon
1 teaspoon baking soda
½ teaspoon cloves
1 cup chocolate chips

In large mixing bowl, cream butter and sugar. Add oil, eggs and zucchini, mixing well after each. Add vanilla to sour milk. Combine all dry ingredients, except cho-

colate chips. Alternately add milk and dry ingredients to zucchini mixture. Mix well. Pour into greased 9 x 13" pan. Top with chocolate chips. Bake at 325° for 40 minutes or until done.

12 to 18 servings

Bill (and Lucy) McCarty, Retired
—Kewaskum

CHOCOLATE ZUCCHINI CAKE

½ cup margarine, softened
½ cup salad oil
1¾ cups sugar
2 eggs
1 teaspoon vanilla
2½ cups flour
¼ cup cocoa
1 teaspoon baking powder
1 teaspoon baking soda
1 teaspoon salt
½ teaspoon cinnamon
½ teaspoon cloves
½ cup sour milk
2 cups shredded zucchini
½ cup chocolate chips
½ cup chopped nuts

Cream margarine, salad oil, sugar, eggs and vanilla. Add all dry ingredients. Mix well. Add sour milk and zucchini. Mix again. Pour into greased 9 x 13" pan. Sprinkle with chocolate chips and chopped nuts. Bake at 325° for 40 to 45 minutes. Let cool and spread powdered sugar glaze over top if desired.

12 to 18 servings

Kitty Krueger, Retired
—Kewaskum

OATMEAL CAKE

1½ cups hot water
1 cup oats
1 cup sugar
1 cup brown sugar
1 cup oil
2 eggs
1⅓ cups flour
1 teaspoon cinnamon
1 teaspoon baking soda
½ teaspoon salt

Icing:
6 tablespoons butter
1 tablespoon evaporated milk
¾ cup brown sugar
1 cup coconut, optional
1 cup chopped nuts, optional

In mixing bowl, pour hot water over oats and let stand. In large bowl, cream sugar, brown sugar, oil and eggs. Sift together last four dry ingredients; combine with creamed mixture. Add oats mixture and beat well. Pour into 9 x 13" pan; bake at 350° for 35 minutes.

In saucepan, combine butter, milk and sugar. Boil for 1 minute and pour over hot cake, or add coconut and nuts and spread over hot cake. Brown lightly in oven or under broiler.

12 to 18 servings

Ruby J. Morrison, Dept. 20
—Jacksonville

SOUR CREAM CAKE

1 18-ounce package Duncan Hines white
  cake mix
¾ cup oil
4 eggs
½ cup sugar
1 cup sour cream
1½ teaspoons brown sugar
1½ teaspoons powdered sugar
2 teaspoons cinnamon
1 cup chopped pecans

Combine cake mix, oil, eggs, sugar and sour cream. Mix well. Add remaining ingredients and mix well. Pour into greased and floured bundt pan. Bake at 350° for 30 to 35 minutes or until done.

12 to 16 servings

Odessa Irvin, Dept. 8400
—Jacksonville

TUTIE FRUITIE CAKE

1½ cups sifted flour
1 teaspoon baking soda
1 cup sugar
½ cup butter or margarine
1 ounce unsweetened baking chocolate,
  melted
1 cup sour milk
½ cup chopped nuts
½ cup raisins

Frosting:
½ cup sugar
2 teaspoons flour
½ cup milk
1 egg
1 tablespoon butter
½ cup raisins
½ cup nuts

Grease and flour two 8" cake pans. Sift together flour and baking soda; set aside. In large bowl, cream sugar and butter; add chocolate. Alternately add flour mixture and sour milk to creamed mixture. Stir in nuts and raisins. Pour into pans and bake at 350° for 30 to 35 minutes. Cool and remove from pans.

In 3-quart saucepan, mix together all frosting ingredients; cook and stir until thickened. Spread between layers of cake, on sides and top.

12 to 16 servings

Gertrude Wondra, Retired
—Kewaskum

POPPY SEED CHIFFON CAKE

¾ cup boiling water
½ cup poppy seeds
2 cups sifted flour
1½ cups sugar
3 teaspoons baking powder
1 teaspoon salt
½ cup oil
7 egg yolks
2 teaspoons vanilla
1 cup egg whites (8 large eggs)
½ teaspoon cream of tartar

Whipped custard frosting:
2 eggs, beaten
½ cup sugar
2 rounded tablespoons flour
1 cup milk
1 cup butter or margarine, softened
4 tablespoons powdered sugar
1 teaspoon vanilla
¼ cup chopped nuts

Pour boiling water over poppy seeds in medium bowl; let stand for 2 hours.

Sift flour, sugar, baking powder and salt into large bowl. Make well in center and add oil, egg yolks, poppy seed mixture and vanilla. Beat with spoon until smooth.

Beat egg whites and cream of tartar in large glass bowl (do not use plastic) with electric mixer at high speed until whites are very stiff. Gradually pour egg yolk mixture over egg whites, gently folding until no streaks of white remain. Pour into ungreased 10" tube pan. Bake at 325° for 1 hour and 10 minutes. Remove from oven and invert pan over funnel or quart-size bottle. Let cool completely.

This cake can also be baked in a 9 x 13" pan and used as a shortcake with berries.

In top of double boiler, combine eggs, sugar and flour and mix well; add milk. Place pan over hot water; cook until thick. Cool. In mixing bowl, cream butter, powdered sugar and vanilla. Add cooled custard mixture to creamed mixture; beat until smooth and creamy. Frost cake and sprinkle with chopped nuts.

12 to 16 servings

Dorothy Jensen, Retired
—Kewaskum

POUND CAKE

½ cup lard or Crisco
1 cup margarine, softened
3 cups sugar
6 eggs
1 cup milk
3½ cups flour
½ teaspoon baking powder
1 teaspoon vanilla
1 teaspoon lemon extract

Mix together all ingredients in order listed. Spoon into greased tube pan. Bake at 325° for 1½ hours.

12 to 16 servings

Michelle Partin, Outlet Store
—Pigeon Forge, TN

THRIFTY POUND CAKE

3 cups flour
½ teaspoon baking powder
½ teaspoon baking soda
¼ teaspoon salt
1 cup butter-flavored Crisco
2 cups sugar
4 eggs
1 teaspoon vanilla
1 teaspoon lemon extract or black walnut extract
1 cup buttermilk

Combine flour, baking powder, baking soda and salt in bowl; set aside. Beat next five ingredients for 2½ minutes. Scrape bowl while beating. Reduce speed of mixer and add flour mixture alternately with buttermilk.

Scrape bowl while beating; beat only enough to blend well, about 3 minutes. Pour batter into well buttered tube pan.

Bake at 350° for 1 hour and 10 minutes. Remove from pan; cool. Frost or serve plain.

This recipe was my mother-in-law's. You couldn't go into her home that she did not offer you a piece of her pound cake. She was a wonderful cook and her pound cake is

fondly remembered by her son and grand-
ildren.

12 to 16 servings

Nancy White, Nationwide Acceptance Corp.
—Arlington, TX

LEMON POUND CAKE

1 18 to 19-ounce package yellow cake
   mix
1 3-ounce package lemon gelatin
⅔ cup oil
⅔ cup water
4 eggs
3 teaspoons lemon extract

Glaze:
2 cups powdered sugar
Juice of 2 oranges
1 teaspoon lemon extract

Mix cake mix with gelatin, oil, water, eggs
and lemon extract. Beat with mixer on
medium speed for 3 minutes. Spoon into
greased and floured bundt pan. Bake at
325° for 1 hour.

Mix together powdered sugar, orange juice
and lemon extract; drizzle over hot cake.

12 to 16 servings

Verna Robinson, Retired
—Jacksonville

LEMON LUSH CAKE

½ cup butter, softened
1 cup flour
½ cup chopped walnuts
¾ cup powdered sugar
1 8-ounce package cream cheese
1 pint whipping cream, whipped
2 3¾-ounce packages instant lemon
   pudding
3 cups milk

Mix together butter, flour and nuts. Press
mixture into lightly greased 9 x 13″ pan.
Bake at 350° for 15 to 20 minutes. Cool
completely. Combine powdered sugar and
cream cheese with 1 cup whipped cream.
Spread over crust. Mix pudding with milk
until thick. Spread over cheese layer. Let
set. Spread remainder of whipped cream on
top and refrigerate.

12 servings

Elvira Schmidt
—Kewaskum

ITALIAN CREAM CAKE

1 18 to 19-ounce package yellow cake
   mix, without pudding
1 3.4-ounce package instant vanilla
   pudding
4 eggs
½ cup oil
1 cup water
¼ cup sugar
1 cup chopped pecans
1 cup chopped coconut

Frosting:
1 8-ounce package cream cheese,
   softened
¼ cup margarine, softened
1 teaspoon vanilla
1 pound (4 to 4½ cups) powdered sugar
1 cup chopped nuts

Mix all ingredients together. Pour into
three or four greased 8″ round cake pans;
bake at 350° for 30 to 35 minutes. Cool on
racks.

Cream together all frosting ingredients
except nuts. Stir in nuts. Spread between
layers and on top of cake.

8 to 12 servings

Janice Thill, Sales
—Kewaskum

LAZY DAISY CAKE

2 eggs
1 cup sugar
1 teaspoon vanilla
1 cup flour
1 teaspoon baking powder
¼ teaspoon salt
½ cup milk
2 tablespoons butter

Frosting:
¾ cup brown sugar
6 tablespoons butter, melted
¼ cup cream
1 cup coconut

Combine eggs, sugar and vanilla; beat until thick. Add sifted dry ingredients. Heat milk and butter to boiling point; add to above mixture. Batter will be thin. Bake in buttered 8" square pan at 350° for 30 to 40 minutes. Remove from oven and frost.

Combine all frosting ingredients; blend well. Spread over hot cake; return to hot oven or broiler to brown.

9 to 12 servings

Cele Schmidt, Administration
—Kewaskum

ICEBOX CAKE

1 cup graham cracker crumbs
1 package lemon gelatin
1 cup boiling water
12 marshmallows
1 cup crushed pineapple, drained
1 cup chopped nuts
1 cup whipped cream or Cool Whip

Line a 9" square cake pan with graham cracker crumbs, reserving 1 tablespoon for top. Dissolve gelatin in boiling water; add marshmallows and stir until melted. Allow gelatin to cool until beginning to set. Add pineapple, nuts and whipped cream or Cool Whip. Mix well; pour over crust. Sprinkle reserved crumbs on top. Refrigerate 12 hours before serving.

9 to 12 servings

Catherine Speer, Dept. 9500
—Jacksonville

FASTEST CAKE IN THE WEST

2 cups flour
1½ cups sugar
½ teaspoon salt
1½ teaspoons baking soda
1½ cups chopped nuts
1 teaspoon cinnamon
1 20-ounce can pie filling (cherry, apple or apricot)
2 eggs, beaten
¾ cup oil

Cream cheese frosting:
1 3-ounce package cream cheese, softened
¼ cup butter, softened
1 teaspoon vanilla
2 cups powdered sugar

In 9 x 13" pan, mix first four ingredients together. Add remaining ingredients. Blend with fork until well mixed. Bake at 350° for 30 minutes. Cool. Top with Cool Whip or cream cheese frosting.

To make frosting, in a small bowl beat together cream cheese, butter and vanilla until fluffy. Gradually add powdered sugar. Whip until smooth.

12 to 18 servings

Carolyn Lessley, Saladmaster, Inc.
—Arlington, TX

FRUIT CAKE DELIGHT

1 18.5-ounce package yellow cake mix
½ cup oil
1 11-ounce can mandarin oranges, drained, reserve juice
4 eggs

Topping:
1 20-ounce can crushed pineapple, with juice
1 3.75-ounce box French vanilla instant pudding
1 8-ounce container Cool Whip, thawed

Combine cake mix, oil, juice and eggs in mixing bowl. Beat 2 minutes at high speed. Stir in mandarin oranges and beat another 20 seconds. Pour into greased and floured 9 x 13" pan. Bake at 325° for 30 to 40 minutes. Cool.

Place pineapple with juice in large bowl. Sprinkle with dry pudding; stir to combine. Fold in Cool Whip. Spread on top of cooled cake. Refrigerate.

12 to 18 servings

Kathy Mielkie, Dept. 15EE
—Kewaskum

SOUR CREAM COCONUT CAKE

2 cups sugar
1 8-ounce can crushed pineapple, with juice
1 16-ounce carton sour cream
1 18-ounce Duncan Hines Pineapple Supreme II cake mix
1 8-ounce container Cool Whip
½ cup coconut

Mix sugar, pineapple with juice and sour cream together. Let stand and prepare cake according to package directions, baking in 9 x 13" pan. Cool cake completely and remove from pan. Using sewing thread, split cake to make two layers. Spread half pineapple mixture between cake layers. Mix remaining pineapple mixture with Cool Whip and frost cake. Sprinkle with coconut.

12 to 18 servings

Betty Bailey, Dept. 2000
—Jacksonville

PIG LICKIN' GOOD CAKE

1 18 or 19-ounce package yellow cake mix
4 eggs, beaten
½ cup oil
1 cup mandarin orange sections and juice

Frosting:
1 12-ounce container Cool Whip
1 3.4-ounce package instant vanilla pudding
1 cup crushed pineapple, drained

Mix together cake mix, eggs, oil, orange segments and juice. Spoon into greased 9 x 13" pan; bake according to package directions. Cool. Mix frosting ingredients together; spread over cooled cake. Refrigerate.

12 to 18 servings

Rita M. Felton, Retired
—Wooster

PUNCH BOWL CAKE

1 18 to 19-ounce package yellow cake mix
1 4.3-ounce package instant vanilla pudding
1 20-ounce can crushed pineapple, drained
1 16-ounce can strawberry pie filling
1 12-ounce container Cool Whip
Chopped nuts, optional

Prepare cake according to package directions using 9 x 13" pan. Cool and break into medium-size chunks. Prepare pudding according to package directions.

In clear glass punch/serving bowl, layer above ingredients in order given using half of each at a time. Repeat second layer of each, topping with chopped nuts if desired. Refrigerate.

16 to 20 servings

Betty Bailey, Dept. 2000
—Jacksonville

FOUR LAYER CAKE

1 9-ounce package Jiffy yellow cake mix
1 3.4-ounce package instant vanilla pudding mix
1½ cups cold milk
1 8-ounce package cream cheese, softened
1 20-ounce can crushed pineapple, drained
1 12-ounce container Cool Whip

Grease and flour 9 x 13" pan. Mix yellow cake mix according to package directions. Bake and cool. In medium bowl, combine pudding mix and milk until dissolved then beat for 2 minutes. Add cream cheese and beat until smooth. Layer cream cheese on top of cake, then drained pineapple and top with Cool Whip.

12 to 18 servings

Laura Hammes, Retired
—Kewaskum

YUMMY YUMMY CAKE

1 18 or 19-ounce package yellow cake mix
2⅔ cups coconut, divided
1 8-ounce cream cheese, softened
2 cups milk
1 3.4-ounce package instant vanilla pudding
1 20-ounce can crushed pineapple, drained
1 12-ounce container Cool Whip

Prepare cake mix according to package directions adding 1⅓ cups coconut; bake in 9 x 13" pan at 350° for 20 minutes or until done. Cool for 10 minutes. Beat cream cheese, milk and pudding on low speed for 2 minutes. Spread mixture over cake. Top with pineapple and Cool Whip. Sprinkle remaining 1⅓ cups coconut over Cool Whip.

12 to 18 servings

Eileen Bonlender
—Kewaskum

THREE DAY LAYER CAKE

1 18-ounce package Duncan Hines Butter Recipe cake mix
2 cups sugar
1 cup sour cream
1 7-ounce package frozen coconut
1 8-ounce container Cool Whip

Bake cake according to package directions in two 8" round cake pans. When cool cut each layer in two, making four layers.

Mix sugar, sour cream and coconut together; fill layers, reserving 1 cup for topping. Mix reserved filling with Cool Whip; frost top and sides of cake. Place in covered container; refrigerate three days before serving. After three days in refrigerator, freeze if desired.

12 to 16 servings

Carol Oberle, Production Scheduling
—Jacksonville

TWINKIE CAKE

8 Twinkies
1 8-ounce package cream cheese, softened
1 8-ounce box instant vanilla pudding mix
1 8-ounce container sour cream
1 cup milk
1 20-ounce can cherry pie filling
1 12-ounce container Cool Whip

Cut Twinkies in half and place cut-side up in 9 x 13" pan. Mix cream cheese, pudding, sour cream and milk together in blender. Spread over Twinkies. Spoon pie filling over first layer; top with Cool Whip.

12 to 18 servings

Gayle Tanner, Dept. 21
—Jacksonville

CREME DE MENTHE CAKE

1 18 to 19-ounce white cake mix
1 16-ounce can Hersheys Chocolate Fudge ice cream topping
1 16-ounce container Cool Whip
1 tablespoon green creme de menthe liqueur (or non-alcoholic ice cream topping)

Bake cake according to package directions for 9 x 13" pan. Place opened can of chocolate fudge topping in pan of boiling water until topping is melted. Let cool. Pour over top of cake, spreading to edges. Refrigerate for 15 minutes until chocolate hardens. Fold creme de menthe into Cool Whip. Spread evenly on top of cake. Refrigerate.

12 to 18 servings

Raymond Fisher, Plastics
—Kewaskum

GLORIFIED CHOCOLATE CAKE

1 18-ounce package chocolate cake mix
1 15-ounce can sweetened condensed milk
1 12-ounce jar caramel ice cream topping
1 8-ounce carton whipped topping
4 Heath candy bars, chopped

Prepare cake mix according to directions and bake in 9 x 13" pan. Cool. Poke holes throughout cake with wooden spoon handle. Pour condensed milk over cake and spread with caramel topping. Spread whipped topping over cake and garnish with chopped candy. Refrigerate.

12 to 18 servings

Diane Schneider, Sales
—Kewaskum

COCOA CHIFFON CAKE

¾ cups boiling water
½ cup cocoa
1¾ cups cake flour
1¾ cups sugar
3 teaspoons baking powder
1 teaspoon salt
½ cup oil
7 egg yolks, unbeaten
1 teaspoon vanilla
¼ teaspoon red food coloring, optional
1 cup egg whites (7 or 8)
½ teaspoon cream of tartar

Hobnail icing:
2 cups sifted, powdered sugar
4 or 5 egg yolks
½ cup milk
6 squares (6 ounces) unsweetened chocolate, melted
2 tablespoons shortening, softened
1 teaspoon vanilla

Combine boiling water and cocoa; stir until smooth and set aside to cool. Measure and sift into mixing bowl, cake flour, sugar, baking powder and salt. Make a well and add in order oil, egg yolks, cooled cocoa mixture, vanilla and food coloring. Beat with spoon until smooth. Set aside.

Whip egg whites and cream of tartar until very stiff peaks form. Do not underbeat. Pour egg yolk mixture gradually over whipped egg whites, gently folding with rubber spatula, just until blended. Do not stir. Immediately pour into ungreased 10" tube pan. Bake at 325° for 55 minutes. Raise oven temperature to 350° and bake an additional 10 to 15 minutes.

Cake may also be baked in 9 x 13" pan at 350° for 45 to 50 minutes or until top springs back when lightly touched.

To make frosting, place mixing bowl in ice water. Mix ingredients in order listed with rotary beater until spreading consistency; 3 to 5 minutes. Spread on top and sides of cake. Make hobnail effect with tip of teaspoon.

12 to 16 servings

Rose Peter (my mother's recipe)
—Kewaskum

SURPRISE CHOCOLATE CAKE

2 cups sifted flour
1 cup sugar
2 teaspoons baking soda
¼ cup cocoa
1 cup cold water
1 teaspoon vanilla
1 cup Miracle Whip salad dressing

Cocoa Fluff frosting:
1 cup whipping cream
½ cup powdered sugar
Dash of salt
¼ cup cocoa

Preheat oven to 350°. Sift together dry ingredients. Add cold water and mix well. Add vanilla and mix. Fold in salad dressing. Grease and flour only bottoms of two 9" round pans or 9 x 13" pan. Bake for 30 to 35 minutes. Cool.

To make frosting, chill mixing bowl in freezer for about 15 minutes. Beat all ingredients well until light and fluffy. Spread frosting between layers, on top and sides of cake.

12 to 18 servings

Cynthia Braun, Dept. 1300
—Kewaskum

CHOCOLATE CAKE

2 cups flour
2 cups sugar
1 cup butter
1 cup water
4 tablespoons cocoa
½ cup buttermilk
2 eggs, beaten
1 teaspoon baking soda
1 teaspoon vanilla

Icing:
½ cup butter
4 tablespoons cocoa
6 tablespoons milk
1 pound (4¼ cups) powdered sugar
1 teaspoon vanilla
1 cup chopped nuts

Sift flour and sugar together. In saucepan, bring to boil butter, water and cocoa. Pour over flour mixture while still hot. Add buttermilk, eggs, baking soda and vanilla. Spoon into greased and floured 9 x 13" pan. Bake at 400° for 20 minutes or until tests done. Cool 10 minutes and spread icing on top.

Bring to boil butter, cocoa and milk. Add powdered sugar, vanilla and nuts. Spread over hot cake.

12 to 18 servings

Goldia Wilkins, Dept. 21
—Jacksonville

SMALL DEVILS FOOD CAKE

When I was young my mother told me to make a cake. I said, "Where's the recipe?" She said, "You don't need one; take one wooden spoon of lard, and about a cup of sugar, use two eggs because they are pullet eggs, a little cocoa and add enough hot water to make a paste." And so on it went. Since then I have revised the recipe as follows:

¾ cup margarine, softened
1 cup sugar
2 eggs, slightly beaten
¼ cup cocoa
1 teaspoon baking soda
1½ cups flour
⅔ cup sour milk

Cream margarine and sugar together, beat in eggs. Sift dry ingredients together, add alternately with sour milk to egg mixture. Pour batter into greased and floured 9 x 9" pan. Bake at 350° for 35 to 40 minutes or until toothpick comes out clean.

Note: You can substitute sweet milk and a "glug", or 1 tablespoon of lemon juice, for sour milk.

9 to 12 servings

Ralph (and Catherine) Strassburg, Retired
—Kewaskum

MEXICAN CHOCOLATE CAKE

½ cup margarine
½ cup oil
1 cup water
¼ cup cocoa
2 cups sugar
2 eggs
½ cup buttermilk
1 teaspoon baking soda
1 teaspoon cinnamon
1 teaspoon vanilla
2 cups flour

Icing:
½ cup margarine
¼ cup cocoa
6 tablespoons evaporated milk
1 pound (4¼ cups) powdered sugar
1 teaspoon vanilla
½ cup chopped nuts

In saucepan, combine margarine, oil, water and cocoa. Bring to boil; cool. Combine sugar, eggs, buttermilk, baking soda, cinnamon, vanilla and flour; mix well. Add cocoa mixture. Mix and pour into greased 9 x 13" pan. Bake at 325° for 35 minutes.

To make icing, combine margarine, cocoa and milk in saucepan and heat until margarine is melted. Add powdered sugar, vanilla and nuts. Mix well and pour over cake as soon as its removed from oven.

12 to 18 servings

Skip Hillary, Sales
—Texas

HO-HO CAKE

1 18.25-ounce devil's food or fudge cake mix
1 5-ounce can evaporated milk
½ cup butter or margarine, softened
⅔ cup Crisco shortening
¾ cup sugar
2 teaspoons vanilla
Pinch of salt
1 16-ounce can ready-to-spread chocolate fudge frosting

Prepare cake mix according to package directions. Spread into greased and floured 10 x 15" jelly roll pan. Bake at 350° for 20 minutes. Cool in pan on rack. In medium bowl, combine evaporated milk, butter, Crisco, sugar, vanilla and salt. Beat 10 minutes until smooth and creamy. Spread over cooled cake. Remove cover and foil from frosting can. Microwave frosting on high power for 1 minute or stand can of frosting in bowl of hot water to soften slightly. Stir just to blend. Spread evenly over creamed layer. Refrigerate until serving.

25 to 36 servings

Diane Schneider, Sales Department
and
Lester (and LaVerne) Schaub, Retired
—Kewaskum

CHOCOLATE SURPRISE CUPCAKES

Filling:
1 8-ounce package cream cheese, softened
⅓ cup sugar
1 egg
1 cup chocolate chips

3 cups flour
2 cups sugar
½ cup cocoa
2 teaspoons baking soda
1 teaspoon salt
⅔ cup oil
2 tablespoons vinegar
2 teaspoons vanilla
2 cups water

Beat together cream cheese, sugar and egg. Add chocolate chips and set aside.

Sift dry ingredients together. Add oil, vinegar, vanilla and water. Beat well. Fill paper-lined muffin pans ½ to ⅔ full. Add heaping teaspoon of cheese mixture in center. Bake at 350° for 30 minutes. Frost when cool.

Makes 36 cupcakes

Joan Meilahn
—Kewaskum

PETER PAUL MOUNDS CAKE

1 Duncan Hines Swiss Chocolate cake
  mix

Filling:
1 cup sugar
½ cup margarine
1 cup evaporated milk
1 14-ounce package coconut
24 large marshmallows

Frosting:
½ cup margarine
⅓ cup cocoa
3 cups powdered sugar
Milk

Bake cake as directed on package in two 9"
round cake pans. Cool. Divide each layer in
half, making four layers. Set aside.

Mix together sugar, margarine and milk
for filling. Bring to a hard boil; boil for 2
minutes. Remove from heat; add coconut
and marshmallows stirring constantly
until cool. When cool spread evenly on
three layers then stack together.

In saucepan, melt margarine and cocoa
together; remove from heat; add powdered
sugar. Mix until smooth and of spreading
consistency; adding milk as needed. Spread
on top and sides of cake.

12 to 16 servings

Doris Russell, Saladmaster, Inc.
—Arlington, TX

HEATH BAR CAKE

½ cup shortening
2 cups brown sugar
2 cups sifted flour
1 egg
1 cup milk
1 teaspoon baking soda
1 teaspoon vanilla
6 Heath bars, chopped

Blend shortening, brown sugar and flour.
Reserve 1 cup for topping. To remaining
mixture, add egg, milk, baking soda and
vanilla. Mix well and put in greased and
floured 9 x 13" pan. Sprinkle reserved

crumb mixture over batter. Top with
chopped candy. Bake at 350° for 30 to 35
minutes.

12 to 18 servings

Carol Heller, Consumer Service Dept.
and
Darlene Pesch, Retired
—Kewaskum

DIRT CAKE

3 3-ounce packages instant vanilla
  pudding
4½ cups milk
2 8-ounce packages cream cheese,
  softened
2 12-ounce containers Cool Whip
2 16-ounce packages Oreo cookies,
  crushed
1 "New" 10-inch flower pot
1 "New" mini-garden shovel

Mix pudding and milk. Add cream cheese.
Fold in Cool Whip. Layer half of crushed
cookies on bottom of flower pot, then
creamed mixture and remaining cookies.

10 to 12 servings

Jill Brennen, Sales Department
—Kewaskum

DIRT CAKE

½ cup butter, softened
1 8-ounce package cream cheese,
  softened
1 cup powdered sugar
2 3.4-ounce packages instant vanilla
  pudding
2 cups cold milk
1 12-ounce container Cool Whip
1 24-ounce package Oreo cookies,
  crushed

Cream together butter, cream cheese and
powdered sugar. In small bowl, mix both
packages of pudding with milk; add Cool
Whip. Combine with cream cheese mixture.

In clean 10" clay or plastic flowerpot, or in bowl shaped like a flower pot, layer half cookie crumbs in bottom; add pudding mixture and top with remaining crumbs. Refrigerate overnight. Before serving, add a pretty silk flower (the stem can be wrapped in foil) and lay a serving scoop beside it for decoration.

8 to 10 servings

> *Gayle Tanner, Dept. 21*
> *—Jacksonville*
> *Lloyd Teeselink, Retired-Shipping Dept.*
> *—Kewaskum*
> *and*
> *Ruthie Stacy, Industrial Engineering*
> *—Jacksonville*

CHERRY TWITZEL TORTE

1 cup butter or margarine, melted
¾ cup sugar
2 cups coarsely ground pretzels (10-ounce bag)
2 8-ounce packages cream cheese, softened
1 cup powdered sugar
1 16-ounce can cherry pie filling
1 8-ounce container frozen whipped topping, thawed

In bowl, combine butter, sugar and pretzels. Reserve 1 cup for topping. Press remaining mixture into ungreased 9 x 9" pan. In another bowl, blend together cream cheese and powdered sugar. Spread on pretzel mixture. Spread cherry pie filling over cream cheese mixture. Spread whipped topping over cherries. Sprinkle reserved pretzels on top. Cover and refrigerate overnight.

9 to 12 servings

> *Ruth Raether, Retired*
> *—Kewaskum*

CHERRY AND BANANA TORTE

6 egg whites
2 cups sugar
1 teaspoon baking powder
1 cup chopped nuts
28 Ritz crackers, finely crushed
3 bananas, sliced
1 20-ounce can cherry pie filling
1 12-ounce container Cool Whip

In large bowl, beat egg whites until stiff. Slowly add sugar, baking powder, nuts and crackers. Mix well. Spread in greased 9 x 13" pan. Bake at 325° for 30 minutes. When cool top with bananas and pie filling. Top with Cool Whip.

12 to 18 servings

> *Mary Ann Miller, Dept. 15WW*
> *—Kewaskum*

FRUIT COCKTAIL TORTE

1¾ cups flour
1 cup sugar
¼ teaspoon salt
1 teaspoon baking soda
1 egg, beaten
1 teaspoon vanilla
1 16-ounce can fruit cocktail, with juice (2 cups)
1 cup brown sugar
½ cup chopped nuts
Whipped cream

Sift flour, sugar, salt and baking soda together. Add egg, vanilla, fruit cocktail and juice. Mix well. Spread in buttered 9 x 13" pan. Sprinkle brown sugar and nuts on top. Bake at 350° for 45 to 50 minutes. Serve with whipped cream.

12 to 18 servings

> *Helene Benzing, Retired*
> *—Kewaskum*

ORANGE "TANG" TORTE

Crust:
1¼ cups flour
1 3-ounce package coconut cream
 pudding
¼ teaspoon salt
½ cup plus 2 tablespoons margarine
1 egg

Filling:
2 cups sour cream
⅓ cup Tang orange drink mix
1 14-ounce Eagle brand condensed milk

Topping:
1 8 or 9-ounce container Cool Whip,
 thawed
1 11-ounce can mandarin oranges,
 drained

Mix crust ingredients to form a stiff dough. Press into 9 x 13" pan and bake at 350° for 12 to 15 minutes.

Combine all filling ingredients and beat 1 minute. Pour over cooled crust. Top with Cool Whip and mandarin oranges. Refrigerate overnight.

12 to 18 servings

Cheri Baird, Finance
—Kewaskum

PEACH TORTE

2 3-ounce packages lemon gelatin
3 cups boiling water
1 quart vanilla ice cream
1 20-ounce can peaches, drained and
 diced
1 9" square graham cracker crust

Dissolve gelatin in boiling water. Spoon ice cream into gelatin and stir until dissolved. Let cool until gelatin mixture mounds. Add peaches. Spoon into graham cracker crust. Let set in refrigerator overnight.

9 to 12 servings

Bonnie Will, Personnel
—Kewaskum

PUMPKIN TORTE

Crust:
2½ cups graham crackers, crushed
⅓ cup sugar
½ cup butter, melted

Filling:
2 eggs, beaten
¾ cup sugar
1 8-ounce package cream cheese,
 softened
2 cups pumpkin
3 egg yolks, beaten
½ cup sugar
½ cup milk
½ teaspoon salt
1 tablespoon cinnamon
1 envelope plain gelatin
½ cup cold water
3 egg whites
¼ cup sugar
1 8-ounce container whipped topping,
 thawed

Preheat oven to 350°. Mix graham crackers, ⅓ cup sugar and butter. Press into 9 x 13" pan. Mix eggs, ¾ cup sugar and softened cream cheese. Pour over crust. Bake for 20 minutes.

Cook pumpkin, egg yolks, ½ cup sugar, milk, salt and cinnamon until mixture thickens. Remove from heat. Dissolve gelatin in cold water and add to pumpkin mixture. Cool. Beat egg whites until stiff with ¼ cup sugar. Fold into pumpkin mixture. Pour over cream cheese layer and top with whipped topping. Refrigerate.

12 to 18 servings

Diane Schneider, Sales Department
—Kewaskum

PUMPKIN TORTE

Crust:
18 graham crackers, crushed
½ cup butter, melted
¼ cup sugar

First layer:
1 8-ounce package cream cheese, softened
2 eggs, beaten
¾ cup sugar

.Second layer:
2 cups pumpkin
3 egg yolks
½ cup sugar
½ cup milk
½ teaspoon salt
1 tablespoon cinnamon
1 envelope Knox gelatin
¼ cup cold water

Third layer:
3 egg whites
¼ cup sugar
Whipped cream, optional

Mix crackers, butter and ¼ cup sugar; line 9 x 13" pan. Set aside.

Beat cream cheese, eggs and ¾ cup sugar until light and fluffy. Pour over crust and bake at 350° for 20 minutes. Cool.

Cook pumpkin, egg yolks, sugar, milk, salt and cinnamon in saucepan until thick. Soften gelatin in cold water. Remove from heat and add gelatin mixture. Mix well. Cool.

Beat egg whites and ¼ cup sugar. Fold into pumpkin mixture and spoon on top of cream cheese layer. May be topped with whipped cream if desired. Refrigerate.

18 to 20 servings

Pat Buechel, 16PR-CDT
—Kewaskum

RASPBERRY TORTE

Crust:
2 cups flour
2 tablespoons sugar
1 cup butter, softened

First layer:
1 cup powdered sugar
1 8-ounce package cream cheese
1 8-ounce Cool Whip

Second layer:
1 6-ounce package raspberry gelatin
2 cups boiling water
2 12-ounce packages frozen raspberries

Topping:
1 8-ounce container Cool Whip

Combine crust ingredients and press into 9 x 13" pan. Bake at 350° for 20 to 25 minutes. Cool. Cream powdered sugar and cream cheese. Add Cool Whip; mix well. Spread on top of crust.

Dissolve gelatin in water. Add raspberries. Stir until melted and thickened. Pour over cream cheese filling. Refrigerate overnight. Top with Cool Whip before serving.

12 to 18 servings

Dorothy Panzer, Dept. 15EE
—Kewaskum

RASPBERRY TORTE

1 pound vanilla wafer cookies
1½ cups powdered sugar
1 egg
½ cup butter, melted
1 quart fresh raspberries
½ pint whipping cream

Grind cookies. Reserve half of crumbs; pat remaining crumbs into 9 x 13" pan. In mixing bowl, combine powdered sugar, egg and butter. Spread in thin layer over crust. Layer raspberries on top. Whip cream until stiff. Spread over berries. Cover with remaining cookie crumbs. Refrigerate for 3 to 4 hours before serving.

12 to 18 servings

Bonnie Clapper, Dept. 15EE
—Kewaskum

RHUBARB TORTE

Crust:
3 cups flour
1 tablespoon sugar
2 teaspoons salt
1 cup oil
4 tablespoons milk

Filling:
4 eggs, beaten
3 cups sugar
½ cup flour
2 teaspoons vanilla
1½ teaspoons salt
1 teaspoon cinnamon
1 teaspoon nutmeg
1½ cups milk
5 to 6 cups chopped rhubarb

In 9 x 13" pan mix flour, sugar and salt. Make well in center; add oil and milk. Mix well; press onto bottom and up sides of pan.

Combine all filling ingredients except rhubarb; mix well. Fold in rhubarb. Pour mixture over crust and bake at 375° for 15 minutes; then reduce heat to 350° and bake until center is firm.

Variation: Use 3 cups chopped rhubarb and 3 cups sliced strawberries in place of rhubarb.

12 to 18 servings

Steven Seefeldt, Maintenance
—Kewaskum

RHUBARB TORTE

Crust:
18 graham crackers, crushed
½ cup butter, melted
¼ cup sugar

First layer:
1½ cups sugar
5 tablespoons cornstarch
6 cups sliced rhubarb
¾ cup water
3 to 4 drops red food coloring

Second layer:
3 cups mini-marshmallows
1 12-ounce container Cool Whip

Third layer:
1 4.3-ounce package vanilla pudding (not instant)

Combine crust ingredients and pat into a 9 x 13" pan. Bake at 350° for 10 minutes. Cool.

In a saucepan, combine sugar, cornstarch, rhubarb and water. Cook and stir until thickened; reduce heat and cook 2 to 3 minutes longer. Add a few drops of red food coloring. Cool and spread on cooled crust.

Fold marshmallows into Cool Whip and spoon over rhubarb. Prepare pudding according to directions. Cool and spread over all. Chill.

Variation: Use strawberries for half the amount of rhubarb.

12 to 18 servings

Pat Buechel, Dept. 16RR
—Kewaskum

RHUBARB TORTE

Crust:
1 cup graham cracker crumbs
2 tablespoons sugar
4 tablespoons butter or margarine, melted

Filling:
1 cup sugar
3 tablespoons cornstarch
4 cups sliced rhubarb
½ cup water
Few drops red food coloring
½ cup whipping cream
1½ cups miniature marshmallows
1 3-ounce package instant vanilla pudding
1¾ cups milk

Mix together crust ingredients. Reserve 2 tablespoons. Pat remainder into 9 x 9" pan. Bake at 350° for 10 minutes. Cool.

Combine sugar and cornstarch. Stir in rhubarb and water. Cook and stir until thickened. Reduce heat; cook 2 to 3 minutes. Add food coloring. Cool. Spread on graham cracker crust. Whip cream; fold in marshmallows and spread on rhubarb mixture. Mix pudding and milk according to package directions. Spread over all. Sprinkle with reserved crumbs.

9 servings

Jewell Zielieke, Sales
—Kewaskum

FROZEN STRAWBERRY TORTE

¾ cup butter or margarine, softened
½ cup brown sugar
1½ cups flour
½ cup crushed nuts
2 egg whites
1 cup sugar
1 tablespoon lemon juice
1 16-ounce package frozen strawberries, partially thawed
1 pint whipping cream

Combine butter, brown sugar, flour and nuts in 9 x 13" pan. Bake at 350° for 20 minutes, stirring occasionally while baking. Cool. Remove ⅓ cup crumbs for top; pat remaining crumbs into bottom of pan.

With electric mixer, beat egg whites, sugar, lemon juice and strawberries in large bowl for 10 to 15 minutes. Beat whipping cream until stiff and fold into strawberry mixture. Pour into crust and sprinkle with reserved crumbs. Cover and freeze.

12 to 18 servings

Ben Ermer, Retired
—Kewaskum

STRAWBERRY TORTE

1 cup flour
¾ cup chopped nuts
¼ cup brown sugar
½ cup butter
3 cups miniature marshmallows
⅔ cup milk
1 cup whipping cream
1 6-ounce package strawberry jello
2 cups boiling water
1 16-ounce package frozen strawberries

Mix flour, nuts, sugar and butter to make pie crust. Pat into 9 x 13" pan. Bake at 350° for 12 to 15 minutes. Cool. Melt marshmallows and milk in double boiler. Cool. Whip cream and add to marshmallow mixture. Spread on crust. Dissolve jello in boiling water; add frozen berries. Let stand until mixture begins to thicken. Spread on top of marshmallow mixture. Refrigerate 3 hours or more.

18 servings

Anna Schaeffer, Dept. 15WW
—Kewaskum

POPPY SEED TORTE

24 graham crackers, crushed
1½ cups butter
¼ cup sugar
1 cup powdered sugar
1 8-ounce cream cheese
2 cups Cool Whip
¼ cup poppy seed
3 cups milk, divided
2 3.4-ounce packages instant vanilla pudding

Mix together graham crackers, butter and sugar. Pat into a 9 x 13" greased pan. Combine powdered sugar, cream cheese and Cool Whip and spread over crust. Mix together 1 cup milk and poppy seed. Set aside. Prepare pudding with 2 cups milk. Combine poppy seed and pudding mixtures. Pour over cream cheese layer. Refrigerate.

12 to 18 servings

Anna Schaeffer, Dept. 15WW
—Kewaskum

POPPY SEED TORTE

Poppy Seed Torte has been a tradition in our family for years. Whenever there's a party, we make this torte.

Crust:
1½ packages graham crackers, crushed (about 30 squares)
½ cup butter, melted
¼ cup sugar

Filling:
½ cup sugar
3 tablespoons cornstarch
¼ cup poppy seeds
3 cups whole milk
4 egg yolks, lightly beaten
¼ cup butter
1 teaspoon vanilla

Meringue topping:
4 egg whites, room temperature
1 7-ounce jar of marshmallow cream

In small bowl, mix crust ingredients with fork. Reserve ¼ cup; pat remainder into bottom and up sides of 9 x 13 x 2″ glass pan.

In heavy 2-quart saucepan, mix together sugar, cornstarch and poppy seeds. Stir in milk. Cook over medium heat, until boiling and slightly thickened, stirring constantly. Spoon some of the hot pudding into egg yolks and mix well. Stir yolk mixture into pudding and continue cooking until thick and bubbly; stirring constantly. Remove from heat and stir in butter and vanilla; stir until butter melts. Cool to room temperature. Spoon into crust.

Preheat oven to 325°. In large bowl, beat egg whites until frothy. Add jar of marshmallow cream. Beat until stiff peaks form. Carefully spoon meringue onto filling, spreading evenly to cover filling to edge of glass pan.

Sprinkle reserved crumbs on top. Bake for 30 minutes until meringue is nicely browned. Cool on rack to room temperature. Refrigerate until serving.

18 servings

Walter Voigt
—Kewaskum

POPPY SEED TORTE

Crust:
1½ cups graham cracker crumbs
1½ cups flour
½ cup chopped nuts
¾ cup butter, melted

Filling:
1½ cups milk
¼ teaspoon salt
1 cup sugar
1 teaspoon vanilla
3 tablespoons cornstarch with ⅛ cup water
5 egg yolks
¼ cup poppy seed
1 package Knox gelatin
¼ cup cold water
5 egg whites
1 teaspoon cream of tartar
½ cup sugar
Whipped cream for topping, optional

Combine all crust ingredients and pat into ungreased 9 x 13″ pan. Bake at 325° for 15 minutes until brown.

In saucepan, combine milk, salt, sugar, vanilla, cornstarch mixture, egg yolks and poppy seeds; cook until thick. Dissolve gelatin in cold water. Beat egg whites until stiff. Gradually add cream of tartar, sugar and gelatin. Fold into custard mixture. Pour into baked crust. Refrigerate overnight. Top with whipped cream if desired.

12 to 18 servings

Linda A. Gehring, Dept. 2000
—Kewaskum

POPPY SEED TORTE

Crust:
1 cup flour
½ cup butter
1 cup ground nuts

First layer:
1 8-ounce package cream cheese
1 cup powdered sugar
1½ cups Cool Whip

Second layer:
**2 3-ounce packages instant vanilla
pudding**
3 cups milk
3 tablespoons poppy seed

Topping:
8 ounces Cool Whip
¼ cup chopped walnuts, optional

Combine flour, butter and nuts; mix well and pat into 9 x 13″ ungreased pan. Bake at 350° for 15 minutes. Cool.

Mix together cream cheese, powdered sugar and Cool Whip; spread on crust. Mix together pudding, milk and poppy seeds; spread over first layer. Top pudding layer with Cool Whip. Sprinkle nuts over top if desired.

12 to 18 servings

*Byrdell Schulz, Retired
—Kewaskum*

POPPY SEED TORTE

3 eggs, separated
2½ cups milk
⅔ cup sugar
½ teaspoon salt
4 tablespoons cornstarch
1 tablespoon butter
1½ teaspoons vanilla
2½ tablespoons poppy seeds
1 9″ square graham cracker crust

Set egg whites aside for meringue. Beat egg yolks slightly with fork. Boil milk hot and fast. Mix sugar, salt and cornstarch in saucepan. Gradually stir hot milk into sugar mixture. Cook over medium heat until thick and boiling. Boil 1 minute. Stir half of mixture into egg yolks, beating well. Stir egg mixture into remaining sugar mixture. Boil 1 minute. Remove from heat. Add butter and vanilla. Let stand until butter is melted. Stir in poppy seeds. Pour into crust and top with

meringue. Broil 3 to 5 minutes until top is brown.

9 servings

*Anne Quackenboss, MIS
—Kewaskum*

ANGEL TORTE

1 10-inch angel food cake
**1 3-ounce package sugar-free instant
vanilla pudding**
**1 8-ounce can crushed pineapple in own
juice**
**1 10-ounce container frozen light
whipped topping, thawed**
**½ pint fresh raspberries, rinsed and well
drained**
1 large banana
1 to 2 kiwi, peeled, sliced
4 to 6 fresh mint leaves, optional

Split cake into two layers, three if very high; place bottom layer on large glass serving plate. In small mixing bowl, stir dry pudding into undrained pineapple, using table fork to blend well. Stir pineapple mixture into whipped topping, using a fork to blend. Spread about ½ cup topping mixture onto bottom layer. Arrange half the unsweetened raspberries on top of filling, followed by banana and 1 kiwi (both quartered and sliced). Spread a thin layer of topping mixture onto underside of top cake layer before placing it on top of the fruit. Frost sides and top of cake with remaining topping mixture. Garnish with remaining raspberries, kiwi slices (halved), and mint leaves if desired.

12 servings

*Adeline Halfmann, Retired
—Kewaskum*

BROCKLE TORTE

3 eggs, well beaten
1 cup sugar
1 cup flour
1 teaspoon baking powder
Pinch of salt
1 cup dates, cut up
1 cup chopped nuts
1 pint whipping cream
½ cup sugar
½ teaspoon vanilla
2 bananas
1 20-ounce can crushed pineapple, well
  drained
Maraschino cherries, optional

In bowl, combine eggs, sugar, flour, baking
powder and salt. Add dates and nuts. Bake
in 9 x 13" pan at 350° for 30 to 35 minutes.
Cool. Break up cake and set aside. Whip
cream with sugar and vanilla. On a re-
cessed torte plate, layer cake pieces,
bananas, spoonfuls of crushed pineapple
and whipping cream, forming a mound.
Decorate with maraschino cherries if
desired.

12 to 14 servings

Marie I. Kleinke, Retired
—Kewaskum

LYNN'S TORTE

2 eggs, well beaten
1 cup sugar
2 tablespoons flour
1 teaspoon baking powder
1 cup chopped nuts
Bananas
Strawberries
Blueberries
Pineapple tidbits, drained
Sweetened whipped cream

Mix first five ingredients together. Put into
9 x 13" pan. Bake at 350° for 30 minutes.
Cool. Break into small pieces and spread on
fancy platter. Cover with sliced bananas,
strawberries, blueberries and pineapple.

Top with sweetened whipped cream or
Cool Whip.

10 to 12 servings

Francis (and Jeane) Gilboy, Retired
—Kewaskum

FROZEN CHEESE TORTE

Crust:
3 cups graham cracker crumbs
½ cup sugar
1 teaspoon cinnamon
½ cup butter, melted

Filling:
2 tablespoons Knox gelatin
½ cup cold water
2 egg yolks
1 cup sugar
½ cup milk
1 pint whipping cream
2 egg whites
1 tablespoon vanilla
1 8-ounce can crushed pineapple, drained
12 maraschino cherries, cut up
2 pounds small curd cottage cheese (???)

Combine all crust ingredients and pat into
9 x 13" pan, reserving 1 cup for topping.

Sprinkle gelatin into cold water. Beat egg
yolks slightly; add sugar and milk and cook
over boiling water in double boiler until
thickened and mixture coats spoon. Add
gelatin to hot mixture and stir until
dissolved. Set aside to cool. Beat cheese
with electric mixer to break up curds.

Whip cream until stiff peaks form. Whip
egg whites until stiff peaks form. Mix
together gelatin mixture, vanilla, pineapple, cherries and cottage cheese. Fold in
whipped cream and egg whites. Pour into
crust and sprinkle on crumb topping.
Refrigerate overnight.

12 to 18 servings

Ken Stuart, Retired, Superintendent
—Kewaskum

PRETZEL TORTE

Crust:
1 cup butter or margarine, melted
¾ cup sugar
2½ cups coarsely crushed pretzels

First layer:
1 8-ounce cream cheese
1 cup powdered sugar
1 cup Cool Whip

Second layer:
2 3-ounce packages instant vanilla pudding
3 cups milk

Third layer:
1 20-ounce can cherry or raspberry pie filling

Topping:
1 8-ounce container Cool Whip

Cream butter and sugar. Add pretzels and mix lightly. Reserve ½ to ¾ cup for top. Press remaining crumbs into ungreased 9 x 13" pan. Do not bake.

Combine cream cheese and powdered sugar. Fold in Cool Whip. Spread on crust and refrigerate. Mix pudding and milk; spread on top of cream cheese mixture. Spread pie filling on top. Spread Cool Whip on top of pie filling; sprinkle with reserved pretzel crumbs. Refrigerate.

12 to 18 servings

Barb Liegl, Purchasing
—Kewaskum

BITTER CHOCOLATE TORTE

Crust:
20 graham crackers, crushed
½ cup butter, melted

Filling:
25 marshmallows
½ cup milk
1 cup heavy cream, whipped (or 8-ounce Cool Whip)
2 squares bitter chocolate, flaked

Mix graham crackers with melted butter. Press in 7 x 11" pan. Bake 15 minutes at 325°. Cool. In double boiler, melt marshmallows with milk. Cool. Combine whipped cream and chocolate; add to cooled marshmallow mixture. Spread on top of crust. Refrigerate several hours.

12 servings

Virginia Wendorff, Retired
—Kewaskum

DEATH BY CHOCOLATE TORTE

1 package fudge brownie mix
1 box sugar-free chocolate mousse (2 packages)
6 Heath bars, crushed
2 9-ounce containers Cool Whip

Bake brownie mix according to directions. Cool. Prepare both packages of chocolate mousse according to directions. Set aside. Break brownies into pieces. Place half of brownie pieces in 9 x 13" pan or decorative bowl. Layer with half of mousse mixture. Reserve 2 tablespoons crushed Heath bars. Top with half of crushed Heath bars and Cool Whip. Repeat second layer with brownies, mousse, crushed Heath Bars and Cool Whip. Sprinkle last layer of Cool Whip with reserved crushed Heath bars. Refrigerate until ready to serve.

12 to 18 servings

Joe (and Kris) Swanson
—Kewaskum

PEANUT PUDDING TORTE

½ cup butter
1 cup flour
⅔ cup dry roasted peanuts, chopped
1 8-ounce package cream cheese, softened
⅓ cup peanut butter
1 cup powdered sugar
2 8-ounce containers whipped topping, thawed, divided
1 3.4-ounce package instant vanilla pudding
1 3.4-ounce package instant chocolate pudding
2¾ cups cold milk
Chopped dry roasted peanuts for garnish
1 1.5-ounce Hershey Bar, shaved

Cut butter into flour as for pie crust. Add chopped peanuts; pat into 9 x 13" pan. Bake at 325° for 20 minutes. Let cool. Combine cream cheese, peanut butter and powdered sugar; beat until smooth and creamy. Gently fold 1 container whipped topping into cream cheese and peanut butter mixture. Spread over cooled crust. Combine instant puddings and milk. Beat until smooth and creamy. Layer over cream cheese and peanut butter mixture. Let set until firm. Top with remaining carton of whipped topping. Garnish with additional chopped peanuts and shaved Hershey candy bar.

12 to 18 servings

Diane Schneider, Sales Department
—Kewaskum

PEANUT TORTE

Crust:
⅔ cup dry roasted peanuts, chopped
1 cup flour
½ cup butter

First layer:
⅓ cup peanut butter, smooth or chunky
1 8-ounce package cream cheese, softened
1 cup powdered sugar
1 to 1½ cups Cool Whip

Second layer:
1 3-ounce package instant vanilla pudding
1 3-ounce package instant chocolate pudding
2¾ cups milk

Third layer:
Cool Whip
Chopped peanuts
Shaved chocolate (Hershey bar)

Mix together crust ingredients and press into 9 x 13" pan. Bake at 350° for 20 minutes. Cool.

Combine peanut butter, cream cheese and powdered sugar; mix until creamy. Fold in Cool Whip. Spread evenly over crust. Mix puddings and milk until smooth and thickened. Spread evenly over cream cheese layer. Spread a generous layer of Cool Whip over pudding layer. Sprinkle with nuts and chocolate for garnish. Chill in refrigerator to set.

10 to 12 servings

Joan Meilahn
—Kewaskum

BUTTER PECAN TORTE

Crust:
1 cup graham cracker crumbs
¾ cup crushed soda crackers
½ cup margarine, melted

Filling:
2 3.4-ounce packages instant vanilla pudding
1 cup milk
1 quart butter pecan ice cream, softened
1 8-ounce container Cool Whip
4 Heath candy bars, crushed

Combine crust ingredients and pat into 9 x 13" pan. Set aside.

Combine pudding and milk; do not over mix. Add to softened ice cream and pour over crust. Top with Cool Whip. Garnish with candy. Refrigerate.

12 to 18 servings

Barb Ebert, Sales Administrator
—Kewaskum

VIENNESE TORTE

1 cup semi-sweet chocolate chips
½ cup butter
¼ cup water
4 egg yolks
2 tablespoons powdered sugar
1 teaspoon vanilla
1 10¾-ounce Sara Lee pound cake

In saucepan, combine chocolate chips, butter and water; heat until melted. Beat egg yolks until light and fluffy. Gradually add to chocolate mixture, beating with electric mixer. Add powdered sugar and vanilla. Beat well. Let cool to spreading consistency.

Cut pound cake horizontally into as many slices as possible. Spread chocolate mixture between layers, on top and sides of cake. Refrigerate.

10 to 12 servings

Merlin (and Gen) Luedtke, Retired
—Kewaskum

VIENNA TORTE

Cake:
6 eggs, separated
1 cup sugar
⅓ cup water
2 teaspoons baking powder
1⅓ cups flour

Custard:
⅓ cup sugar
⅓ cup cornstarch
1 egg, beaten
2 cups milk
1 teaspoon vanilla
1 cup butter, softened
1 cup powdered sugar
¼ to ½ cup cocoa

For cake, beat egg yolks until thick. Add sugar and water. Beat well. Sift baking powder and flour; add to egg yolk mixture. Beat well. Beat egg whites until stiff; fold in egg yolk mixture. Pour into three greased and floured 8" layer pans; bake at 350° for 25 to 30 minutes.

In saucepan, combine sugar, cornstarch, egg, milk and vanilla. Cook until thick stirring occasionally. Put into refrigerator to cool.

Beat butter. Gradually add powdered sugar and cocoa. Beat into cooled custard mixture. Spread between layers, on top and sides.

12 to 16 servings

Heide Ewerdt, Dept. 1400
—Kewaskum

BAKED CHEESE TORTE

Crust:
2 cups graham crackers, crushed
½ cup chopped walnuts
½ cup butter, softened
1 teaspoon cinnamon

Filling:
3 eggs
2 8-ounce packages cream cheese, softened
1 cup sugar
3 cups sour cream
1 teaspoon vanilla

Combine crust ingredients and press into greased 9" springform pan. Combine filling ingredients and beat until smooth. Pour onto crust. Bake at 350° for 1 hour.

12 to 16 servings

Jan Kumrow, Retired
—Kewaskum

BAKED CHEESECAKE

2 cups cottage cheese
2 cups sour cream
1 8-ounce package cream cheese,
  softened
4 eggs
1½ cups sugar
⅓ cup butter, softened
⅓ cup cornstarch
1 teaspoon vanilla
1 tablespoon lemon juice
Graham cracker crust for 9 x 13" pan

Blend all ingredients in blender until smooth. Pour into crust and bake at 350° for 1 hour.

12 to 18 servings

Michael Hendricks, Dept. 700
—Kewaskum

IRISH CREAM CHEESECAKE

Crust:
2 cups finely crushed chocolate cookie
  wafers, about 36
¼ cup sugar
6 tablespoons butter or margarine,
  melted

Filling:
4½ 8-ounce packages cream cheese,
  softened
1⅔ cups sugar
5 eggs
1½ cups Irish Cream liqueur
1 tablespoon vanilla
1 cup semi-sweet chocolate chips

Topping:
1 cup whipping cream
2 tablespoons sugar
½ cup semi-sweet chocolate chips,
  melted

Preheat oven to 325°. Combine crust ingredients. Press into bottom and 1" up sides of greased 10" springform pan. Bake 7 to 10 minutes.

Beat cream cheese until smooth. Add sugar and eggs, beating until fluffy. Add liqueur and vanilla, mixing well. Sprinkle chocolate

chips over crust. Spoon filling over chips. Bake 1 hour and 20 minutes or until center is set. Cool completely in pan. Remove sides of pan.

For topping, beat cream and sugar in large, chilled bowl until stiff. Continue to beat while slowly adding chocolate. Spread mixture over cooled cake. Refrigerate until ready to serve.

12 to 16 servings

Albert (and Ann) Oak
Exec. Vice President of Manufacturing
—Kewaskum

CHEESECAKE

1½ cups graham crackers, crushed
½ cup butter, melted
½ cup brown sugar
1 package Dream Whip
1 8-ounce package Philadelphia cream
  cheese, softened
1 cup powdered sugar
1 16-ounce can cherry pie filling,
  optional

Mix graham crackers, butter and brown sugar in a bowl. Press into 8 or 9" square pan. Prepare Dream Whip according to package instructions; set aside. Beat cream cheese and powdered sugar; blend with Dream Whip. Spread on top of graham cracker crust. Cover with pie filling and chill for 24 hours.

9 to 12 servings

Gord McLauchlin, Vice President of Sales
—Canada

CHEESECAKE
The Best in Ohio

Crust:
1¼ cups graham cracker crumbs
3 tablespoons sugar
⅓ cup margarine, melted

140

Filling:

3 8-ounce packages cream cheese
1 cup sugar
1 tablespoon vanilla
1 16-ounce container Cool Whip, thawed
1 20-ounce can cherry pie filling

Combine graham crackers and sugar in medium-size bowl. Stir in margarine until thoroughly blended. Pack mixture firmly in 9 x 13" pan. Chill 1 hour.

Cream together cream cheese, sugar and vanilla. Add Cool Whip and mix well. Pour over graham cracker crust. Top with pie filling.

12 to 18 servings

Naoma P. Butts
—Wooster

CHOCOLATE-WALNUT PEAR CHEESECAKE

Crust:
1 cup chocolate wafer crumbs
2 tablespoons sugar
3 tablespoons butter or margarine, melted

Chocolate walnuts:
1 cup chocolate chips
¼ cup white syrup
1 cup toasted walnuts, coarsely chopped

Filling:
3 8-ounce packages cream cheese, softened
1¼ cups sugar
1½ teaspoons vanilla
4 eggs
1 cup sour cream
1 cup heavy cream
1 32-ounce can pears, drained thoroughly; cut into bite-sized pieces

Topping:
Whipping cream, optional

Heat oven to 325°. Mix crumbs, sugar and butter; press onto bottom of 9" springform or cheesecake pan. Bake on lowest rack in oven for 10 minutes. Set aside.

Melt chocolate chips with white syrup in small saucepan. Stir in nuts to coat. Set aside.

Beat cream cheese, sugar, vanilla and 1 egg until very smooth. Add remaining 3 eggs, sour cream and heavy cream; beat until smooth. Gently fold in chocolate-walnut mixture and pears. Pour into prepared crust.

Bake on lowest rack of 325° oven for 1 hour and check. May need to bake longer until set. Cool and refrigerate for at least 8 hours. Remove rim of pan and top with whipped cream.

12 to 16 servings

Kaye Hunnewell, Sales
—California

ELEGANT CHEESECAKE

1½ cups fine Zwieback crumbs*
2 tablespoons butter
2 tablespoons sugar
½ cup sugar
2 tablespoons flour
¼ teaspoon salt
2 8-ounce packages cream cheese, softened
1 teaspoon vanilla
4 egg yolks
1 cup light cream
4 egg whites, stiffly beaten

Blend Zwieback crumbs with butter and 2 tablespoons sugar. Press into bottom of 9" springform pan. Blend ½ cup sugar with flour, salt and cream cheese. Add vanilla. Stir in egg yolks and mix well. Add cream, blend thoroughly. Fold in egg whites. Pour mixture on top of crumbs. Bake at 325° for 1½ hours or until set in center.

*Zwieback toast is usually found with the baby food.

8-10 servings

Anne Quackenboss, MIS
—Kewaskum

REGAL CHEESECAKE

This original recipe was found at a famous "smorgasbord" in Stow, Ohio about the year 1955 and has been made by our family and friends ever since. Our holidays are never complete without this cheesecake.

Filling:
6 8-ounce packages "Philly" cream cheese, softened
10 eggs, 5 medium and 5 large or 10 medium
2 cups sugar
3 teaspoons vanilla

Crust:
2 cups crushed graham crackers, (about 36)
2 tablespoons sugar
2 tablespoons butter or margarine

Topping:
3 pints sour cream
1 cup sugar
3 teaspoons vanilla

With electric mixer, beat cream cheese alternately with eggs, one at a time. Add sugar and vanilla. Mix well.

In large bowl, combine graham cracker crumbs, sugar and butter. Line bottom of one 4-quart or two 9 x 13" glass baking dishes with crumb mixture. Slowly pour cream cheese batter over crust, filling each pan half full. Bake at 300° for 1 hour.

Mix together sour cream, sugar and vanilla. Gently pour on top of baked cake; return to oven. Bake at 300° for 5 minutes. When cool, place in refrigerator overnight to set.

24 to 36 servings

Phyllis Stroh (Wife of Fred Stroh, deceased), Retired, Production Inventory Control
—Wooster

MOM'S APPLE PIE

2 9" pie crusts
4 to 5 apples, peeled and sliced (Granny Smith, MacIntosh or Jonathan)
1 cup sugar
1 stick butter or margarine
1 teaspoon cinnamon

Pile apple slices into one of the crusts. Pour sugar over apples. Cut butter or margarine into slices and scatter over top of apples. Sprinkle cinnamon, to taste, over top. Place remaining pie crust on top and seal edges with fork; cut 4 slits in top. Bake in middle of oven on cookie sheet at 350° for 1 hour or until top is golden brown.

6 to 8 servings

Gail Smart
Data Processing Dept., Saladmaster, Inc.
—Arlington, TX

GOLDEN DELICIOUS APPLE PIE

This recipe is simply a family favorite and good when served warm with vanilla ice cream!

Crust for 9" pie:
1½ cups flour
1 teaspoon salt
½ cup butter-flavored shortening
4 to 5 tablespoons cold apple juice

Filling:
4 large yellow Delicious apples
1 cup water
½ cup sugar
½ cup packed light brown sugar
3 tablespoons cornstarch
¼ teaspoon salt
½ teaspoon apple pie spice
½ teaspoon cinnamon
½ teaspoon cardamom
1¼ cups apple juice

Crumb topping:
½ cup flour
3 tablespoons sugar
2 tablespoons packed light brown sugar
3 tablespoons margarine
¼ cup chopped pecans

Mix flour and salt. Cut in shortening until mixture resembles coarse crumbs. Add apple juice, 1 tablespoon at a time. Gather dough with fork until ball forms. Roll on floured surface. Place in pie plate; shape, trim and flute edges. Set aside. Reserve leftover dough.

Peel, core and slice apples. Cook in water until barely tender. Drain and set aside.

Mix dry filling ingredients together in 2-quart saucepan. Add apple juice; mix well. Cook until sauce begins to thicken. Add apples; mix and pour into crust. For topping mix flour, sugars and margarine together with pastry cutter. Add nuts.

Sprinkle topping over the apples. Use left-over dough to make cut-out apples and leaves; arrange on top of crumbs. Bake at 450° for 10 minutes. Reduce heat to 350° and bake for 30 to 35 minutes or until golden brown.

6 to 8 servings

Jack (and Betty) Stivers, Purchasing Agent
—Jacksonville

FRIED APPLE PIES

1 quart bag dried apple slices, about 4
  cups
2 cups water
½ cup sugar
½ teaspoon cinnamon
Pastry for double crust pie

Rinse apples. Add water and cook in sauce-pan for 25 minutes. Mash with potato masher. Add sugar and cinnamon.

On lightly floured surface, roll pastry to about ⅛" thick. Cut out circles the size of a saucer, about 6". Place 2 tablespoons apples on one-half of circle. Moisten edges with water. Fold over, pinch edges together and prick with fork. Fry in hot shortening or oil until light brown on both sides (or until dough is cooked).

Makes 10 large pies

Rose Ketter, Retired
—Kewaskum

BLENDER COCONUT PIE

4 eggs
1 teaspoon coconut flavoring
¼ cup margarine, softened
¾ cup sugar
½ cup flour
2 cups milk

Put all ingredients in blender. Blend 10 to 12 seconds until well mixed. Pour into greased 9" pie pan. (Do not put in pie shell as it will make crust as it bakes.) Bake at 350° for 45 minutes. Cool completely before cutting.

6 to 8 servings

Linda Hodges
—Pigeon Forge, TN

COMPANY LEMON PIE

2 cups flour
1 cup margarine, softened
2 tablespoons sugar
1½ cups powdered sugar
2 8-ounce packages Philadelphia cream
  cheese, softened
2 cans "Thank You" brand lemon pie
  filling
Cool Whip

Mix together flour, margarine and sugar. Pat crumbs into ungreased 11 x 17" pan; bake at 350° for 15 minutes. Check while baking so it does not get too brown. Cool.

Mix powdered sugar and cream cheese together and spread on baked crust. Spread pie filling over cream cheese mixture. Top with Cool Whip. Refrigerate.

20 servings

Carolyn Jackson, Retired
—Wooster

LEMON ICE BOX PIE

1 14-ounce can Eagle Brand condensed
   milk
½ cup fresh lemon juice
Grated rind of 1 lemon or ¼ teaspoon
   lemon extract
2 eggs, separated
1 tablespoon sugar
1 9" graham cracker crust

Blend milk, lemon juice, lemon rind and egg yolks. Pour into unbaked crumb crust. Beat egg whites and sugar until stiff. Spread over top of filling. Bake at 350° until meringue is browned. Chill before serving.

6 to 8 servings

Bill Garlington, Sr. Industrial Engineer
—Jacksonville

COUSIN KARIN'S PEACH PARFAIT PIE

3½ cups sliced peaches, reserve juice
1 3-ounce package lemon gelatin
½ cup cold water
1 pint vanilla ice cream
1 baked 9" pie shell
½ cup whipping cream, whipped

Drain peaches, reserving syrup. Add water to syrup to make 1 cup; heat to boiling. Add gelatin, stir until dissolved. Add cold water. Cut ice cream into 6 pieces. Add to hot liquid and stir until melted. Chill until mixture mounds slightly, 20 minutes. Fold in peaches reserving 3 or 4 slices for garnish. Pour into pastry shell. Chill until firm, 45 minutes for cream pie, several hours for firmer filling. Top with whipped cream and peaches.

6 to 8 servings

Christine Catalino, Sales Office
—New Jersey

COOL AND CREAMY PUMPKIN PIE

Crust:
½ cup butter or butter-flavored Crisco
¼ cup sugar, scant*
1 egg yolk
1¼ cups flour
1 teaspoon salt

Filling:
1 16-ounce can pumpkin (2 cups)
1 12-ounce container whipped topping,
   thawed
1 box instant vanilla pudding (4-serving
   size)*
1 teaspoon pumpkin pie spice

Cream butter, sugar and egg yolk. Using a pie blender, add flour and salt. Put into a buttered 11½ x 7" pan, patting into bottom and working up the sides. Bake at 400° until golden brown. Cool.

In large mixing bowl, combine pumpkin, ½ container whipped topping, pudding and spice. Beat at low speed until well blended, 1 to 2 minutes. Spread onto baked crust. Top with remaining whipped topping. Refrigerate until ready to serve.

* For a diabetic, eliminate sugar in crust and use sugar-free pudding.

12 servings

Betty Backhaus, Retired
—Kewaskum

IMPOSSIBLE PUMPKIN PIE

¾ cup sugar
½ cup Bisquick
2 tablespoons butter
2 eggs, beaten
1 16-ounce can pumpkin
1 teaspoon cinnamon
½ teaspoon vanilla
1 13-ounce can evaporated milk

Beat all ingredients until smooth, 1 minute in blender at high speed or 2 minutes with hand mixer. Pour into lightly greased 10" pie pan. Bake at 350° for 50 to 55 minutes.

8 to 12 servings

Rita M. Felton, Retired
—Wooster

SUGAR-FREE STRAWBERRY PIE

Glaze:
1 3-ounce package sugar-free vanilla pudding (not instant)
1 0.3-ounce package sugar-free strawberry gelatin
2½ cups cold water

4 cups sliced or whole strawberries
1 9" pie shell, baked
Whipped cream

In saucepan, mix pudding, gelatin and water. Stir over medium heat until mixture comes to full boil. Remove from heat. Cool in refrigerator until slightly thickened. Arrange strawberries in pie shell. Pour cooled mixture over fruit. Chill until set. Serve with whipped cream.

6 to 8 servings

Sally Mielke
—Kewaskum

PECAN PIE

3 eggs
½ cup sugar
1 cup white Karo syrup
¼ cup butter, melted
1 teaspoon vanilla
1 cup chopped pecans
Pinch of salt
1 9" unbaked pie shell

Mix eggs, sugar, syrup, butter, vanilla, pecans and salt. Pour into pie shell. Bake at 350° for 50 to 60 minutes.

6 to 8 servings

Stella Russell, Dept. 8200
—Jacksonville

MAPLEY PECAN PIE (Diabetic)

1½ cups "Lite" pancake syrup
¼ cup margarine
¼ cup Sugar Twin
1½ cups pecan halves or chopped pecans
1 unbaked 9" pie shell
3 eggs, slightly beaten
1 teaspoon vanilla
Dash salt

Combine syrup, margarine and Sugar Twin in 2-quart saucepan; heat to boiling. Boil gently, uncovered 5 minutes, stirring occasionally. Cool slightly.

Place pecans in pie shell. Mix eggs, vanilla and salt in large bowl. Gradually stir in cooled syrup mixture. Pour over pecans in pie shell.

Bake at 375° for 35 to 40 minutes or until knife inserted near center comes out clean. Cool on wire rack.

8 servings

LaVern Geidel, Retired
—Kewaskum

J.C.'S PECAN PIE

1 9" pie shell, unbaked
1¼ cups sugar
½ cup butter
½ cup light corn syrup
3 eggs, slightly beaten
1 teaspoon vanilla
1½ cups pecans

Preheat oven to 375°. Prebake pie shell 3 to 4 minutes. Remove and set aside. In medium saucepan, heat sugar, butter and corn syrup over low heat until butter melts. Do not boil. Cool slightly. Stir in eggs, vanilla and nuts. Pour into pie shell and bake 40 to 45 minutes. Center should be soft.

6 to 8 servings

Jim (and Helen) Portmann, Sales, Retired
—Minneapolis

BUTTERMILK PIE

½ cup butter, softened
1 cup sugar
2 teaspoons flour
Dash of salt
3 eggs
1 cup buttermilk
1 teaspoon vanilla
9" unbaked pie shell

In bowl, cream butter and sugar until light and fluffy. Mix in flour, salt, and eggs one at a time. Add milk and vanilla. Beat until well mixed. Pour into unbaked pie shell and bake at 325° for 50 minutes.

6 to 8 servings

Nancy White, Nationwide Acceptance
—Arlington, TX

ANGEL PIE

Meringue:
6 egg whites
1 cup sugar
1 teaspoon vinegar
½ teaspoon cream of tartar

Lemon filling:
3 cups sugar
⅔ cup cornstarch
3 cups water
½ cup lemon juice
6 egg yolks, beaten
6 teaspoons butter
1 teaspoon lemon rind

Place egg whites and sugar in bowl. Beat until stiff. Add vinegar and cream of tartar. Mix well. Spread meringue in buttered 9 x 13" pan. Bake at 325° for 1 hour. Leave in oven to cool.

In saucepan, mix sugar and cornstarch with water. Bring to boil over low heat, stirring constantly. Slowly add lemon juice, egg yolks, butter and lemon rind. Cook until thick. Cool. Pour filling on top of meringue. Chill and serve.

Serve within 6 hours as lemon filling will become rubbery.

12 to 18 servings

Lloyd Gatzke, Industrial Engineering
—Kewaskum

MARGARITA PIE

Crust:
2 cups cinnamon graham cracker crumbs
½ cup butter, melted

Filling:
1 envelope plain gelatin
½ cup freshly squeezed lime juice
4 eggs, separated
1 cup sugar, divided
¼ teaspoon salt
1 teaspoon grated lime rind
⅓ cup tequila
3 tablespoons triple sec or other orange-flavored liqueur

Topping:
1 cup whipping cream
2 tablespoons sugar
1 lime thinly sliced for garnish

Mix together graham cracker crumbs and melted butter. Press into 9" pie pan. Chill.

Sprinkle gelatin over lime juice; let stand until softened. Beat egg yolks and ½ cup sugar in top of double boiler until lemon colored. Add gelatin mixture. Cook, stirring constantly, over boiling water until slightly thickened. Do not boil. Remove from heat.

Stir in salt and grated lime rind. Whisk in tequila and liqueur. Pour into bowl, cover. Refrigerate to chill slightly, about 10 minutes; do not allow to jell.

Meanwhile, beat egg whites with ½ cup sugar until stiff but not dry. Fold into chilled mixture. Pour mixture into chilled crust. Chill pie until set, about 6 to 8 hours or overnight.

For topping, beat cream, adding 2 tablespoons sugar gradually and beating until soft peaks form. Spread over top of pie. Decorate with lime slices.

6 to 8 servings

Skip Hillary, Sales
—Texas

CHOCOLATE PIE

Crust:
1½ cups Crisco shortening
3 cups flour
1 teaspoon salt
1 tablespoon vinegar
½ cup ice water

Chocolate filling:
1 tablespoon flour
2 tablespoons cocoa
1 cup sugar
1 cup milk (canned vegetable milk -
   Milnot makes a creamier pie)
3 eggs, separated
1 teaspoon vanilla
1 teaspoon butter or margarine
5 to 6 large marshmallows (this makes
   the pie richer and smoother)

Meringue:
3 egg whites
½ teaspoon vanilla
¼ teaspoon cream of tartar
6 tablespoons sugar

For crust, cut shortening into flour and salt until mixture is in small pieces. Combine vinegar and water; pour liquid into flour mixture. Mix until ingredients form a ball. Divide into thirds and roll out on floured pastry sheet; place in pie pan. Bake at 350° until lightly browned (Or freeze two crusts for later use.) Makes three 9" pie crusts.

For filling, combine flour, cocoa and sugar; add enough milk to mix flour mixture thoroughly. Add 3 slightly beaten egg yolks into mixture and stir in remaining milk and vanilla. Cook over medium heat in 3-quart saucepan until thickened; stirring constantly. Add butter and marshmallows; stir until marshmallows are completely melted. Remove from heat and let cool. Pour into baked 9" pie crust. Top with meringue.

For meringue, in 3-quart mixing bowl, beat egg whites with vanilla and cream of tartar until soft peaks form. Add sugar gradually and beat until stiff peaks form. Completely cover pie filling with meringue. Bake at 350° for 12 to 15 minutes.

6 to 8 servings

Doris Russell, Data Processing Dept.
Saladmaster, Inc.
—Arlington, TX

DRUM STICK PIE

Crust:
2 cups graham crackers, crushed
½ cup butter, melted
⅔ cup crushed Spanish peanuts

First layer:
2 8-ounce packages cream cheese,
   softened
⅓ cup peanut butter
1 cup powdered sugar
2 cups Cool Whip

Second layer:
2 3.4-ounce packages instant chocolate
   pudding
3 cups milk

Third layer:
2 cups Cool Whip
⅓ cup crushed peanuts

Combine crust ingredients and pat into 9 x 13" pan. Bake at 350° for 10 minutes. Cool. For first layer, combine cream cheese, peanut butter and sugar. Fold in Cool Whip. Pour over cooled crust. For second layer, combine pudding and milk and spread over cream cheese mixture. For third layer, combine Cool Whip and peanuts and spread over top. Refrigerate 3 to 4 hours before serving.

15 servings

Heide Ewerdt, Dept. 1400
—Kewaskum

FRUIT PIZZA

1 8-ounce package crescent rolls
1 8-ounce package cream cheese,
   softened
1 7-ounce jar marshmallow cream
Crushed pineapple, drained
Strawberries
Grapes
Any other fruit desired

Spread crescent rolls out on cookie sheet. Bake at 375° until light brown, about 8 minutes. Cool. Beat together cream cheese and marshmallow cream. Spread on crust. Arrange fruit over topping.

20 to 24 servings

Eileen Bonlender
—Kewaskum

FRUIT PIZZA

1 20-ounce package Pillsbury
  refrigerated Sugar Cookie dough
1 7-ounce jar marshmallow cream
1 8-ounce package cream cheese
1 pint strawberries, halved
1 kiwi, sliced
1 banana, sliced
Fresh or canned peach slices

Glaze:
½ cup orange juice
½ cup sugar
¼ cup water
1 tablespoon cornstarch
Dash of salt

Spread cookie dough onto pizza pan. Bake at 350° until light brown. Cool.

Cream together marshmallow cream and cream cheese; spread over cooled cookie crust. Arrange fruit on top of cream mixture.

In small saucepan, over medium heat, mix all glaze ingredients. Cook until thick and clear, stirring constantly. Cool and pour over fruit. Refrigerate.

About 12 servings

John Howard, Draftsman
—Jacksonville

FLAN

Caramel:
1 cup sugar
¼ cup water

Custard:
3 small navel oranges
1 quart (4 cups) milk
2 4-inch cinnamon sticks
1 teaspoon vanilla
6 eggs
2 egg yolks
1½ cups sugar

In small saucepan, bring sugar and water to boil over high heat, stirring until sugar completely dissolves. Reduce heat to moderate and cook briskly without stirring, but gently tipping pan back and forth until syrup turns deep golden brown, 10 minutes or more.

The moment syrup reaches desired color, remove pan from heat and quickly pour about 1 tablespoon into each of 8 flan or custard cups. Tip and swirl syrup evenly around bottom and then set aside.

Remove peel from oranges without cutting into the white pith. Add to milk and cinnamon sticks in a 2-quart pan. Bring almost to a boil over moderate heat. Remove pan from heat, discard orange peel and cinnamon sticks. Stir in vanilla.

Whisk eggs and yolks with sugar until well blended. Stirring constantly, pour hot milk mixture in thin stream into eggs. Fill cups with custard. Place in shallow baking dish. Pour in enough boiling water to come halfway up sides of cups. Bake at 350°, lowering oven temperature if water in pan begins to boil, for about 45 minutes, or until knife inserted in center of custard comes out clean.

Remove cups from water and refrigerate for at least 3 hours. Run knife around edge of flan, invert onto serving plate and with a quick downward motion, unmold flan onto plate.

8 servings

Kim Peterson
—Kewaskum

FLAMING CREPES SUZETTE

4 eggs
1 cup milk
¾ cup flour
Dash of salt
2 tablespoons sugar
2 tablespoons plus 1 cup butter, divided
½ cup powdered sugar
Grated rinds of 1 lemon and 1 orange
½ cup Cointreau (orange liqueur)
½ cup brandy

Beat eggs until foamy. Beat in milk. Gradually add flour, salt and sugar. Allow batter to stand for 1 hour. Lightly butter bottom of 6" skillet. Spoon 2 tablespoons batter into heated skillet. Rotate pan quickly to spread batter over the entire bottom of pan. Fry over medium heat until edges of crepe are brown. Loosen edges, invert pan and remove crepe; brown on other side. Stack crepes with piece of waxed paper between each one. Refrigerate or freeze until ready for use. (If frozen, allow to defrost for 1 hour at room temperature before using.) Make two 6" crepes. Fold crepes into quarters. Melt 1 cup butter in large skillet. Add powdered sugar, grated lemon and orange rinds and Cointreau. Heat until mixture bubbles. Add folded crepes; turn several times to coat well. Heat brandy and pour over crepes. Set aflame.

8 servings

Colleen Fisher, Dept. 8400-1
—Kewaskum

PERFECT ENDING SPICED BANANAS

¼ cup butter
½ cup brown sugar
1 teaspoon cinnamon
2 tablespoons lemon juice
2½ tablespoons dark rum
4 bananas, peeled and cut into ¼"
   diagonal slices
Sour cream or ice cream
Cinnamon

In skillet, melt butter over medium-high heat. Stir in brown sugar, cinnamon, lemon juice and rum. Bring to boil while stirring constantly. Reduce heat to low and stir in bananas. Stir gently until bananas are well coated and heated through. Serve in four individual dishes with a dollop of sour cream or ice cream. Sprinkle with cinnamon.

4 servings

Kurt and Sallie Myers
—Orangeville

STRAWBERRY REFRIGERATOR DESSERT

Crust:
1 cup flour
¼ cup brown sugar
½ cup chopped nuts
½ cup butter, melted

Filling:
30 marshmallows
⅔ cup milk
1 8-ounce package cream cheese,
   softened
½ cup sugar
1 cup whipping cream

Topping:
2 3-ounce packages strawberry gelatin
2 cups boiling water
2 10-ounce packages strawberries

Mix crust ingredients like pie crust. Pat into 9 x 13" pan. Bake at 350° for 12 minutes. Cool.

Combine marshmallows and milk. Cook over low heat or in double boiler until marshmallows melt. Cool. Beat cream cheese and sugar. Whip cream until stiff; fold into cream cheese mixture. Add to marshmallow mixture and spread over crust. Chill until set.

Combine gelatin and boiling water, stirring until dissolved. Add frozen berries. Chill until slightly thickened. Spoon over filling. Chill several hours or overnight.

12 to 18 servings

Diane Schraufnagel, Dept. 8300-1
—Kewaskum

BANANA SPLIT

1½ cups boiling water
2 3-ounce or 1 6-ounce package Jello brand gelatin, any red flavor
2 cups cold water
2 cups vanilla ice cream, softened
Cool Whip, thawed
1 banana, sliced
1 pint strawberries, halved
1 20-ounce can pineapple chunks, drained
Chopped nuts

Stir boiling water into gelatin in large bowl for 2 minutes or until completely dissolved. Add cold water. Stir in ice cream until smooth. Pour into 3- or 4-quart serving bowl. Refrigerate 3 hours until firm. Garnish with Cool Whip, fruits and nuts.

8 servings

Marianne Wondra
—Kewaskum

CHOCOLATE MOUSSE

3 tablespoons sugar
3 tablespoons water
2 egg yolks, optional
1 6-ounce semi-sweet chocolate chips, melted
1½ cups Cool Whip
Raspberries

Heat sugar and water over low heat to dissolve sugar, swirling occasionally. Bring to a boil. Whisk yolks in large bowl. Using mixer, beat in syrup in thin stream. Beat until cool and triples in volume. Beat in melted chocolate. Fold in Cool Whip. Refrigerate. Serve with raspberries on top.

4 servings

Dick (and Jean) Myers, Retired
—Kewaskum

BAKED LEMON PUDDING

This baked pudding is very easy to make and can be served warm or cold. Be sure to use fresh lemon juice for best flavor. While pudding is baking, it separates into a thin bottom layer of lemon sauce with a fluffy cake-like layer on top.

¾ cup sugar, divided
5 tablespoons flour
¼ teaspoon baking powder
⅛ teaspoon salt
2 eggs, separated
3 tablespoons fresh lemon juice
Grated rind of 1 lemon
1½ tablespoons butter, melted
1 cup milk

Preheat oven to 375°. Combine ½ cup sugar with flour, baking powder and salt. Beat egg yolks until light; add lemon juice, rind, butter and milk. Beat well with a spoon. Stir in dry ingredients until smooth. Beat egg whites until foamy; gradually beat in remaining ¼ cup sugar until stiff but not dry. Fold into flour mixture.

Transfer mixture to 1-quart baking dish. Put baking dish in a larger pan filled with warm water. Bake at 375° for 40 to 45 minutes until top is firm and nicely browned.

6 servings

Phyllys von Garlem, Secretary
—Chicago Sales Office

MICROWAVE VANILLA PUDDING/CUSTARD

¾ cup sugar
2 tablespoons cornstarch
¼ teaspoon salt
2 cups milk
2 egg yolks, beaten
2 tablespoons butter
1 teaspoon vanilla

Combine sugar, cornstarch, salt and milk in 4-cup microwave-safe dish; beat together with wire whisk. Microwave 4 minutes. Slowly add beaten egg yolks and stir. Microwave at 2 minute interals, stirring with wire whisk after each. When mixture has thickened, add butter and vanilla; stir. Cool and serve.

Can be used for pies or filling for cakes.

4 servings

Mrs. Allen Koepke
—Kewaskum

CHOCOLATE GRAVY

4 tablespoons flour
2 cups sugar
4 tablespoons cocoa
2 cups milk
4 tablespoons butter

Mix flour, sugar and cocoa together in bowl. Add milk and mix well. In saucepan, melt butter; add remaining ingredients. Boil until thickened. Pour over cake or a sweet bread.

Makes 3 cups

Ed Jackson, Outlet Store
—Pigeon Forge, TN

CHOCOLATE GRAVY

1 to 2 cups sugar
⅔ cup cocoa
⅓ cup flour
3 cups milk

In medium saucepan, combine all ingredients. Cook over low to medium heat until gravy thickens. Serve over biscuits.

Makes about 4 cups

Cherie Peets, Dept. 8400
—Jacksonville

APPLE DUMPLINGS

12 sheets puff pastry
2 to 3 tablespoons melted butter
6 McIntosh apples, cored
½ cup dark seedless raisins
⅓ cup coarsely chopped walnuts, optional
6 teaspoons sugar

Sauce:
⅔ cup sugar
3 tablespoons butter
1 cup water
¼ teaspoon nutmeg
2 to 3 drops red food coloring, optional
1 teaspoon vanilla

Lightly brush a sheet of puff pastry with butter; place another sheet on top (or use your favorite pie crust recipe, rolled ⅛" thick and cut into 10" squares). Center apple on top of pastry. Fill center of apple with raisins, nuts if desired, and 1 teaspoon sugar. Bring pastry up and around apple, twisting top slightly to make a pouch. Place dumpling in 9 x 13" baking pan. Repeat with remaining apples and pastry. Heat oven to 425°.

In small saucepan, over medium heat, mix all sauce ingredients except vanilla. Bring to boil; boil 3 minutes. Stir in vanilla. Pour hot sauce over dumplings. Bake in preheated oven 40 to 55 minutes until apples are tender but not mushy and pastry is lightly browned. Serve warm or cold.

6 servings

Adeline Halfmann, Retired
—Kewaskum

MASHED POTATO DONUTS

1 cup hot mashed potatoes
2 tablespoons butter
¾ cup sugar
½ teaspoon vanilla
1 egg, slightly beaten
1½ cups flour
3 teaspoons baking powder
½ teaspoon salt
⅛ to ¼ teaspoon nutmeg
¼ to ½ teaspoon cinnamon
½ cup milk

Put hot mashed potatoes, butter, sugar and vanilla in bowl. Mix until blended; add egg. Mix flour, baking powder, salt, nutmeg and cinnamon. Stir into potato mixture alternately with milk. Cover and chill in refrigerator at least 1 hour. Roll out dough and cut donuts. Fry donuts in hot oil (375°).

Makes 18 to 24 donuts

Judy Bowater, Sales Department
—Kewaskum

REGAL WARE, INC.

Corporate Headquarters

Kewaskum, Wisconsin

Manufacturing Facilities

Kewaskum, Wisconsin
Jacksonville, Arkansas
Orangeville, Ontario, Canada
Bogota, Colombia, S.A.
Caracas, Venezuela, S.A.

Sales Offices

Chicago, Illinois
Dallas, Texas
Portland, Oregon
Secaucus, New Jersey
Orangeville, Ontario, Canada
Nagoya, Japan
Seoul, Korea

Subsidiaries

Saladmaster, Inc., Arlington, Texas
Nationwide Acceptance Corp., Arlington, Texas

INDEX